The Man/Food Equation

KU-731-406

Young plant, symbol of man's food, needs man's cultivation before it can sustain man.

Hand, symbol of man and the need of awareness that the answer lies in man's own hands.

Department of Social and Administrative Studies,
Barnett House,
Wellington Square,
Oxford.
WITHDRAWN

The Man/Food Equation

Proceedings of a Symposium held at the Royal Institution London, September, 1973

Edited by

F. STEELE *and* A. BOURNE

Council for Environmental Science and Engineering London, England

Department of Environmental Sciences, Lancaster, England

1975

ACADEMIC PRESS

London · New York · San Francisco

A Subsidiary of Harcourt Brace Jovanovich, Publishers

ACADEMIC PRESS INC. (LONDON) LTD.
24/28 Oval Road,
London NW1

United States Edition published by
ACADEMIC PRESS INC.
111 Fifth Avenue
New York, New York 10003

Copyright © 1975 by
ACADEMIC PRESS INC. (LONDON) LTD.

All Rights Reserved
No part of this book may be reproduced in any form by photostat, microfilm, or any other means, without written permission from the publishers

Library of Congress Catalog Card Number: 75–29716
ISBN: 0–12–664850–6

Printed in Great Britain by
ROYSTAN PRINTERS LIMITED
Spencer Court, 7 Chalcot Road
London NW1

Contributors

Chairman of Symposium	ARTHUR BOURNE
Chairmen of Sessions	P. JEWEL GEORG BORGSTROM GERALD LEACH S. J. HOLT R. E. BOOTE (closing discussion)

BOOTE, R. E. *Nature Conservancy Council, London, England.*

BORGSTROM, GEORG *Department of Food Science and Human Nutrition, Michigan State University, East Lansing, Michigan, USA.*

*BOURNE, ARTHUR *Department of Environmental Sciences, University of Lancaster, Lancaster, England.*

BURKITT, DENIS P. *Medical Research Council (External Staff), London, England.*

CRAWFORD, M. A. *Nuffield Institute of Comparative Medicine, The Zoological Society of London, London, England.*

DIMBLEBY, G. W. *Department of Human Environment, Institute of Archaeology, University of London, London, England.*

FEINGOLD, BEN F. *Department of Allergy, Kaiser Permanente Medical Center, San Francisco, California, USA.*

HOLT, S. J. *International Ocean Institute, The Royal University of Malta, Msida, Malta.*

JEWEL, P. *Department of Zoology, Royal Holloway College, University of London, London, England.*

LEACH, GERALD *Science Policy Research Unit, University of Sussex, Brighton, Sussex, England.*

* Now care of Academic Press.

NARAIN, R. D. *Statistics Division, FAO, Rome, Italy.*

PAINTER, N. S. *The Manor House Hospital, London, England.*

PIRIE, N. W. *Department of Biochemistry, Rothamsted Experimental Station, Harpenden, Hertfordshire, England.*

RIVERS, J. P. W. *Nuffield Institute of Comparative Medicine, The Zoological Society of London, London, England.*

**SUKHATME, P. V. *Gokhale Institute of Politics and Economics, Poona, India.*

WHEELER, ERICA F. *Department of Human Nutrition, London School of Hygiene and Tropical Medicine, London, England.*

WILLIAMS, J. T. *Department of Botany, University of Birmingham, Birmingham, England.*

WORGAN, J. T. *National College of Food Technology, University of Reading, Weybridge, Surrey, England.*

**Now care of Maharashtra Association for the Cultivation of Science, Poona, India

Foreword

I very much welcome the initiative that was taken in organizing the Man/Food Equation Symposium.

It brought together authoritative contributions on various aspects of the issue from a number of scientific disciplines. It also represented an attempt to bring before the public a considered analysis by certain highly-qualified individuals of some of the basic problems facing mankind. While it is the responsibility of national governments, together with international organizations such as FAO, to formulate measures to improve the quality of life—particularly for the huge numbers of people in the underprivileged regions of the world—private individuals and societies have an essential part to play by helping to clarify these problems.

The prospects for the future of human society have reached a critical stage. With the world's population increasing at its present rate, there will be twice as many mouths to feed by the year 2000. Most of this increase will occur in those parts of the world which are already densely populated and where malnutrition is most widely spread. To meet the needs, agricultural production will have to double every 18 years—a rate never before achieved over a sustained period by our present affluent societies. But this rate of growth must be pursued in full awareness of the necessity of maintaining a balance between the increasing demands for food and the demands of the environment from which it comes.

I am confident that the world can in fact meet this challenge, provided that there is more enlightened management of its resources than hitherto. In the general endeavour to achieve this, contributions of knowledge such as those that were made at the Man/Food Equation Symposium are of more than passing value.

A. H. BOERMA
Director-General
Food and Agriculture Organization
of the United Nations

Acknowledgements

The chairman and organisers would like to acknowledge the financial support given them by the Biostrath Foundation—in particular Mr F. Pestalozzi—in sponsoring this Symposium, and the help and encouragement received from Mr and Mrs Michael Van Straten and their staff. Without their support the Symposium would not have been possible.

We would also like to thank the Director, Managers and staff of the Royal Institution, and Mr Alan Massam for their help, and to acknowledge our indebtedness to Mr Boerma, the Director-General of FAO, for his interest and for writing the foreword to this book.

Contents

The Alternatives
CHAIRMAN: S. J. HOLT

The Cost: Health
CHAIRMAN: GERALD LEACH

Introduction

The disparity between the needs of an increasing global population and decreasing food resources poses one of the most intractable problems mankind has ever faced. Even a superficial survey of the world presents us with a picture of growing food shortages, and although the worst hit areas are to be found in the Third World, the shortages are having an increasing impact on the wealthier industrial communities. Proposals for solving the problem have been legion and all, even if they have not been actual failures, have fallen short of their predicted successes.

Much of the blame, I believe, for this failure lies in our way of looking at the major problems of the world community. Our world picture is fragmented by the disparate ways in which we view it; our personal, political, religious and economic differences prevent us from recognizing the fundamental relationships that bind us together and force us to face a common problem. This fragmentation is further distorted by the narrow specialist view of the "experts", a situation that provides little or no help in our predicament or guidance to the world leaders.

The idea for this Symposium was born of necessity, a need to clarify, to understand the nature of this the most pressing of the human predicaments. Somehow or other mankind must find a solution to the Man/Food Equation. It is possible that we do not know all the factors that have to be put into the Equation and if that is so then we cannot solve it, but by understanding the nature of the Equation we should know what those missing factors are and hopefully where to look for them. What, then, are the realities of the situation? Can we solve the Equation?

So far our attempts at solving it have been lamentably poor because we have not taken and still do not take sufficient account in our calculations of the natural restraints that the environment imposes upon us. If these restraints are the reason for our failures to achieve a solution, the question of our ability to meet the needs of a growing world population immediately presents itself. It is patently obvious that the human species cannot go on increasing indefinitely, sooner or later brakes will be applied either by the environment or by society. The only question then to arise will be which will be the first, the environment or society, and will it be sooner or later than we think?

It is inconceivable that we will come up with the answers to these questions in this Symposium, but even if we can only manage to clear away some of the mythological undergrowth that has accumulated over the years, we shall have a clearer understanding of the problems and in understanding them we may be able to suggest means of tackling them.

The subject matter of this Symposium is wide and it would be impossible to cover more than a few particular aspects. Therefore we have brought together four representative themes that provide a logical progression from one to another and highlight the major areas of concern. In the first of these themes we pose the question of whether we can ever feed adequately the present human population and if so for how long, and can we justifiably extrapolate from this whether we will be able to meet the needs of tomorrow's population. The second examines in both a contemporary and historical context the natural restraints that restrict the supply of food, and in so doing we include the very real problem of that other limited resource, energy. We then look at the alternative methods that might open up another option for Man and these are laid alongside the physiological needs of the human animal and the cost of changing our feeding habits.

Man in common with all other animals is dependent on his food supply and although he has increased his control over the environment and thereby the carrying capacity of the land, there is an upper limit to this and experience is showing us that that upper limit has been, or has almost been reached. One of the consequences of our not being able to grasp this fact of life has led to the generation of a number of myths, among them that science and technology can provide indefinitely for the needs of the growing and consuming human population. One hope born of this myth was the so-called Green Revolution which for a little while lived up to its promise but which was doomed in the long run to failure. In our situation short-term palliatives are the long-term catastrophes. There are no cornucopeias left.

However, it is not just a matter of growing or producing enough food, it is also a matter of what kind of food—the dietary requirements of one human are not necessarily those of another. The physiological needs of the human body are many, yet emphasis is put on some of these at the expense of others, for example a myth has grown up around the significance of protein to which a disproportionate importance has been attached. This situation has brought confusion, not only to nutritionists but to those who try to plan the harvests. We hear from one authority that there is a serious protein shortage and from another that there is plenty of protein if only it is distributed fairly. Somewhere along the line of argument the fact that people eat not just protein but *food* has been lost.

Millions of our own kind are condemned never to realise their full potential as men and women because of inadequate food supplies. If we cannot provide for these our contemporaries, it seems unlikely that we shall provide for tomorrow's people, and tomorrow is very near.

ARTHUR BOURNE

Population and Resources

Population and Food Supply

R. D. NARAIN

Food and Agriculture Organization of the United Nations

Summary

The paper is mainly concerned with recent trends in food/population relations and medium-term prospects. It shows that food production at the world and regional level during the last two decades has increased faster than population growth. However, production in a number of countries has lagged behind population growth and in many more behind effective demand for food. The growth rates of food production in the developing countries need to be considerably stepped up to meet the targets for the agricultural sector of the Second Development Decade (DD2). Even if these targets are met, the magnitude of the nutritional problems would remain at approximately present levels in terms of the number of people inadequately nourished in spite of projected world cereal surpluses.

Short-term fluctuations in food production due to seasonal and climatic conditions will continue, necessitating procedures for concerting national and international food stock policies in order to protect the world against the worst consequences of food scarcities due to crop failures. The Director-General of the Food and Agriculture Organization (FAO) is proposing to Governments the acceptance of a meaningful concept for this purpose.

The technical possibility for bringing about considerable increases in agricultural production exists, but its realization is dependent upon availability of modern inputs and related institutional and structural measures. Much of this requires investment beyond the capacity of many developing countries hence calling for international measures both in the field of trade and aid.

This paper is based on the material assembled and studies being carried out in the FAO in connection with the preparation for the Fourth World Food Survey. The views expressed in this paper, however, do not necessarily represent the stated policy of the FAO.

Nutritional problems are largely a function of poverty and therefore their solution requires measures for the creation and redistribution of income. Such measures are inhibited by a rapidly increasing population, the consequent pressure on land and the continuing high proportion of agricultural workers in the total labour force. Whatever conceivable rates of growth are assumed for the non-agricultural sector, agriculture must continue to absorb a large proportion of new entrants into the labour force. The ability of the agricultural sector to cope with this necessity and the possible consequences on income creation and redistribution and on levels of nutrition are serious problems, the solution of which is vital to the success of any developmental efforts.

The size of the population and its rate of growth have certainly a major influence on these problems. A population policy itself, therefore, becomes a major component of food and agricultural policies.

Population Growth

At the beginning of the Christian Era the population of the world is estimated to have been about 250 million people. This doubled in the next sixteen centuries, reaching 500 millions about the year 1650. The next doubling of the population required only two centuries. The subsequent doubling took just 80 years. Thus there were two billion people by 1930. Currently the world population continues to grow at 2% a year and the developing countries have an average growth rate of 2·5%. Appendix I presents the estimates of population for 1950, 1960 and projected 1980 of the different regions and sub-regions of the world together with the implied rates of growth. Asia experienced a rate of population growth of about 2% a year in the 1950s, and this increased to 2·2% in the last decade. Its population is expected to continue to grow at about this rate in the 1970s. A significant reduction in fertility is considered likely to occur thereafter, leading to a decline in the population growth rate. In Africa, declining mortality rates combined with stable and even rising fertility rates resulted in an acceleration of the population growth rate to 2·5% between 1960 and 1970. It is projected that during the period 1970–1980 the rate of population growth in Africa will increase to 2·9%, with many countries exceeding 3% per year, and no marked decline is expected this century. The Latin American region in the last decades has had a higher rate of population growth than all the other regions of the world. The population is currently increasing at 2·9% per year, and the rate will remain high despite declining fertility. The current rates of population growth in the developed part of the world, except Oceania, are around 1%.

It is against the background of this demographic situation that the current and future food supply must be assessed.

Trends in Food Production

In the 1950s world food production increased at an annual rate of 3·2% against a population growth of just under 2% (see Table 1). The rate of growth of food production in all regions exceeded population growth. *Per capita* food production increased fastest in the developed countries, followed by Asia. In the 1960s the rate of growth of food production showed a significant decline in all regions except in Latin America. Population growth in the developing countries increased during the 1960s, but growth of food production, nevertheless, continued to more than match population growth, although the margin between the two rates considerably narrowed, except in Latin America. The decline in the rate of growth in food production in the richer countries largely resulted from official policies of restricting production.

Although food production at the global and regional level outpaced population growth, the picture at the national level was not so good. Out of 106 countries for which detailed information is available for the period 1952–1971, population growth outstripped food production in 27 (See Appendix II), while in the more recent period the figure is even larger. The national

TABLE 1

Rate of growth of population and food production

Region	1952–1960			1960–1970		
	Population	Food production total	Food production *per capita*	Population	Food production total	Food production *per capita*
	% per year					
Africa	2·2	2·8	0·6	2·5	2·6	0·1
Asia	2·0	3·4	1·4	2·2	2·7	0·5
Latin America	2·8	3·2	0·4	2·9	3·5	0·6
USA, Canada Europe and Oceania	1·3	3·2	1·9	1·1	2·6	1·5
World	1·8	3·2	1·4	2·0	2·8	0·8

Source: FAO Index Numbers of Food Production; United Nations Population Estimates.

figures are shown in graphic form in Fig. 1. For countries below the diagonal line the population growth rate was higher than that of food production.

Out of the 79 countries where food production grew faster than population, in 22 food production failed to keep pace with the effective demand.* (It is

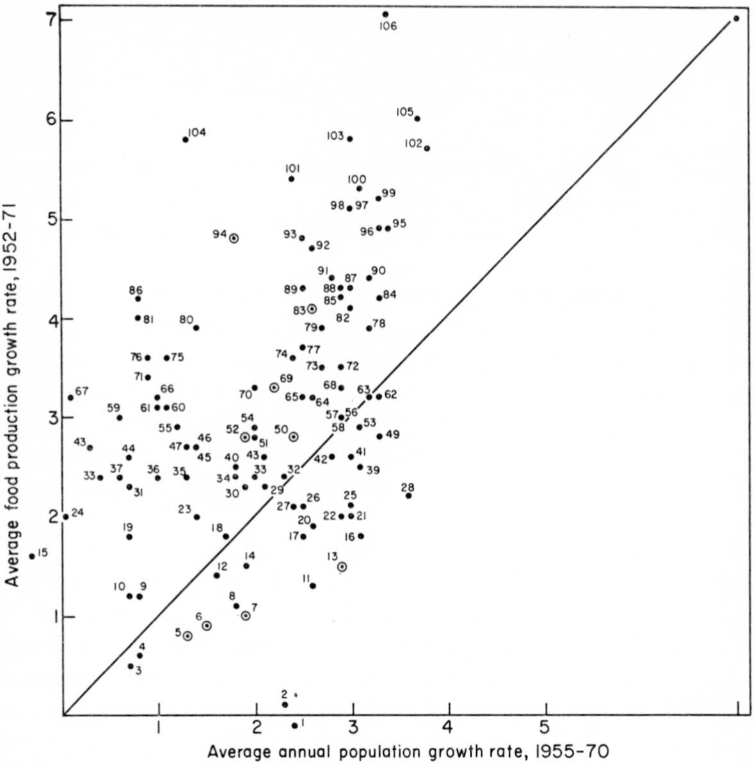

Fig. 1. Distribution of countries according to growth rates of their food supply and population.

Food production increased as much as or more than estimated demand

79 Ghana	84 Honduras	88 Sudan
96 Ivory Coast	98 Nicaragua	104 Cyprus
101 Togo	95 Mexico	103 Lebanon
46 Angola	93 Bolivia	77 Egypt
70 Cameroon	82 Brazil	97 Malaysia
76 Gabon	99 Ecuador	74 Sri Lanka
65 Tanzania	105 Venezuela	100 Thailand
92 Malawi	102 Costa Rica	
78 Rhodesia	85 Guatemala	

Continued p. 7

*The effective demand for food was estimated by taking into account the growth rates of population and *per capita* income given in Columns 2 and 3 of Appendix II and the estimates of farmgate elasticity given in the FAO Commodity Projections, 1970–1980.

23 USA	51 Australia	80 USSR
43 Canada	54 New Zealand	86 Bulgaria
		19 Czechoslovakia
37 Belgium-Luxembourg		15 Germany, Democratic Republic
61 France		18 Hungary
36 Germany, Federal Republic		55 Poland
31 Italy		60 Romania
47 Netherlands		
38 Austria		106 Israel
44 Finland		89 South Africa
81 Greece		
40 Iceland		
24 Ireland		
67 Malta		
71 Spain		
59 UK		
75 Yugoslavia		

Food production increased less than estimated demand but more than population

58 Morocco	90 Panama	64 Turkey
34 Mauritania	63 Columbia	68 Iran
35 Sierra Leone	57 Peru	32 India
30 Ethiopia	18 Argentina	56 Pakistan
87 Zambia		33 Burma
45 Mozambique		91 Korean Republic
		79 China
		73 Khmer
10 Portugal		
9 Denmark		
66 Japan		
72 Albania		

Food production increased less than population

1 Algeria	82 Dominican Republic	53 Saudi Arabia
21 Nigeria	14 Jamaica	22 Syria
2 Zaire	20 Trinidad and Tobago	49 Iraq
41 Kenya	26 Chile	16 Jordan
11 Mauritius	39 Guyana	27 Indonesia
17 Uganda	42 Paraguay	62 Philippines
8 Tunisia	25 El Salvador	
4 Norway		
3 Sweden		
12 Switzerland		

Countries having negative income growth rate

13 Dahomey	7 Haiti
83 Niger	5 Uruguay
69 Senegal	
94 Upper Volta	
52 Central African Republic	
6 Chad	
50 Madagascar	

estimated that in the developing countries about 70% of the increase in effective demand is accounted for by population growth.) Countries with large populations, such as China and India, fall into this category. Only in 25 developing countries was the growth of food production increasing faster than effective demand. Because demand exceeded supply, many countries were forced to increase their dependence on cereal imports. In many cases, this import dependence was considerable in the late 1960s (See Appendix II). For some countries the reason is that a part of their limited arable land is devoted to export crops. In other countries a high man-land ratio may be a contributory factor in their dependence on imports. In some richer countries the import dependence is further increased owing to the high feed requirements for livestock. For instance, in the second half of the last decade four countries, United Kingdom, Japan, Federal Republic of Germany and Italy with a total population of less than 300 million imported 31 million tons of cereals *per annum,* whereas India and China with a population almost five times larger imported an average of only 11 million tons *per annum.*

While a high import dependence is not necessarily a cause for concern to countries with plentiful sources of foreign exchange earnings, for many developing countries food imports cut into scarce foreign exchange resources that are badly needed to finance capital investment. Bilateral and international food aid has provided some relief from this constraint.

Current Food and Nutrition Situation

The previous sections were mainly concerned with a review of past trends of population and food production. Current levels and patterns of food consumption and their adequacy in terms of energy and protein requirements are now analysed. The analysis at the regional and national level is based on food balance sheets available to FAO for more than 100 countries and covering different periods in the late 1960s. These estimate food supplies by taking into account not only food production but also external trade, changes in stocks and non-food utilization. The results of recent food consumption surveys also are used to throw light on the distribution of food within countries.

Table 2 gives the present pattern of the availability of food by regions (for more detailed figures by sub-region see Appendix III). It will be noted from these tables that most developing countries derive their energy intake (calories) mainly from cereals. In Asia, 67% of the calories come from

TABLE 2

% Contribution of different foods to the total intake of calories and protein

Regions	Cereals		Starchy roots		Sugar		Pulses and nuts		Fruit and vegetables		Meat, eggs fish, milk		Fats and oils	
	calories	protein	calories	protein	calories	protein	calories	protein	calories	protein	calories	protein	calories	protein
Asia	67	59	7	3	6	–	6	17	3	3	7	18	4	–
Africa	53	55	19	9	5	–	7	14	3	3	7	19	6	–
Latin America	39	39	11	5	17	–	7	16	3	3	16	37	7	–
Europe	38	39	7	6	12	–	2	3	4	5	23	47	14	–
North America	20	16	3	2	16	–	3	4	6	5	35	73	17	–
Oceania	25	24	3	3	17	–	2	2	5	4	37	67	11	–

Source: FAO Food Balance Sheets.

cereals. Although cereals account for more than one-half of the calorie supply in Africa, in some parts of Central and Western Africa starchy roots are the main source of calories. In Latin America, the food intake is more diversified, almost as much as in the developed countries, but quantitatively the levels of consumption in the developed regions are higher.

A comparison of calorie and protein intakes with nutritional requirements shown in Appendix III suggests that all sub-regions of Asia, with the exception of Japan and Israel, have deficits in calories, and this also is true for Africa, excepting Eastern Africa and South Africa. Latin America is better able to meet calorie requirements. Nearly all sub-regions have *per capita* protein supplies that appear to be adequate on the basis of the new recommendations for protein requirements (FAO/WHO, 1973).

Appendix IV shows the calories and protein availability by country together with the corresponding requirements. It appears that 44 of the countries shown have calorie supplies that are less than the calorie requirements, and in 16 of these countries the deficit exceeds 10%; *per capita* protein supplies are in excess of requirements for all countries.

The appraisal of the problem of nutritional inadequacy on the basis of national averages, as summarized in the preceding paragraph, generally underestimates the size of the food problem, because even in developed countries food is never distributed in accordance with nutritional requirements. In fact, available food is invariably unevenly distributed owing to the inequality of income, rural-urban differences, etc. Distribution may also vary widely between seasons, regions and even between individuals in a family. Thus, even where the average *per capita* supply of energy and nutrients are adequate or even in excess, there may well be serious problems of undernutrition* and malnutrition†.

To study the incidence of nutritional deficiencies information is needed on distribution of calories, proteins and other nutrients between individuals and between households, in different socio-economic groups and ecological zones. Only food consumption surveys supplemented by clinical surveys can provide this information.

---

*Undernutrition means inadequacy in the quantity of the diet, i.e. calorie intake which, continued over a long period, results in either loss of normal body activity or reduction in physical activity, or work. This definition is strictly appropriate to adults, not to children. For children, the consequences of low calorie intake are unsatisfactory growth and physical development and a reduction of the high degree of activity characteristic of healthy children.

†Malnutrition means inadequacy of the nutritional quality of the diet, which if made good enables a person to lead a healthy active life. More precisely, it denotes inadequacy of a particular nutrient or several essential nutrients. Serious shortages of nutrients may result in clinical signs of deficiency diseases; a minor degree of deficiency can contribute to poor general health.

At present such information is limited in coverage. The assessment made in FAO's 1963 Third World Food Survey on the basis of such data as were then available indicated that at least 20% of the population in the less developed areas was undernourished.

The main nutritional problem is one of protein/calorie malnutrition, which occurs when the quantity of food ingested does not meet protein requirements or when the available protein is adequate but not properly utilized due to a lack of calories. The latter is the most common form of protein/calorie malnutrition, as in most diets, even in poorer countries, protein needs are met if the quantity of food consumed adequately meets calorie requirements. However, in cases where calorie requirements are derived largely from roots and tubers, protein malnutrition may occur even though the consumption of calories meets requirements.

TABLE 3

Daily calorie intake per capita *by income*

Country	Urban/ rural	Income group[a,b] 1	2	3	4	5	6
Brazil, North-East	Urban	1400	2100	2400	3000	4000	4300
	Rural	1600	2000	2300	2000	2900	2900
Brazil, East	Urban	1400	2000	2200	2700	3300	3800
	Rural	1700	2400	2700	3000	3000	4100
Brazil, South	Urban	1600	2000	2400	2600	3100	3200
	Rural	2600	2700	3000	3400	4100	4800
Pakistan West	Urban	1700	1800	1800	1800	2100	2000
	Rural	2000	2100	2200	2500	2100	2500
Pakistan, East[c]	Urban	1500	1700	1700	1800	1800	1800
	Rural	2000	2200	2400	2600	2600	3100
Madagascar	Rural	2200	2300	2400	2400	2300	2500
Gabon	Rural	1500	1700	2200	2200	2400	2500
Trinidad and Tobago	Urban	2700	2600	2800	2900	3400	3500
	Rural	3000	3000	3200	3100	3000	2900

The surveys in the countries shown from which these figures were extracted were taken during the early 1960s.

[a]Income is shown classified into six groups ranging from the lowest income group to the highest. The actual income range for each group varies from country to country.

[b]In some cases the levels of consumption appear to be on the high side. This may be in part due to the omission from the household of guests, visitors, labourers and the increasing amount of plate waste as income rises.

[c]Now Bangladesh.

The most important cause of nutritional deficiency is poverty and inequality of income distribution, often aggravated by social, ecological and other factors. Food consumption surveys indicate that at lower levels of income calorie consumption is positively correlated with income; at higher levels of income the calorie intake reaches a plateau, as is the case with high income groups in developing countries and at nearly all levels in developed countries.

Table 3 shows the average calorie intake *per capita* by income group for a few developing countries for which recent data are available.

The general picture is clear: calorie intake is not only closely correlated with income but is often grossly inadequate at the lower end of the income scale. Rural/urban differences are also revealed by the data in Table 3, urban households tending to have lower intakes than rural households with the same income. These differences seem to disappear with rising incomes. Regional differences also can be noted from the data.

For the developed countries the incidence of undernutrition is negligible. In fact, the available evidence indicates that large sections of population consume in excess of requirements, and in consequence the incidence of obesity and other effects of over-eating is fairly common.

The fact that the under- and malnourished are found among the poverty-stricken underlines that if the problem is to be tackled, it must be by raising income levels of the poorer sections of the population and improving the distribution of available food supplies within a country.

Future Food Supply and Requirements

Prospects of supply and demand for the 1970s are given in FAO's Agricultural Commodity Projections for 1980.

Table 4 summarizes the likely picture for cereals in 1980. According to these figures the world production of cereals, barring short-term fluctuations mainly resulting from the vagaries of Nature, will increase from 1,080 million tons in 1970 to 1,427 million tons in 1980. This would represent a growth rate of 2·9% per year—well above the likely population growth. The rate of growth of cereal production will be somewhat faster in developing countries, in particular in Latin America and Asia, reflecting the anticipated spread of high-yielding varieties. Despite the measures being taken to restrict production in developed countries, world production of cereals is likely to exceed projected demand in 1980 creating a surplus of nearly 62 million tons.

However, projected production may fail to meet projected demand for other foods, for example, beef and veal, mutton and lamb, fish and milk (FAO Agricultural Commodity Projections).

TABLE 4

Estimated production, demand and balance for cereals in 1970 and 1980

Regions	Production (million tons) 1970	Production (million tons) 1980	Demand (million tons) 1980	Balance (export availabilities or import requirements)
	Million metric tons			
World	1080·1	1427·42	1365·69	−61·73
Surplus regions				
Australia	12·86	19·22	6·82	−12·40
North America	214·09	301·42	312·97	−11·55
USSR	160·43	181·37	176·50	− 4·87
Eastern European countries	55·86	79·97	77·76	− 2·21
Other developed countries	8·78	14·55	11·27	− 3·28
Latin America	65·27	98·85	82·41	−10·44
Deficit regions				
Western Europe	126·93	163·75	181·01	17·26
Japan	13·05	11·84	34·91	23·07
Africa	43·43	59·79	62·67	2·88
Near East	38·76	50·54	57·93	7·39
Asia and Far East (excl. China)	169·32	232·65	236·20	3·55
China	163·65	210·38	215·51	5·13

Source: FAO/Agricultural Commodity Projections, 1970–1980.

A word of caution is, however, necessary here. These projected surpluses and deficits may not reflect the real situation. An export surplus in a country, as assessed in the FAO Study, simply suggests that demand at the current price is less than the supply at that price, as the FAO projections have not taken into account the effects of possible price changes. Furthermore, no explicit account has been taken of the possible changes in the distribution of income. Recent FAO studies (1972 a, b) indicated that attempts at a more egalitarian distribution of income would raise the total demand for food (and also change its composition) substantially above the level projected for 1980.

TABLE 5

Projected food demand

Region and sub-region	Food demand 1970–1980						Required growth rate of food supply (% per year compound) 1970–1980	
	Calories (No. *per capita* per day)			Protein (g *per capita* per day)				
	1970	1980T	1980H	1970	1980T	1980H	T	H
ASIA								
South Asia	2010	2163	2241	48·8	52·3	54·0	3·6	4·2
East and South-East Asia	2060	2114	2161	48·8	50·6	52·1	3·6	4·0
Japan	2470	2611	2611	76·9	81·4	81·4	1·9	1·9
China	2000	2122	2200	56·6	60·1	62·5	2·9	3·6
Asian centrally planned economies (excluding China)	2130	2256	2313	59·3	63·7	66·7	3·6	4·4
Near East in Asia	2320	2415	2452	65·9	68·4	69·5	3·8	4·0
Israel	2990	3080	3080	91·5	96·8	96·8	3·3	3·3
Average	2050	2176	2243	54·5	57·5	59·3	3·1	3·6
AFRICA								
North-Western Africa	2118	2179	2222	60·1	61·7	62·9	3·4	3·7
Western Africa	2257	2374	2444	59·0	63·4	65·7	3·7	4·2
Central Africa	2112	2232	2284	45·1	48·2	50·2	2·9	3·3
Eastern Africa	2103	2190	2256	59·6	62·3	64·7	3·3	3·8
South Africa	2761	2816	2816	78·6	81·0	81·0	2·9	2·9
Near East in Africa	2597	2704	2730	73·2	76·5	77·4	3·6	4·0
Average	2264	2363	2417	61·0	64·3	66·2	3·5	3·9
LATIN AMERICA								
Central America	2452	2518	2535	62·3	63·3	64·1	4·6	4·8
Caribbean	2381	2466	2540	58·0	60·5	63·0	3·5	4·0
South America	2648	2751	2794	67·1	70·0	71·3	2·8	3·1
Average	2579	2669	2707	65·2	67·5	68·8	3·2	3·5
NORTH AMERICA, EUROPE AND OCEANIA								
Western Europe	3110	3127	3127	88·2	91·9	91·9	1·0	1·0
Eastern Europe	3150	3226	3226	90·9	93·2	93·2	1·1	1·1
North America	3290	3329	3329	98·2	100·6	100·6	1·7	1·7
Oceania	3190	3209	3209	94·4	95·4	95·4	2·2	2·2
Average	3169	3214	3214	91·7	94·6	94·6	1·2	1·2

Source: FAO/Agricultural Commodity Projections, 1970–1980.

T = Trend assumption per income
H = High assumption for income

For instance, it has been estimated that a moderate redistribution of income in 10 Latin American countries would result in an additional demand in 1980 of 9·0 to 9·5%.

Two alternative projections of demand for food are shown in Table 5. The first is the trend (T) alternative that assumes that income will increase broadly in accordance with past trends over the period 1955 to 1968 as interpreted by FAO. The other is the high (H) alternative that assumes that the targets of economic growth established by the United Nations for the Second Development Decade will be met.

Table 5 shows the *per capita* calorie and protein levels for 1980 as implied by the FAO demand projections. It would seem that the regional level calorie and protein consumption might match requirements, but major shortages in many countries would still exist. It is estimated that in 1980 there would still be approximately 40 countries where energy intake would remain below average *per capita* requirement. Indications are that in 1980 there would be no substantial reduction in the absolute numbers of people suffering from undernutrition. This existence of serious nutritional deficiencies, despite the considerable acceleration of the rate of growth of food production and in the face of projected cereal surpluses in the world, will remain a reality in the 1970s.

The rates of growth in food production required to meet the FAO demand projections in the 1970s are shown in the last two columns of Table 5. A comparison with Table 1 shows that the rates of growth in food production required to meet food demand in the developing regions are much higher than those achieved in the last decade, particularly so under the high (H) assumption for income growth.

Targets for the Second Development Decade of the United Nations (DD2)

The Second Development Decade of the United Nations contemplates a 4% rate of growth of agricultural production in the developing countries as a whole. In fact this is the only quantitative agricultural target specified in the international strategy for the DD2.

It is based, however, on the production objectives up to 1975 and 1985 proposed for 62 individual countries in FAO's Provisional Indicative World Plan for Agricultural Development (IWP) and related studies, and shown in Appendix II. A recent analysis indicates that from 1961–1963 (the base period on the IWP) to 1971 the rates of growth proposed for the period up to 1975 were attained in only 21, or one-third, of the 62 countries (FAO, 1973). Although these proposed objectives obviously have no operational significance for the countries concerned, it is noteworthy that they are often lower than the targets in national development plans, while the most frequent criticism of them is that they are too low—thus the shortfall from government objectives is generally even greater.

Actually DD2 has got off to a bad start in the agricultural sector mainly because of wide-spread unfavourable weather. In 1971 agricultural production in the developing countries as a whole increased by only about 1% and in 1972 there was no increase at all. Thus, to meet the target of an average annual rate of growth of 4% in the agricultural production of the developing countries during the decade as a whole, much higher rates are now needed in the remaining eight years.

What are the pre-requisites for accelerating the rate of growth of food production in the developing countries? All that is possible in this paper is to outline certain general considerations. The deepening pool of knowledge which can be made available to farmers in the developing countries, with some adaptive research, provides the potential for increases in food and agricultural production. But the wider use of available technology requires, first, the allocation of resources to produce domestically or import the necessary inputs such as chemical fertilizers and pesticides, etc. and second, an adequate organization to ensure distribution of these inputs. Third, there is a need for an intensified programme of education for farmers, including improvements in the extension services. The fulfilment of these conditions requires the creation of new types of institutions to provide adequate incentives and services to the farmers, as well as the strengthening of the infrastructure for the efficient marketing and distribution of agricultural products.

Directing attention only towards increasing supply in aggregate terms largely ignores basic issues involving distribution of food between individuals, regions and seasons. Scarce inputs and trained manpower have tended to be concentrated in the more favoured agricultural areas and have not always reached the small farmer, thus accentuating disparities both between regions and between individuals within regions. Such efforts, therefore, fail to alleviate under- and malnutrition. Because of the differences in ecological conditions some regional disparities in the rate of agricultural development are inevitable, as in the case of arid areas. Nutritional adequacy will not be easy to attain in such areas unless supported by special welfare measures. Similarly, attention must be paid to seasonal variations in income and consumption levels that require provision of employment opportunities in slack agricultural seasons, if a reasonable minimum nutritional level is to be attained throughout the year.

Annual and seasonal fluctuations in food supplies call for procedures for concerting national and international food stock policies. The need for such reserves* was highlighted recently when many countries, including developed ones, suffered bad harvests due to unfavourable climatic conditions. The Director-General of FAO is proposing to Governments the acceptance of a meaningful concept of minimum world food security against which to assess the adequacy of stock-holding by individual nations.

It is necessary to consider also the international aspects of agricultural development strategy. Even the modest improvement in the food and nutritional situation by 1980 implied by the FAO Commodity Projections is conditional on the ability of many countries to finance food imports, or imports of agricultural inputs needed to produce the food domestically. The needed foreign exchange earnings would in some countries have to come largely from agricultural exports.

Trends in the value of agricultural exports of the developing countries as a whole over the last decade showed an annual rate of increase of 3·3% although the performance of many countries has been less satisfactory. This was accompanied, however, by a decline in the share of the developing countries in total world agricultural trade from 40 to 34% (FAO, 1973). Furthermore, the real value of agricultural exports has continued to decline relative to manufactures, and the terms of trade have moved steadily against developing countries. The difficulties that many countries are now facing in financing their imports and, indeed, their domestic investment are accentuated when they are largely dependent on a single cash crop, the price of which may be susceptible to wide fluctuation.

The situation is further aggravated by the existence of trade barriers and the export subsidising policies of the developed countries. Technological changes in developed countries which result in the replacement of agricultural products create more difficulties. Therefore, agricultural planning and policy-making in developed countries has to be viewed in the light of the needs of the developing countries. Nor will a policy of reducing tariff barriers alone greatly help the developing countries, since the chief beneficiaries will generally be exporters in the developed countries who tend to be more competitive and better organized. A system has to be formulated in which future agricultural planning in developed countries, including agricultural adjustments, is carried out in a manner that will, on the one hand, reduce the need for support measures in the developed countries and, on the other, will increase the developing countries' share in world agricultural exports (FAO, 1972c).

---

*Another effect of population growth has been to increase substantially the size of food reserve that is needed.

The development assistance situation has not been satisfactory either. For the achievement of the DD2 targets, it was considered necessary for developed countries to increase official development assistance on concessional terms to 0·7% of their GNP by 1975. It now seems unlikely that it will reach even half of this target. To make matters worse the terms of such assistance have hardened with the decline in the share of grants in total development assistance.

Agricultural Population and Employment

In the developing countries, agriculture is the mainstay of the bulk of the population. They not only produce their own food but meet their other needs as well from the income earned on farms. The percentage of the population dependent on agriculture is given in Table 6. In Asia, this dependence is estimated for 1970 at 65%. In Africa, the dependence on agriculture is slightly higher at 70%, whereas for Latin America it is only 42%. In contrast to the above, the proportion of the population dependent on

TABLE 6

Mid-year estimates of agricultural population and its share in the total population

	Population dependent on agriculture					Share of agricultural population in total population				
	1950	1960	1970	1980	1985	1950	1960	1970	1980	1985
	Millions					Per cent				
Asia	1069·7	1178·3	1327·3	1473·9	1531·0	78·9	71·6	64·6	57·1	53·3
Africa	171·3	200·0	239·3	290·0	318·4	78·9	74·5	69·5	63·5	60·1
Latin America	87·1	102·6	117·9	130·6	135·2	53·6	48·1	41·6	34·6	31·1
Western Europe	85·4	70·9	57·1	42·8	35·4	28·3	21·7	16·1	11·2	8·9
Eastern Europe	143·0	128·4	109·1	82·2	68·3	53·0	41·1	31·3	21·3	16·8
North America	21·7	14·3	10·0	7·1	6·5	13·0	7·2	4·4	2·7	2·3
Oceania	3·6	4·0	4·3	4·5	4·6	28·9	25·1	22·1	18·8	17·3
World	1581·8	1699·2	1865·0	2031·1	2099·5	63·6	57·0	51·3	45·5	42·4

Source: United Nations Population Estimates; ILO Labour Force Projections 1971; Schulte *et al.* (1972).

agriculture in developed countries of North America, Western Europe and Oceania is significantly lower, ranging from 4 to 22%. Eastern Europe including the USSR, is in an intermediate position with 31% of the population dependent on agriculture. There is a decreasing trend in the percentage dependence both in developed and developing countries. The agricultural labour force follows the same trend as the population dependent on agriculture. The important point to note however is that whereas in the developed countries there has been a decline in the absolute size of the agricultural labour force from 109 to 89 million between the 1960s and 1970s, in the developing countries it continued to rise from 629 to 682 million (Appendix V). Argentina, Chile, Cuba, Gabon, Jamaica and Uruguay are among the few developing countries where the agricultural labour force was already falling in absolute numbers by 1970.

Table 7 shows estimates of the maximum labour force in agriculture and the year when this would be reached in each of the developing regions and in sub-regions. In this calculation, it is assumed that rates of growth in both the total and non-agricultural labour force continue after 1985 at the rates projected for 1980–1985. For the world the maximum labour force in agriculture of 837 million would be reached in 1994. The estimates for the various regions range from 1991 in Latin America to 2004 in Africa, but for some individual countries the maximum will not be reached under these assumptions until well into the next century.

The timing of this turning point depends mainly on the rate of population growth, the initial proportion of the agricultural labour force in the total, and the rate at which non-agricultural employment can be created. The rate of population growth has a very powerful influence, and a faster rate not only delays the time when the agricultural labour force ceases to grow, but also results in a higher maximum level. As compared with the development period of the countries that are now industrialized, population growth in the developing countries is much more rapid, while modern industry absorbs progressively much less labour per unit of output. There are now obvious limits to the rate of expansion of employment in industrial-cum-urban sectors due to the usual constraints on the possible rates of economic growth, the capital-intensive bias of industrialization, and, last but not least, the high rate of increase of the urban population itself.

Much of the burden of the rapidly growing labour force in the rural areas will have to be borne by the agricultural sector, where already a high level of underemployment, both open and disguised, is widespread and is, in many places, spilling over into the towns through migration.

It is no doubt imperative to adopt all possible measures to increase employment opportunities in the rural-cum-agricultural sector, but the task of creating additional jobs commensurate with the increase in the rural labour

TABLE 7

Maximum economically active population in agriculture

	1985				Average Annual rate of Growth 1980–1985			Year when EAA is maximum	Population when EAA is at maximum		
	P	EA	EAA	EAA/ EA	EA	EAA	EA/ EAA		EA	EAA	EAA/ EA
	millions			%				AD	millions		%
ASIA	2874	1146	606	52·9	2·0	0·6	3·8	1992	1316	632	48·0
South Asia	1067	383	217	56·7	2·5	1·1	4·3	2001	572	242	42·3
East and South-East Asia	479	177	98	55·3	2·7	1·2	4·6	2001	270	110	40·7
China	965	440	244	55·5	1·5	0·2	3·3	1987	454	245	54·0
Other Asian centrally planned economies	51	25	14	55·3	2·3	0·7	4·6	1991	29	15	51·7
Near East in Asia	187	59	27	46·9	2·8	0·7	4·7	1992	71	28	39·8
AFRICA	530	187	117	62·3	2·5	1·4	4·5	2006	315	156	49·5
North-Western Africa	58	14	6	44·7	3·3	1·5	4·8	2001	24	7	30·6
Western Africa	155	60	38	63·6	2·4	1·4	4·1	2012	116	49	42·1
Central Africa	52	20	13	67·0	2·1	0·8	2·4	2011	34	16	47·1
Eastern Africa	149	60	43	71·4	2·6	1·4	5·6	2002	92	49	53·6
Southern Africa	4	2	1	70·0	2·1	0·9	4·9	1998	2	1	57·2
South Africa	30	9	2	25·4	2·2	1·0	2·7	2006	15	3	20·3
Near East in Africa	81	22	12	55·9	2·9	2·0	4·0	2029	78	29	37·2
LATIN AMERICA	435	130	40	31·1	2·7	0·5	3·7	1991	153	41	26·9
Central America	112	31	11	35·8	3·3	0·8	4·7	1991	39	11	29·7
Caribbean	36	13	5	38·3	2·3	0·9	3·2	2004	20	5	27·4
South America	287	86	24	28·3	2·6	0·4	3·5	1990	99	25	25·0
WORLD	4948	1957	820	41·9	1·9	0·4	3·0	1994	2308	837	36·3

P = Total population
EA = Total economically active population
EAA = Population economically active in agriculture.

force will prove formidable, if not impossible, unless the growth of their number can be arrested earlier than the projected dates by slower population growth.

The large and still increasing agricultural labour force of the developing countries has to share a small and only slowly growing market for agricultural products. The domestic demand is limited because of the low incomes of a larger proportion of the people, while the growth of the export market is also limited. It is obviously essential to do all that is possible to increase the demand for agricultural products, through measures such as income re-distribution and the reduction of trade barriers, and to increase production up to the ceiling imposed by demand.

The wide variations in labour requirements per hectare of the different crops would seem to offer scope for increasing employment opportunities by influencing the product-mix or pattern of production. However, although changes in the product-mix can have a substantial effect on employment, it is difficult to influence it deliberately in the interests of employment-creation, since it must be largely determined by the patterns of demand.

The main way in which agricultural employment can be affected is through measures influencing the type of technology used to produce a given output. If production is increased by extending the cultivated area, employment is increased in similar proportion, but the possibilities of doing this are becoming steadily less, since even where there is still much unused land it is increasingly inaccessible and costly to open up. More and more of the increase in production, as said before, has to come from higher yields per hectare, and much depends on the methods used to increase yields. Improvements such as irrigation and the use of better seeds, fertilizers and pesticides reduce labour requirements per unit of yield, but raise them for hectare if the yield increase is big enough.

Large increases in the productivity of labour, such as are made possible by mechanization, are not appropriate when a small and only slowly expanding market for agricultural products has to be shared among an increasing and largely underemployed agricultural labour force. If too great increases in productivity are made by certain favoured members of the labour force, this must result in worse underemployment for many of the rest, since they cannot move quickly enough into non-agricultural jobs.

Governments can affect the technology used to increase production by influencing the relative prices of the different factors of production. The recent break-through in cereal crops has introduced labour-using bias into technical progress by making possible intensification of land use, which is neither related to size of holding nor to a high degree of mechanization.

Even with such measures, it is clearly not possible for agriculture to provide jobs for all the new entrants into the rural labour force while the present rapid growth of population continues; considerable attention is also needed to the provision of full-time and part-time employment opportunities in non-agricultural activities in rural areas. Public work programmes could use the non-utilized labour resources to help build irrigation works, roads, communications systems, schools, hospitals, etc. It is also important to take maximum advantage of the possibilities of village industries, particularly processing industries of agricultural commodities, for which larger agricultural production envisaged in development plans offers considerable scope for expansion.

The above are only some of the suggestions made to accommodate the expanding labour force within the rural sectors. To what extent the measures or programmes taken up to implement them can cope with the problem of employment, it is difficult to foresee. It is quite likely that some of them may turn out "make-work" schemes which, as such, are not economically feasible. As it appears now, the problem of employment would seem, as the FAO IWP study stated, to be far more intractable than that of food supply. In a sense the two are inter-related. It is the unemployed and under-employed who do not get adequate food, and paradoxically the majority of them are engaged on food production as their main activity, i.e. small farmers, landless workers. The overall balance between food supply and requirement can be attained with any foreseeable rate of population growth, but it is the rural poor who cannot equate their food requirement with the available supply, and improve their standard of living for lack of gainful employment. Their growing number makes it difficult to reap the benefits of technological advances in agriculture.

References

FAO (1971). "Agricultural Commodity Projections, 1970–1980". Vol. 1, pp.42–89. Rome.

FAO (1972a). *Monthly Bull. Agric. Econ. Stat.* **21,** 3 (March), 1–11.

FAO (1972b). "Perspective Study of Agricultural Development for South America" (provisional version). Chapter III, p.14. Rome.

FAO (1972c). "Agricultural Adjustment in Developed Countries". Rome.

FAO (1973). *Monthly Bull. Agric. Econ. Stat.* **22,** 4 (April), 1–17.

FAO/WHO (1973). "Energy and Protein Requirements", Report of a Joint FAO/WHO Ad Hoc Expert Group. p.74. Rome.

Schulte, W., Naiken, L. and Bruni, A., (1972). FAO *Monthly Bull. Agric. Econ. Stat.* **21,** 1, 1–10.

APPENDIX I

Mid-year estimates and projections of the population and rate of growth

Region and sub-region	Total population 1950	1960	1970	1980	Annual rates of growth (compound) 1950–1960	1960–1970	1970–1980
	millions				%		
ASIA	1355·3	1645·3	2055·8	2581·0	2·0	2·2	2·3
South Asia	451·5	552·2	715·3	938·9	2·0	2·6	2·8
East and South-East Asia	188·8	239·4	314·5	416·2	2·4	2·8	2·8
Japan	82·9	93·2	103·5	116·3	1·2	1·1	1·2
Asian centrally planned economies	556·3	663·5	795·9	939·5	1·8	1·8	1·6
China	532·9	635·9	759·6	893·9	1·8	1·8	1·6
Other Asian centrally planned economies	23·4	27·6	36·3	45·6	1·6	2·8	2·2
Near East in Asia	70·6	90·1	117·3	157·6	2·5	3·7	3·0
Israel	1·3	2·1	2·9	3·6	5·3	3·2	2·2
Others	3·9	4·8	6·4	8·9			
AFRICA	217·3	269·5	344·5	456·8	2·2	2·5	2·9
North-Western Africa	20·8	26·4	35·1	49·4	2·4	2·9	3·5
Western Africa	64·2	79·5	101·3	133·4	2·1	2·5	2·8
Central Africa	24·8	29·4	35·9	45·8	1·7	2·0	2·5
Eastern Africa	62·5	77·1	97·9	128·8	2·2	2·4	2·8
Southern Africa	1·9	2·2	2·7	3·4	1·7	2·0	2·4
South Africa	12·5	15·9	20·1	26·0	2·5	2·4	2·6
Near East in Africa	30·6	39·0	51·5	70·0	2·5	2·9	3·1
LATIN AMERICA	162·4	213·4	283·3	377·2	2·8	2·9	2·9
Central America	35·3	48·1	67·3	94·5	3·2	3·4	3·5

Continued

Appendix I contd.

Region and sub-region	Total population				Annual rates of growth (compound)		
	1950	1960	1970	1980	1950–1960	1960–1970	1970–1980
	millions				%		
Mexico	26·3	36·1	50·7	71·4	3·2	3·4	3·4
Other Central American countries	9·0	12·0	16·6	23·1	3·0	3·2	3·4
Caribbean	15·5	19·0	23·8	29·9	2·0	2·3	2·3
South America	110·2	144·6	190·0	250·3	2·8	2·8	2·8
Brazil	52·0	69·7	93·0	123·7	3·0	2·9	2·8
River Plate countries	20·6	25·1	29·6	34·5	2·0	1·7	1·5
Other South American countries	37·6	49·8	67·4	92·1	2·8	3·1	3·2
Others	1·4	1·7	2·2	2·5	2·0	2·1	1·7
WESTERN EUROPE	302·2	326·2	355·9	381·8	0·8	0·9	0·7
EEC	213·2	229·5	250·3	267·4	0·7	0·9	0·7
Scandinavian countries	14·3	15·5	16·6	17·8	0·8	0·7	0·6
Other Western European countries	72·3	78·7	86·5	94·3	0·9	0·9	0·9
Others	2·4	2·5	2·5	2·3	0·3	−0·1	−0·6
EASTERN EUROPE	269·8	312·6	348·9	385·9	1·5	1·1	1·0
USSR	180·1	214·2	242·6	270·7	1·8	1·2	1·1
Other Eastern European countries	89·7	98·4	106·3	115·2	0·9	0·8	0·8
NORTH AMERICA	166·1	198·7	227·6	260·7	1·8	1·4	1·4
OCEANIA	12·6	15·8	19·4	24·0	2·3	2·1	2·2
WORLD	2485·7	2981·5	3635·4	4467·4	1·8	2·0	2·1

Source: UN Population division.

APPENDIX II

Indicators of population and food situation with IWP targets

Country	Population	*Per capita* income	Total food demand[a]	Total food production	Agricultural productivity IWP objectives[b]		Net food cereal imports 1966–1970 ('000 tons)	Imports as percentages of domestic production	Persons per ha of agricultural land
	1955–1970			1953–1971	1961/3–1975	1975–1985			
DEVELOPING COUNTRIES									
Food production increased as much as or more than estimated demand									
Gabon	0·9	4·8	2·7	3·6	1·4	1·3	–	–	–
Cyprus	1·3	3·8	2·5	5·8	–	–	85	53·7	1·5
Angola	1·4	2·2	2·6	2·7	–	–	−71	–	6·1
Cameroon	2·0	1·7	2·7	3·3	2·9	2·7	60	7·5	0·8
Togo	2·4	0·3	2·5	5·4	2·8	3·8	–	–	–
Sri Lanka	2·4	1·6	3·0	3·6	4·3	4·1	1013	69·8	6·3
Bolivia	2·5	0·8	2·9	4·8	3·1	3·2	186	38·3	1·6
Tanzania	2·5	1·1	3·1	3·2	3·6	3·0	28	2·7	–
Egypt	2·5	2·3	3·7	3·7	3·2	2·9	1558	21·3	11·7
Malawi	2·6	2·5	3·8	4·7	3·3	3·4	−55	–	1·5
Ghana	2·7	0·8	3·0	3·9	3·1	3·4	124	20·3	3·1
Sudan	2·9	1·7	3·9	4·3	3·6	3·7	158	7·9	2·2
Guatemala[e]	2·9	2·3	4·1	4·2	–	4·4	83	10·6	3·5
Lebanon	3·0	0·7	3·3	5·8	3·7	3·7	462	669·6	8·4
Nicaragua	3·0	2·1	3·9	5·1	–	5·3[e]	49	14·2	2·3
Malaysia	3·0	2·1	4·1	5·1	–	–	650	42·0	1·8

Continued

Country	Population	*Per capita* income	Total food demand[a]	Total food production	Agricultural productivity IWP objectives[b]		Net food cereal imports 1966–1970 ('000 tons)	Imports as percentages of domestic production	Persons per ha of agricultural land
	1955–1970			1953–1971	1961/3–1975	1975–1985			
Food production increased as much as or more than estimated demand									
Brazil	3·0	3·0	4·0	4·1	2·5	3·0	1434	6·6	3·1
Thailand	3·1	3·2	4·6	5·3	4·4	4·3	2602	–	3·1
Rhodesia	3·2	1·4	3·9	3·9	–	–	–	–	2·9
Ivory Coast	3·3	1·0	3·7	4·9	4·7	3·3	122	19·3	0·6
Ecuador	3·3	1·2	4·0	5·2	2·7	3·3	77	13·6	1·6
Honduras[e]	3·3	1·7	4·2	4·2	–	5·3[e]	9	2·1	3·1
Mexico	3·4	2·8	4·3	4·9	4·0	4·3	—1229	–	2·1
Venezuela	3·7	1·5	4·2	6·0	3·6	4·2	717	77·3	2·1
Costa Rica	3·8	2·7	4·8	5·7	–	5·1[e]	87	46·0	1·8
Food production increased less than estimated demand but more than population									
Sierra Leone	1·3	4·2	3·2	2·4	–	–	69	14·5	0·7
Mozambique	1·4	2·8	2·9	2·7	–	–	45	5·4	2·8
Argentina	1·7	1·9	2·0	1·8	2·5	2·5	—846	–	0·9
Mauritania	1·8	4·1	2·8	2·4	2·7	3·4	–	–	–
Ethiopia	1·9	2·1	3·1	2·3	2·5	2·9	35	0·6	2·0
Burma	2·0	2·6	3·1	2·4	–	–	—650	–	1·7
China	2·1	0·7	2·6	2·3	–	–	3566	1·8	7·7
India	2·3	1·6	3·2	2·4	3·4	3·9	6546	6·1	3·4
Turkey	2·6	2·7	3·7	3·2	–	–	318	1·9	1·3

Khmer	2·7	2·1	4·2	3·5	–	–	−228	–	2·4
Korea Republic	2·8	4·7	4·8	4·4	3·4	2·4	1470	19·0	14·0
Morocco	2·9	0·6	3·2	3·0	3·5[d]	3·6	469	10·0	2·8
Peru	2·9	1·7	3·9	3·0	2·9	3·1	601	43·5	4·8
Pakistan	2·9	1·8	4·1	3·0	4·1	4·6	1314	4·8	4·6
Iran	2·9	6·1	6·5	3·3	3·8	3·8	151	2·4	2·5
Zambia	3·0	3·9	4·9	4·3	5·0	4·8	−110	–	0·9
Colombia	3·2	1·4	3·8	3·2	3·1	3·6	260	13·6	4·0
Panama	3·2	3·9	4·8	4·4	–	–	45	19·0	2·6
Food production increased less than population									
Tunisia	1·8	2·0	3·2	1·1	3·4[c]	4·0	352	66·7	1·1
Jamaica	1·9	3·0	3·3	1·5	–	–	236	3367·1	8·3
Zaire	2·3	0·4	2·6	0·1	2·7	3·4	156	32·5	2·4
Indonesia	2·4	0·1	2·5	2·1	–	4·3[d]	811	4·3	3·8
Algeria	2·4	1·5	3·4	−0·1	3·2[c]	4·6	576	28·9	2·0
Uganda	2·5	1·6	3·3	1·8	3·9	2·9	34	2·8	1·7
Chile	2·5	1·8	3·3	2·1	2·6	3·2	484	26·2	2·1
Mauritius	2·6	0·8	3·0	1·3	–	–	121	–	8·0
Trinidad and Tobago	2·6	4·6	4·9	1·9	–	–	162	1247·7	7·6
Paraguay	2·8	1·0	3·1	2·6	3·2	2·5	70	24·2	2·5
Syria	2·9	2·9	4·5	2·0	3·3	3·7	214	16·4	1·0
Nigeria	3·0	1·6	3·7	2·0	3·1	3·4	178	2·3	3·1
El Salvador	3·0	1·9	4·1	2·1	–	3·7[e]	87	18·1	5·5
Kenya	3·0	2·9	4·7	2·6	3·8	3·9	−134	–	6·5
Guyana	3·1	1·1	3·7	2·5	–	–	−43	–	0·9
Jordan	3·1	5·4	6·5	1·8	3·1	4·0	162	92·6	1·7
Saudi Arabia	3·1	5·5	5·7	2·9	3·6	3·9	448	178·7	6·5
Philippines	3·3	1·7	4·3	3·2	4·2	4·6	648	9·4	4·5
Iraq	3·3	2·9	5·2	2·8	3·4	4·3	39	1·8	1·3
Dominican Republic	3·6	0·6	3·9	2·2	–	–	100	43·5	4·1

Continued

Country	Population	*Per capita* income	Total food demand[a]	Total food production	Agricultural productivity IWP objectives[b]		Net food cereal imports 1966–1970 ('000 tons)	Imports as percentages of domestic production	Persons per ha of agricultural land
	1955–1970			1953–1971	1961/3–1975	1975–1985			
Countries having negative income growth rate									
Uruguay	1·3	−0·8	1·2	0·8	2·6	3·1	−90	–	1·5
Chad	1·5	−1·5	0·6	0·9	2·7	3·0	8	1·0	0·5
Upper Volta	1·8	−1·4	1·2	4·8	2·4	2·9	23	2·2	1·0
Central African Republic	1·9	−1·7	1·2	2·8	2·8	2·5	–	–	–
Haiti	1·9	−0·1	1·8	1·0	–	–	36	7·9	13·2
Senegal	2·2	−2·2	1·2	3·3	3·2	3·2	244	33·1	0·7
Madagascar	2·4	−0·5	2·1	2·8	3·1	3·1	−4	–	2·1
Niger	2·6	−1·4	2·0	4·1	3·0	3·2	–	–	0·3
Dahomey	2·9	−3·5	0·7	1·5	3·4	3·4	17	6·1	1·8
DEVELOPED COUNTRIES									
Food production increased as much as or more than estimated demand									
Germany, Democratic Republic	−0·3	5·4	0·8	1·6	–	–	2216	31·1	3·6
Ireland	0·03	3·1	0·3	2·0	–	–	470	34·1	2·6
Malta	0·1	4·0	1·2	3·2	–	–	93	2317·4	20·0

Hungary	0·3	4·8	1·7	2·7	–	–	−7	–	1·8
Austria	0·4	4·2	1·1	2·4	–	–	448	14·0	4·4
UK	0·6	2·1	0·8	3·0	–	–	8155	58·6	7·7
Belgium-Luxembourg	0·6	3·3	1·2	2·4	–	–	2573	131·8	11·0
Finland	0·7	3·7	1·0	2·6	–	–	48	1·8	1·7
Czechoslovakia	0·7	4·2	1·7	1·8	–	–	1695	22·7	2·8
Italy	0·7	4·8	2·3	2·3	–	–	6478	41·2	3·6
Greece	0·8	5·4	2·3	4·0	–	–	8	0·3	2·5
Bulgaria	0·8	6·8	2·8	4·2	–	–	−270	–	1·7
Spain	0·9	5·0	3·0	3·4	–	–	2024	17·6	1·7
Germany, Federal Republic	1·0	4·1	1·9	2·4	–	–	5402	28·7	7·3
France	1·0	4·4	2·0	3·1	–	–	−8287	–	2·6
Yugoslavia	1·1	5·0	2·3	3·6	–	–	−33	–	2·5
Romania	1·1	5·6	2·7	3·1	–	–	−1181	–	1·9
Poland	1·2	4·8	2·1	2·9	–	–	2052	11·6	2·1
Netherlands	1·3	3·3	1·7	2·7	–	–	3081	193·1	15·0
USA	1·4	2·0	1·5	2·0	–	–	−39752	–	1·2
USSR	1·4	5·6	2·9	3·9	–	–	−2817	–	1·7
Iceland	1·8	1·8	1·9	2·5	–	–	–	–	–
New Zealand	2·0	1·8	2·1	2·9	–	–	818	12·5	3·7
Australia	2·0	3·0	2·3	2·8	–	–	−7254	–	0·3
Canada	2·1	2·4	2·4	2·6	–	–	−11775	–	0·5
South Africa	2·5	2·7	3·3	4·3	–	–	−1098	–	–
Israel	3·4	5·2	4·9	7·6	–	–	998	443·9	7·0
Food production increased less than estimated demand but more than population									
Denmark	0·7	3·9	1·3	1·2	–	–	259	3·9	1·8
Portugal	0·8	4·6	2·5	1·2	–	–	744	43·4	2·2

Continued

Appendix II contd.

Country	Population	*Per capita* income	Total food demand[a]	Total food production	Agricultural productivity IWP objectives[b]		Net food cereal imports 1966–1970 ('000 tons)	Imports as percentages of domestic production	Persons per ha of agricultural land
	1955–1970			1953–1971	1961/3–1975	1975–1985			
Food production increased less than estimated demand but more than population									
Japan	1·0	9·4	3·6	3·2	–	–	12554	66·2	18·5
Albania	2·9	4·3	4·7	3·5	–	–	67	11·6	3·8
Food production increased less than population									
Sweden	0·7	3·4	1·0	0·5	–	–	−409	–	3·9
Norway	0·8	3·5	1·2	0·6	–	–	699	91·3	4·8
Switzerland	1·6	2·5	2·0	1·4	–	–	1262	192·4	15·6

[a]Calculated on the basis of the growth rates of population and *per capita* income for 1955–1970 given in Columns 2 and 3 and the estimates of farmgate elasticity of demand for food given the FAO Agricultural Commodity Projections, 1970 1980 (FAO, 1971).

[b]Based on the targets proposed in the Indicative World Plan for Agricultural Development (IWP) (FAO, 1969) on the basis of a detailed assessment of the economic and technical feasibility of production increases. It should be noted that the IWP objectives relate to agricultural production comprising food and non-food items; the growth rates for food and agricultural production, particularly for developing countries, are however usually of similar magnitudes. –: Not covered by IWP.

[c]1965–1975

[d]1970–1980, from "Perspective Study of Agricultural Development (Provisional) for Indonesia 1970–1980, FAO Rome, 1972.

[e]Projected growth rates 1970–1990 of "Trend variant with high export growth" from the FAO Perspective Study of Agricultural Development for Central America.

APPENDIX III

Current levels of per capita *food consumption in relation to nutritional requirements*

Region and sub-regions	Cereals		Starchy roots		Sugar		Pulses and nuts		Fruits and veg		Meat, eggs fish and milk		Oils and fats		Total supply		Total requirements	
	C	P	C	P	C	P	C	P	C	P	C	P	C	P	C	P	C	P
ASIA																		
South Asia	1405	32·3	37	0·5	173	0·5	157	8·6	35	0·6	120	6·3	86	–	2010	48·8	2230	37·0
East and South-East Asia	1396	28·7	178	1·6	108	0·1	95	5·5	63	2·0	120	10·9	88	–	2060	48·8	2210	35·0
Japan	1238	25·8	114	0·7	282	–	148	12·7	145	5·9	314	31·8	229	–	2470	76·9	2340	36·1
China	1340	31·8	217	2·9	42	–	126	10·8	39	2·2	165	8·8	67	0·1	1000	56·6	2360	38·4
Asian centrally planned economies	1547	33·7	172	2·3	20	–	124	10·1	79	3·3	163	9·8	26	0·1	2130	59·3	2240	36·9
North-East in Asia	1502	45·1	33	0·6	100	–	91	4·7	157	3·3	168	12·2	183	–	2320	65·9	2460	46·7
Israel	1067	34·6	79	1·8	430	–	126	4·8	241	6·0	593	44·3	452	–	2990	91·5	2570	37·8
Average	1380	31·7	136	1·7	114	0·2	131	9·0	54	1·6	153	9·7	90	–	2050	54·4	2300	37·8
AFRICA																		
North-West Africa	1386	44·4	23	0·5	224	–	57	3·3	93	2·0	138	9·9	197	–	2118	60·1	2410	50·8
West Africa	1010	30·3	677	10·1	43	–	152	7·9	33	1·1	95	9·6	187	–	2257	59·0	2320	41·1
Central Africa	636	14·6	1036	9·7	53	–	217	11·1	71	1·3	104	10·2	93	–	2112	45·1	2280	37·3
East Africa	1123	30·3	330	2·9	94	–	218	12·7	101	1·8	164	11·9	73	–	2103	59·6	2320	40·1
South Africa	1562	42·9	33	0·7	398	–	53	3·2	55	1·5	492	30·3	178	–	2761	78·6	2450	37·2
North-East in Africa	1662	47·4	161	1·6	169	0·1	87	5·5	124	4·7	217	13·8	180	0·1	2597	73·2	2460	43·2
Average	1176	33·3	441	5·2	114	–	152	8·5	76	1·9	158	12·1	145	–	2262	61·0	2350	41·5

Continued

Appendix III contd.

Region and sub-regions	Cereals		Starchy roots		Sugar		Pulses and nuts		Fruits and veg		Meat, eggs fish and milk		Oils and fats		Total supply		Total requirements	
	C	P	C	P	C	P	C	P	C	P	C	P	C	P	C	P	C	P
LATIN AMERICA																		
Central America	1243	31·6	48	0·5	418	0·2	195	11·9	99	2·0	371	22·8	218	–	2381	58·0	2280	35·6
Mexico	1270	33·2	36	0·4	452	0·2	220	13·3	110	2·1	281	15·9	198	–	2562	65·1	2330	38·1
Others	1161	26·7	86	0·9	314	0·1	120	7·7	64	1·5	213	16·7	163	–	2121	53·6	2250	35·8
Caribbean	888	21·4	262	3·3	405	–	141	8·3	96	2·2	371	22·8	218	–	2381	58·0	2280	35·6
South America	928	22·7	373	4·2	432	0·1	181	10·6	88	1·9	446	27·5	200	0·1	2648	67·1	2420	38·0
Brazil	984	22·9	464	3·9	494	0·1	297	17·3	63	1·2	359	21·3	163	0·1	2820	66·8	2390	38·9
River Plate countries	932	26·5	242	4·2	349	–	38	2·4	147	3·4	946	57·4	322	0·1	2976	94·0	2630	38·8
Others	850	21·0	305	4·8	382	–	84	4·9	96	2·3	347	22·7	196	–	2260	55·7	2370	36·5
Average	1000	24·8	287	3·2	426	0·1	181	10·7	91	1·9	396	24·5	198	–	2579	65·2	2380	37·7
NORTH AMERICA																		
EUROPE and OCEANIA																		
Europe	1202	34·6	209	5·1	381	–	67	3·0	133	4·3	695	42·2	433	0·3	3130	89·5	2570	40·0
West Europe	902	27·0	176	4·3	377	–	76	2·9	186	5·2	827	48·5	562	0·3	3110	88·2	2570	40·0
EEC	829	24·7	174	4·2	404	–	67	2·5	178	5·1	904	52·7	610	0·3	3170	89·6	2570	39·7
Scandinavian countries	664	20·7	173	4·2	454	–	35	1·2	122	2·0	968	54·9	484	0·2	2900	83·2	2690	40·6
Others	1156	34·9	184	4·5	285	–	109	1·2	220	6·2	581	35·3	440	0·2	2970	85·3	2510	41·0
East Europe	1505	42·3	242	5·9	385	–	58	3·2	79	3·4	560	35·8	323	0·3	3150	90·9	2570	40·0
USSR	1544	43·6	265	6·4	412	–	60	3·5	68	2·9	540	35·6	293	0·2	3180	92·2	2560	39·3

Others	1416	39·3	190	4·6	323	–	55	2·6	104	4·5	611	36·2	392	0·6	3090	87·8
North America	650	15·9	102	2·4	540	0·1	101	4·1	179	4·9	1141	70·7	573	0·1	3290	98·2
Oceania	818	22·6	100	2·4	552	–	58	2·2	147	3·5	1143	63·4	369	0·3	3190	94·4
Average	1063	29·9	182	4·4	422	–	75	3·2	144	4·4	809	49·3	473	0·3	3170	91·7

Others	2590	41·4
North America	2640	39·8
Oceania	2660	38·9
Average	2590	39·8

C = Calories *per capita* per day

P = Grams of protein *per capita* per day

Source: FAO food balance sheets, some constructed for a period around 1970, some extrapolated to 1970 from 1964–1966 and the rest for the most recent year available varying between 1965–1970.

APPENDIX IV

Daily per capita *calories and protein supplies and requirements by country*[a]

Country	Calories			Protein		
	Supply[b] (No. *per capita* per day)	Requirements (No. *per capita* per day)	Supply/ requirements %	Supply[b] (g *per capita* per day)	Requirements (g *per capita* per day)	Supply/ requirements %
Food production increased as much or more than estimated demand						
DEVELOPING COUNTRIES						
Ghana	2070	2300	90	43·0	36·5	118
Ivory Coast	2440	2310	106	55·2	35·7	115
Togo	2320	2300	101	53·8	37·6	143
Angola	1980	2350	84	41·5	38·0	109
Cameroon	2340	2320	101	60·8	38·1	160
Gabon	2210	2340	94	55·7	34·9	160
Tanzania	1700	2320	73	42·5	37·3	114
Malawi	2400	2320	103	63·1	50·2	126
Rhodesia	2620	2390	110	74·8	42·8	175
Honduras	2200	2260	97	55·0	36·8	149
Nicaragua	2330	2250	104	63·2	36·7	172
Mexico	2560	2330	110	65·1	38·1	171
Bolivia	2000	2390	84	49·7	38·7	128
Brazil	2820	2390	118	66·8	38·9	172
Ecuador	1970	2290	86	45·5	38·4	118
Venezuela	2430	2470	98	59·7	36·7	163

Costa Rica	2370	2240	106	62·0	34·3	181
Guatemala	2020	2190	92	50·2	34·8	144
Egypt	2770	2510	110	79·9	45·7	175
Sudan	2220	2350	94	60·1	38·0	158
Cyprus	2660	2480	107	85·5	39·4	217
Lebanon	2360	2480	95	69·9	41·3	169
Malaysia	2230	2240	100	50·1	34·0	147
Sri Lanka	2390	2220	108	49·1	35·5	138
Thailand	2220	2220	100	50·5	34·4	147
DEVELOPED COUNTRIES						
USA	3300	2640	125	98·6	39·7	248
Canada	3200	2660	120	95·8	35·9	267
Belgium-Luxembourg	3230	2640	122	91·6	40·9	224
France	3270	2520	130	102·6	38·7	265
Germany, Federal Republic	3180	2670	119	83·0	41·4	200
Italy	3020	2520	120	87·9	38·6	228
Netherlands	3200	2690	119	85·0	40·9	208
Austria	3230	2630	123	86·3	40·9	211
Finland	2940	2710	108	90·2	37·8	239
Greece	2920	2500	117	97·9	38·5	254
Iceland	2890	2660	109	97·9	39·8	246
Ireland	3510	2510	140	96·4	38·3	252
Malta	2810	2480	113	88·4	40·6	218
Spain	2770	2460	113	79·9	38·7	206
UK	3170	2520	126	86·8	39·1	222
Yugoslavia	3130	2540	123	91·6	46·3	198

Continued

Appendix IV contd.

Country	Calories			Protein		
	Supply[b] (No. *per capita* per day)	Requirements (No. *per capita* per day)	Supply/ requirements %	Supply[b] (g *per capita* per day)	Requirements (g *per capita* per day)	Supply/ requirements %
DEVELOPED COUNTRIES						
Australia	3240	2660	122	97·9	39·9	245
New Zealand	3380	2640	128	108·4	34·5	314
USSR	3210	2560	125	94·6	39·3	241
Bulgaria	3180	2500	127	90·9	45·8	198
Czechoslovakia	3100	2470	126	86·8	37·8	230
Germany, Democratic Republic	3160	2620	121	81·1	41·4	196
Hungary	3190	2630	121	97·9	41·4	236
Poland	3160	2620	121	95·4	40·8	234
Romania	3000	2650	113	87·2	45·2	193
Israel	2990	2570	116	91·1	37·8	241
South Africa	2760	2450	113	78·6	37·2	211
Food production increased less than estimated demand but more than population						
DEVELOPING COUNTRIES						
Morocco	2220	2420	92	62·2	46·7	133
Mauritania	2110	2310	91	77·2	35·2	219
Sierra Leone	2250	2300	98	49·9	38·8	129

Ethiopia	1980	2330	85	66·4	39·9	166
Zambia	2330	2310	101	70·8	39·3	180
Mozambique	2210	2340	94	43·4	41·7	104
Panama	2370	2310	102	59·2	35·2	168
Colombia	2140	2320	92	50·0	35·1	142
Peru	2320	2350	99	61·1	37·3	164
Argentina	3050	2650	115	97·3	39·0	249
Turkey	2760	2520	110	77·9	48·2	162
Iran	2030	2410	84	55·2	43·9	126
India	1940	2210	88	47·9	36·8	130
Pakistan	2350	2310	102	53·5	38·2	140
Burma	2010	2160	93	44·1	34·6	127
Korea, Republic of	2510	2350	107	69·0	40·0	172
China[c]	2000	2360	85	56·6	38·4	147
Khmer	2230	2220	100	57·7	35·4	163
DEVELOPED COUNTRIES						
Portugal	2920	2450	119	81·8	39·4	208
Denmark	3180	2690	118	89·7	41·4	217
Japan	2470	2340	106	76·9	36·1	213
Albania	2400	2410	100	74·2	39·6	187
Food production increased less than population						
DEVELOPING COUNTRIES						
Algeria	1980	2400	82	55·9	55·8	100
Nigeria	2290	2360	97	59·9	42·9	140

Continued

Appendix IV contd.

Country	Calories			Protein		
	Supply[b] (No. *per capita* per day)	Requirements (No. *per capita* per day)	Supply/requirements %	Supply[b] (g *per capita* per day)	Requirements (g *per capita* per day)	Supply/requirements %
	Food production increased less than population					
DEVELOPING COUNTRIES						
Zaire	2030	2220	91	34·4	37·6	91
Kenya	2200	2320	95	68·0	38·8	175
Mauritius	2360	2270	104	47·7	36·5	131
Uganda	2050	2330	88	60·4	37·3	162
Tunisia	2200	2390	92	64·8	50·2	129
Dominican Republic	2140	2260	95	48·5	36·9	131
Jamaica	2330	2240	104	59·7	33·1	180
Trinidad and Tobago	2440	2420	101	66·8	36·9	181
Chile	2560	2440	105	65·9	36·5	180
Guyana	2080	2270	92	46·5	33·6	138
Paraguay	2540	2310	110	65·4	35·7	183
El Salvador	1850	2290	81	45·2	37·2	122
Saudi Arabia	2080	2420	86	56·2	47·5	118
Syria	2450	2480	99	69·2	46·8	133
Iraq	2050	2410	85	57·8	42·5	136
Jordan	2400	2460	98	64·8	45·8	141
Indonesia	1750	2160	81	38·2	36·1	106
Philippines	2040	2260	90	53·2	33·3	160

DEVELOPED COUNTRIES						
Norway	2940	2680	110	81·9	41·6	197
Sweden	2850	2690	106	80·0	41·7	192
Switzerland	3190	2690	118	85·8	41·4	207
COUNTRIES HAVING NEGATIVE INCOME GROWTH RATE						
Dahomey	2260	2300	98	52·2	39·6	132
Niger	2240	2350	95	79·3	39·2	202
Senegal	2380	2380	100	65·5	34·7	189
Upper Volta	2100	2370	89	71·1	45·2	157
Central African Republic	2190	2260	97	47·5	36·0	132
Chad	2250	2380	94	76·6	39·5	194
Madagascar	2240	2270	99	51·2	36·6	140
Haiti	2000	2260	88	46·5	36·0	129
Uruguay	2740	2670	103	90·8	39·6	229

[a]Based on FAO Food Balance Sheets, some constructed for 1970, some extrapolated to 1970 from 1964–1966 and the rest of as recent years as available varying between 1965 to 1970. In general, the above figures reflect the present situation.

[b]Based on the most recent FAO/WHO standards (formulated by the FAO/WHO Expert Committee on Energy and Protein Requirements, Rome, (report in press).

[c]There is considerable uncertainty about the figures for China in these tables. The *per capita* supply of calories has, according to some experts' opinion, been underestimated by at least 5%.

APPENDIX V

Mid-year estimates of economically active population in agriculture and related rates of growth

Region and sub-region	1950	1960	1970 millions	1980	1985	Average annual growth rate (compound) 1950–1960	1960–1970 %	1970–1980	1980–1985
ASIA	450·68	512·36	550·60	587·49	606·46	1·3	0·7	0·6	0·6
South Asia	156·86	167·83	186·38	205·51	216·89	0·7	1·1	1·0	1·1
East and South-East Asia	60·49	69·46	79·98	91·35	97·16	1·4	1·4	1·3	1·2
Japan	17·51	14·37	10·76	6·88	5·36	−2·0	—2·8	−4·4	−5·0
Asian centrally planned economies	193·55	236·66	247·48	255·90	258·25	2·0	0·4	0·3	0·2
China	183·43	225·59	235·35	242·49	244·38	2·1	0·4	0·3	0·2
Other Asian centralled planned economies	10·12	11·07	12·13	13·41	13·87	0·9	0·9	1·0	0·7
Near East in Asia	21·12	22·87	24·74	26·51	27·39	0·8	0·8	0·7	0·7
Israel	0·09	0·11	0·11	0·09	0·08	1·8	0·2	−1·7	−2·5
Others	1·06	1·06	1·15	1·25	1·33	0·1	0·8	0·8	1·2
AFRICA	74·50	83·32	95·07	108·85	116·68	1·1	1·3	1·4	1·4
North-Western Africa	4·47	4·63	5·03	5·79	6·23	0·4	0·8	1·4	1·5
Western Africa	24·96	27·29	31·20	35·70	38·35	0·9	1·3	1·4	1·4
Central Africa	9·96	10·95	11·92	12·88	13·43	0·9	0·9	0·8	0·8
Eastern Africa	25·84	29·79	34·54	39·85	42·70	1·4	1·4	1·4	1·4
Southern Africa	0·88	10·98	1·07	1·17	1·23	1·1	1·0	0·9	0·9

South Africa	1·59	1·83	2·04	2·27	2·39	1·4	1·1	1·1	1·0
Near East in Africa	6·80	7·85	9·27	11·19	12·35	1·4	1·7	1·9	2·0
LATIN AMERICA	30·05	33·56	36·60	39·23	40·32	1·1	0·9	0·7	0·5
Central America	7·13	8·36	9·57	10·66	11·10	1·6	1·3	1·1	0·8
Mexico	5·12	5·97	6·67	7·24	7·45	1·5	1·1	0·8	0·6
Other Central American countries	2·01	2·39	2·90	3·42	3·65	1·8	1·9	1·6	1·3
Caribbean	3·57	3·81	4·10	4·45	4·67	0·7	0·7	0·8	1·0
South America	19·12	21·18	22·71	23·91	24·34	1·0	0·7	0·5	0·4
Brazil	10·34	11·72	12·53	12·99	13·13	1·2	0·7	0·3	0·2
River Plate countries	2·21	2·10	1·93	1·75	1·66	−0·5	−0·8	−1·0	−1·0
Other South American countries	6·57	7·36	8·25	9·17	9·55	1·1	1·1	1·1	0·8
Others	0·23	0·21	0·22	0·21	0·21	−0·8	0·1	−0·1	−0·7
WESTERN EUROPE	41·90	33·17	25·69	18·73	15·71	−2·3	−2·5	−3·1	−3·5
EEC	23·77	16·81	11·72	7·52	6·02	−3·4	−3·6	−4·3	−4·4
Scandinavian countries	1·94	1·47	1·11	0·75	0·62	−2·8	−2·8	−3·8	−3·8
Other Western European countries	16·13	14·85	12·84	10·44	9·06	−0·8	−1·5	−2·1	−2·8
Others	0·06	0·04	0·02	0·02	0·01	–	–	–	–
EASTERN EUROPE	76·91	68·10	57·33	43·98	36·15	−1·2	−1·7	−2·6	−3·8
USSR	52·33	46·48	39·27	30·25	24·66	−1·2	−1·7	−2·5	−4·0
Other Eastern European countries	24·58	21·62	18·06	13·73	11·49	−1·3	−1·8	−2·7	−3·5
NORTH AMERICA	8·64	5·53	3·91	2·86	2·64	−4·3	−3·4	−3·1	−1·6
OCEANIA	1·70	1·78	1·90	1·97	2·00	0·5	0·6	0·4	0·2
WORLD	684·38	737·82	771·10	803·11	819·96	0·8	0·4	0·4	0·4

Source: Schulte *et al.* (1972).

Neglected Aspects of the World Food Issue

GEORG BORGSTROM

Department of Food Science and Human Nutrition, Michigan State University

Summary

The full complexity of the dynamic relationship between food and people has been poorly recognized in post-war action programmes. The debate around these issues needs to be broadened. This paper is an attempt to bring clearly into focus the neglected historical, biological and geographical dimensions. An effort is made to formulate a survival hexagon covering six basic criteria for indispensable co-ordination of any food programme. Emphasis is placed on the urgency of fully incorporating nutrition into agricultural pursuits and of acknowledging the resource basis as manifested in soils and water. Most designs for the future have failed to apprehend the deeply disruptive forces of urbanization.

Hunger has been Man's persistent companion since the dawn of history. He was always forced to eke out an existence in a harsh struggle against the constraints of Nature. History records innumerable hardships with hunger frequently erupting into starvation, famine, and death—most devastating in the populous centres of human settlements such as China, India and parts of the Middle East. Wars were presumably the outlet not only for the Mongolians of the Central Asian steppes, striking east, west and south, but also in the Maorian fight for survival in New Zealand and in the continuous sequence of confrontations between the many American Indian tribes and not least in the nation-collisions of Europe. Behind the power struggles lay the need for securing more land, water and food.

It has been said that all this belongs to history. The magic wand of technology is claimed to have lifted Man in a definitive manner out of this bondage and Western history is supposed to be the convincing proof of this turn of events. Westerners were so sure about the validity of this interpretation that a quarter of a century ago they launched a Technical Aid Program predicated on the basic notion that what the world needed was only a little technical oiling here and there. Their "know-how" was to be put to work on a global scale, and the accomplishments were magnificent, sometimes almost breathtaking. They have every reason to point proudly to their gigantic irrigation dams, their plant and animal breeding endeavours, their potent chemical weapons in fighting pests and diseases, as well as many more achievements along these lines.

The success is incontrovertible. Both agriculture and fisheries showed gains in production far in excess of any population increases (Table 1). Seemingly, Man was winning the overall race between himself and food.

But despite these impressive accomplishments and energetic endeavours, there has been a general failure to take adequate care of the 2,000 million people added to the globe since 1900. The global figures in Table 1 are

TABLE 1
Gains in production
annual averages in million metric tons

Commodities	1948–1952	1970–1971	Gain %
Total cereals	692·1	1,258·9	83
wheat	171·2	330·5	93
rice	167·5	307·5	83
corn	139·9	283·9	101
millet and sorghum	47·4	97·1	103
Sugar	37·8	83·6	121
Potato	247·6	308·8	24
Sweet potato and yams	69·6	142·3	104
Legumes	50·9	62·5	23
Oilseeds	84·3	120·8	45
Milk	258·3	359·7	55
Meat (excl. poultry, horse)	40·7	80·8	98
Poultry meat	4·9	17·1	249
Eggs	10·2	21·3	249
Fish and shellfish	22·6	69·5	207
POPULATION (million)	2,497.6	3,760.9	50

Source: FAO Production Yearbooks

merely averages masking several ugly realities. When calculated in calories the biggest gains are in sugar and fats, less in protein. Most importantly such overall figures do not reflect the discrepancies between the "satisfied world" and the "Hungry World." Feed grains (cereals and soya beans) provide a larger share of the increases than food grains. Oilseeds are predominantly earmarked for use in the satisfied world which is receiving a far greater share of fat and still more of protein.

On the whole, the *per capita* food production in the hungry world has not shown advances ahead of population growth corresponding to those in the satisfied world (Table 2). The Far East figure is rather high but this is because it includes Japan which actually belongs to the satisfied world.

TABLE 2

Per capita *production of food (satisfied world and hungry world)*
(percentages with 1952–1956 taken as a standard)

	1948–1952	1952–1956	1961–1965	1970–1971
Satisfied world	92	100	113	127
Western Europe	87	100	118	135
USSR and Eastern Europe	87	100	123	148
North America	88	100	101	108
Oceania	102	100	118	124
Hungry world	94	100	106	108
Latin America	97	100	100	101
Near East	90	100	94	107
Far East[a]	94	100	94	107
Africa	93	100	102	98

[a]Inclusive of Japan
Source: FAO Production Yearbooks

These data furthermore overlook the fact that the current food production in the hungry world actually would need to be doubled if the present human population were to be provided with those minimum quantities modern nutrition considers indispensable. An equal sharing throughout the world of the food available would consequently lead to universal hunger.

Fisheries have faired even better than agriculture, an achievement often proudly emphasized by spokesmen for this sector of food production. However, close to half of the marine catch of fish (1970–1971) was channelled away from direct human consumption and utilized as meal and oil, the major portion of the latter going into the margarine industry of Western Europe.

The meal, now as then, is almost exclusively used as feed for broilers, egg-layers and pigs in Europe and North America; some is purchased by Japan for similar purposes. Most of the anchoveta landings from the Peruvian Current (taken off Peru and Chile) and the pilchard catches of the Benguela Current off South-West Africa move into reduction plants. Good food-fish like herring, sand launce, and capelin are in Europe, to a major degree, converted into meal and oil.

Percentage figures blur the picture in more than one way. Animal production seemingly has gained equally in both the satisfied and hungry worlds, but milk has gained even more in the hungry world (Table 3).

TABLE 3

Gains in animal production (satisfied world and hungry world)

	Annual averages 1948–1952 (million metric tons)	Annual averages 1970–1971 (million metric tons)	Gain (million metric tons)	Gain (%)	Population (1000 million)	Gain (kg *per capita*)	Protein (kg *per capita*)
MILK							(3·2%)
Total	258·3	399·7	141·4	55	3·8	37·3	1·19
Satisfied world	209·9	318·1	108·2	52	1·3	83·5	2·68
Hungry world	48·5	81·6	33·0	69	2·5	13·3	0·43
MEAT							(15%)[a]
Total	40·7	80·3	40·4	99	3·8	10·6	1·6
Satisfied world	28·6	56·4	27·8	93	1·3	21·3	3·2
Hungry world	12·4	23·9	11·5	93	2·5	4·6	0·7
China	4·2	11·3	7·1	169	0·86	8·3	1·2
Hungry world minus China	8·2	12·6	4·4	54	1·6	2·7	0·41

[a]Percentage of protein in milk and meat respectively

However, the tonnage gain in the satisfied world is three times higher for milk and twice as large for meat as compared to that in the hungry world with twice as many people. Taking into account the glaring exception of China, with its big build-up in subsistence-raising of pigs and poultry, the major part of the hungry world has made extremely modest gains in meat. *Per capita* the gap between the satisfied and hungry worlds has widened. Currently one-third of the human race is disposing of two-thirds of what is produced from both land and water in terms of food and feed.

Despite much popular writing to the contrary, the bulk of food and feed originates from agriculture and fisheries. Synthetic food represents a trifle in global terms. Vitamins are almost exclusively channelled to the well-fed world, also to its livestock. Nine-tenths of the world's food, measured in calories, consists of vegetable products, of which four-fifths are starchy foods, either grains or tubers such as potato, sweet potato, cassava, yams, etc.

TABLE 4

Gains in crop production (in percentages) 1948–1952 to 1969–1970

	Production	Yield per hectare	Acreage
Wheat	93	57	24
Rice	84	40	31
Corn	103	63	25
Barley	146	60	54
Millet and sorghum	105	64	20
Dry beans	97	32	51
Potato	25	25	–
Sweet potato and yams	104	26	61
Cassava	80	28	41

As is evident from Table 4, the gains are still to no small degree due to expanded acreages under cultivation: for the crops listed above, 150·8 million hectares have been added which is 11% of the world acreage. These added acreages are generally less suitable for cropping than lands previously in use. Gain in yield (production per unit area) is largely a characteristic feature of the satisfied world and a few selected countries or regions of the hungry world. For example, double cropping—mostly with irrigation and a heavier use of appropriate fertilizers—has allowed a higher output per cultivated hectare in Taiwan, Indonesia, parts of the Philippines, India, and Pakistan.

Only in recent years, mainly since 1968, has the introduction into the hungry world of high-yielding varieties, the so-called Green Revolution, initiated a trend towards greater returns per hectare, although not to the degree generally assumed, since in most of the countries involved, 40% to 60% of the gains are to be ascribed to expanded acreages.

Many sweeping and misleading statements are made about agricultural conditions in "developing" countries. This latter term in itself is fallacious. In general, it is assumed that agricultural production is universally neglected and that yields fall far behind those of "developed" nations. This is not in accordance with fact. Several such lands show yields well matching those in the satisfied world.

The USSR is the only major country that shares with the United States the advantage of having more tilled land *per capita* to feed its people than most countries of the globe. The Soviet Union, however, has a more adverse climate with far more vagaries, in particular frost and drought, than the United States. Each American has at his disposal 2·2 acres of tilled land (0·6 acres goes into net export) and in addition 3·5 acres of rangeland. This brings us back to the assumption on which the Technical Aid Program was footed. Despite indisputable successes its failure to remove the "hunger gap" raises doubts about the validity of the diagnosis then made. In particular two basic dimensions were lacking—the historic and the biological ones. A review of the comments surrounding President Truman's speech to the United Nations General Assembly launching the Program reveals almost universal acceptance of its basic premises, clearly mirrored in the term "underdeveloped'. At the time there were few reminders that this other world which was to be helped had in effect carried all advanced civilizations in the past, and as a consequence was in many parts *over*developed with far too many people. This had pushed their quest for food and feed far beyond the limits of prudency and thus overtaxed their resources of soil, forests, water, etc. resulting in major soil erosion, denuded forestlands, tapped groundwaters and a persistent expansion of the globe's deserts.

Far more critical was the lack of historical perspective. The Western world just stood at the end of its grand Golden Age (1850–1950) during which it had brought almost the entire globe within its action sphere and utilized its remaining lands, not to feed the needy world, but to support the big European population explosion. This peaked just after the turn of the century, which upsurge is generally attributed to the medical advances in the Western world thereby reducing infant mortality. Most textbooks emphasize such sanitary measures as the creation of waterworks, improved sewage disposal, mass vaccination and compulsory pasteurization of milk. Unquestionably each one of these measures drastically reduced mortality and particularly among infants. The survival of more individuals does not, however, in itself explain the population upsurge, far less its explosive nature. This was largely determined by quite different factors, primarily whether the surviving millions could be fed. Four major factors then became decisive:

1. large scale migration—the greatest in history and with global repercussions (100 million people left and 25 to 30 million returned home);
2. transportation technology creating transoceanic and transcontinental deliveries of food and feed—based on the discovery of liquid fuel and of the combustion engine;
3. introduction of new methods of preserving food (canning, freezing, and refrigeration);

4. application of science to agriculture, thereby raising the yields per acre and reversing the ongoing decline in soil productivity.

All this lifted the survival ceiling for Western Man. In the North American prairies a supporting colony was created which in terms of tilled acreage, forestlands, and mineral wealth was far bigger than that of all Europe.

The long distance hauling of food and feed made hunger vanish from the Western scene, and it became for the first time in history feasible to sustain cities of a million inhabitants and more. This is one of the roots of the current ecology crisis. The urbanized millions of Europe and of the United States have lost sight of the wide expanses on which their survival depended.

This has grave repercussions not the least of which have been in the nutritional sphere. Greater affluence has in most instances resulted in two contrasting trends: one reflected in a greater intake of empty calories, chiefly in the form of sugar and fats, the other in a mounting consumption of protein-rich animal products (meat, milk and eggs). Only the Western world with its own land resources and also access to land in other parts of the world could allow themselves this extravagance. Yet serious imbalances resulted due to a lack of purchasing power or faltering education. Excess fat and sugar still victimize many through metabolic disturbances.

This leads to the most critical shortcoming, namely, Man's thinking and conceptualizing around the food issue both on the international and national scene. In turn this reflects in his programmes and actions. Food is analysed and discussed in very simplified specialist categories. More attention is paid to tactics than to strategy. Man is so enamoured of his techniques that he childishly believes that by willing these means he automatically should attain his goals. This is the real reason he has failed on so many counts. It all looks so simple. Food shortages are countered by producing more, but much greater gains could be made by paying attention to the current huge losses. The problem of too many people is met by a drive for contraceptives. Nutritional deficiencies are remedied by filling in the voids. Dietary absurdities are countered by multipurpose foods. Food technologists evolve procedures towards perfection in nutritional fulfillment. Yet action on each one of these matters requires in order to succeed, concomitant and co-ordinated measures as analysed below.

More than twenty years were lost in taking one little first step, namely the move from the one-dimensional notion that it was all a question of producing more food. The goal was seen as the banishing of hunger from the Earth. A whole generation of presidential rhetoric from F. D. R. Roosevelt onwards reflects this myopia. Only in the latter part of the 1960s was the decision taken to introduce a second dimension and look to the other end of the ledger—the population numbers. Many still believe this was all that was needed. Yet history repeatedly shows how without special precautions more food inevitably means more people. The Western world has been made to believe it is the other way round; namely that more people almost automatically do find ways of raising more food. But this is only true when there is a margin available and history explains why. Yet today Western Man enjoys far greater resources and less constraints than others and takes the lion's share of the ocean catches and what moves into the world market of food and feed. Europe currently imports more plant protein than is consumed either by India or the total African continent.

The history of Western Man, particularly during the glorious hundred years referred to above as his Golden Age, is a grand scale demonstration of how the European population explosion came about through a world-wide scramble not to feed the world but to feed the Europeans. World trade still follows the pattern then laid down: moving largely between the well-to-do, and to a considerable degree depending on the prairies via grain and soya beans. US soya beans and African peanuts are basic not only to the milk production of Western Europe and Canada but also to their margarine production. The "butter mounds" of Europe are further glaring evidences of the basic need for coordinating agricultural production and nutrition. On the whole, short range profitability and quantitative acrobatics are of little avail if nutritive deficits accrue or disease risks mount. Any number of examples could be brought forward to show the urgent need for co-ordination of Man's efforts. This is long overdue. It is necessary to formulate a valid strategy and abandon Man's shortsighted tactical manoeuvrings. Such co-ordination needs to harness together many fields, but primarily the following six:

1. more food;
2. less people;
3. better storage and utilization (of food and feed);
4. nutritional requirements;
5. diseases;
6. resources.

Each measure taken to readjust the Man/Food Equation needs to be co-ordinated or related to all these six basic ramifications. This is a "hexagon for survival".

Only a few illustrations in the field of nutrition will be added here. On the whole, quality needs to be superimposed upon quantity. High yielding varieties are of questionable value unless the protein barrier is maintained. US grain surpluses could in themselves not raise a single litter of pigs. Protein content needs to be brought in as a main pricing index of cereals as well as of milk. Beans are the main compensators of deficient cereal proteins to hundreds of millions and far cheaper than any amino-acid supplementation. India has seen its pulse protein intake drop ever since the mid-1950s and at an accelerated pace after the Green Revolution. The battle for the protein front is most intense in the tuber-eating tropical regions of Brazil, West Africa, India and Indonesia. Cassava is further the source of destructive liver defects and tumour growth. Better processing of the tubers into flour for removal of hydrocyanic acid is needed.

In summary, all these factors interplay decisively in the Man/Food Equation and have not been given sufficient attention. Far less have they been properly placed into the equation of a humankind, which has added one thousand million beings to itself in little more than a decade. Yet, superimposed upon all this is the huge influx into cities. Food is taken for granted by planners, futurologists and food scientists, and this goes for both the satisfied and hungry worlds. Nonetheless, this is a most crucial issue, involving as it does the two most basic matters of all: food and water. During the 1970s six hundred million people will be added to the world's cities and more than two-thirds of them will move in from overpopulated rural areas in the hungry world, where farms have dwindled in size to below one to two acres per family. No agricultural miracles are capable of increasing their output many times over on such a diminutive basis. Moving the dependants to distant cities with the ensuing cumbersome and costly transfer of the all too small output does not absolve them from the excruciating burden of subsistence.

Food is in many ways also the key to the pollution issue, chiefly due to this very same congestion induced by urbanization. In the United States a far higher polluting load has been created through intensified animal production, and in addition almost as big a load as that of human sewage comes from the food industries. Little has this, the most potent force in pollution, been heeded, and yet it is critically affecting the safety and the quality of both food and water.

Several of the issues discussed in this paper have been notably absent in the debate surrounding the Man/Food Equation. Most critical, however, is Man's piecemeal approach in development programmes. Far better coordination is urgently needed, particularly so since mankind is swiftly moving to a major crisis of imbalance.

References

Borgstrom, G. (1973). "Focal Points". Macmillan, New York.

Borgstrom, G. (1973). "The Food and People Dilemma". Duxbury Press, North Sciutate, Mass.

Borgstrom, G. (1973). "World Food Resources". Intertext, Aylesbury, Bucks.

Human Protein Needs and the Relative Role of Energy and Protein in Meeting Them

P. V. SUKHATME

*Gokhale Institute of Politics and Economics, India**

Summary

The persistent and widespread malnutrition exhibited in developing countries continues to be attributed to an insufficiency of good quality protein in their diets. The United Nations, for example, urges countries to increase the supplies of protein using modern technology and to distribute them to the vulnerable members of their populations through nationwide feeding programmes. However examination of the available data suggests that there is no evidence to support the thesis that diets common in developing countries are deficient in protein. Rather, the limiting factor is calories to utilize the protein eaten and not the protein itself. It is not surprising therefore that the current programmes have proved ineffective in tackling the problem of malnutrition.

I believe that there are three broad reasons for this lack of success; firstly, representation of the problem simply as one of the deficiency of a single nutrient irrespective of whether the diet can meet the energy cost of synthesizing and retaining the nutrient; secondly, the erroneous interpretation placed on nutrient requirements in the study of intake data; and thirdly, a lack of attention paid to the need to provide an adequate socio-economic framework to solve the problem. These points are discussed in this paper, and to support my view that calorie deficiency is the more important factor contributing to malnutrition I draw upon recent data from India.

* Now care of Maharashtra Association for the Cultivation of Science, India.

Introduction

Many erroneous ideas about diet have been advanced over the years to explain the persistent and widespread malnutrition in the developing countries. The most recent one concerns protein. It is held that an insufficiency of good quality protein in the diet is at the heart of the problem of malnutrition. So acute is this deficiency that no less than the United Nations and its Agencies have warned countries of the "impending crisis", while proposing at the same time an appropriate strategy and programmes to overcome it. In particular, countries are urged to increase the supplies of protein using modern technology and to distribute these to vulnerable classes through nationwide feeding programmes. However, if the available data is examined, there is no evidence to support the thesis that diets common in the developing countries are deficient in protein. What are lacking are calories to utilize the protein actually eaten. It is therefore hardly surprising that the current programmes have proved ineffective in tackling the problem of malnutrition.

Broadly there are three reasons for the lack of success. Firstly, the problem is presented simply as one of the deficiency of a single nutrient regardless of whether the diets are adequate in meeting the energy cost of synthesizing and retaining the nutrient. The second reason can be traced to the erroneous interpretation placed on the meaning of nutrient requirements in the study of intake data. This has made the problem appear primarily as one of gross deficiency in protein and hence one of supply. And thirdly, far too little emphasis is placed on the need to provide an adequate socio-economic framework to solve the problem. It will be the purpose of this paper to state what Man's needs for protein are, to evaluate the available intake data, to ascertain how far these needs are satisfied, and to examine the extent to which the new interpretation of the concept of requirements has contributed to the current myth about lack of protein in the diet. Also the socio-economic background involved in the solution of the problem will be briefly touched upon. The paper will mainly draw upon recent data for India.

Calorie and Protein Needs

Human needs vary with age, sex, weight, physical activity, environmental conditions and other factors. They are defined separately for each one of several age–sex groups. Calorie needs are based on measurements of energy intake and/or expenditure in healthy active subjects; needs for protein are based on obligatory losses on a no-protein diet supplemented by the results of nitrogen-balance studies. Both calorie and protein needs are simply expressed as rates per kilo of body weight as in the latest FAO/WHO report on energy and protein requirements (1971). Used in conjunction with information on reference body weight and activity, the rates provide the means of calculating the requirements of individuals for satisfactory growth and maintenance of health.

For calories, the requirements are defined as average *per capita* needs of specified age–sex groups. It is recognized that individuals within a group may need calories which may be below or above the suggested average. But the principal concern is with establishing averages and not with variations within age–sex groups. The magnitude of individual variability is estimated at approximately 15%.

Unlike calories, requirements for protein are based on the consideration of the individual as well as of the group. The earlier report on protein requirements by FAO/WHO (1965) defined needs at three levels namely, average, (average + 20%), and (average − 20%). The upper level, which is placed at a distance of twice the standard deviation above the average protein needs, is expected to cover the requirements of all but a very small proportion of the population. In other words the probability that a healthy individual will have a requirement exceeding the upper level will be very small. The lower level is placed at twice the standard deviation below the average and represents the level below which protein deficiency may be expected to occur in all but a few individuals. In other words, the probability that a healthy individual will have a protein need below the lower level will be very small. The magnitude of individual variability was estimated at 10%.

The 1971 report does not continue the practice of defining protein requirements at three levels. Instead the requirements are now based on the consideration of an individual, and are defined *at the upper level* only, namely average plus twice the standard deviation ($m + 2\sigma$). The estimate of σ has been revised upwards to 15% of the mean. The requirement so defined is called "recommended intake" or "safe level of intake". It is recognized that an individual eating below ($m + 2\sigma$) is not necessarily malnourished. However, a corollary is added to the effect that as the intake falls below ($m + 2\sigma$), the probability of dietary deficiency increases. It is emphasized that an individual should aim to eat at a level above ($m + 2\sigma$).

By way of an example, Table 1 gives the new recommended levels for calories and protein for a pre-school child and an adult living in India. Protein requirements are shown both in terms of egg as well as dietary protein. Available data show that the net protein utilization (NPU) of the average

TABLE 1

Recommended levels of nutrient intake for a pre-school child and an adult in India (FAO/WHO, 1971, approximate only).

Age (yrs)	Weight in kg	Cal/kg	Total calories	Protein as egg g/kg	Total protein as egg g	Protein/cal concentration %	Dietary protein of NPU relative to egg = 67 g	Dietary protein as recommended by ICMR[a] (1968) g
1–3	12	100	1200	1·25	15	5·0	22·5	18
Adult	55	46	2550	0·57	32	5·0	48·0	55

[a] Indian Council of Medical Research

cereal pulse diet relative to egg is approximately two-thirds in the case of children, and 90% in the case of adults. However, the difference will be ignored and a uniform value of two-thirds assumed for NPU. The recommended levels of dietary protein so calculated will slightly overestimate adult need but will be on the safe side. They are shown in the table. It is seen that the cereal pulse diet on average will have to provide 48g of dietary protein to meet the recommended needs of an adult, and about 22·5g to meet the recommended requirements of a child of age 1–3 years.

Three points need to be made about Table 1. The recommended levels of protein for adults are much lower than previously used. In part this is due to the protein quality of diet relative to egg being higher in adults than previously assumed, and in part due to a higher value for the nitrogen losses on the no-protein diets previously used. Clearly, protein needs are very low compared to what is eaten in the rich countries. The explanation appears to be that people with high and rising incomes must find it difficult not to eat more tasty animal foods when they can afford to do so.

The second point concerns the general belief that a child needs much more protein relative to his energy needs compared with an adult. This is however not borne out on current evidence. The table shows that if a diet has 5% of its calories from good quality protein, such as in egg, the individual's needs for protein will be met regardless of whether the individual is a pre-school child or an adult man provided the individual eats enough to meet his energy needs. It nevertheless is true that dietary protein is less efficiently utilized by a child than by an adult, so that relative to energy a child will undoubtedly need more dietary protein than an adult. However, as long as a diet has an equivalent of 5% good quality protein such as in egg, a child's needs may usually be expected to be met, infants excepted. Even human milk contains only 5–6% of its calories as protein and yet it is an ideal infant food.

The third point is that requirements for protein are valid only when calorie needs are met.

The So-called Protein Gap

Figures for average requirements are now compared with what people eat. Such a comparison is given in Table 2. Side by side with figures for protein are given figures for calories. This has been done because an overriding condition in the comparison of protein intake with requirements is that the

TABLE 2

Energy and protein supply compared with respective requirements
(Micro-comparison on per capita *basis)*

Year	Energy in calories			Protein in grams				
	Supply	Requirement	% Gap	Supply	Requirement	Recommended	% Supply/ requirement	% Supply/ recommended
1963–1965	2000	2200	10					
1965–1967	1900	2200	15					
1970–1971	2100	2200	5					
1971–	2000	2200	10	50	30	36	166	140

calorie needs of an individual must be met. Table 2 shows that the protein supply averages about 50g per person per day as against an average requirement of only some 30g. Far from there being a gap, the protein supply is seen to exceed the average requirement by over 60%. It must be concluded that unless protein intake is very unevenly distributed it must be rare to find protein deficiency occurring; however that this does occur is confirmed by data from nutrition surveys. As an example, a study of some 5000 children under five years of age conducted with the assistance of the WHO showed that some 2000 of them suffered from states of protein malnutrition, ranging from serious retardation in growth and extreme emaciation, to other associated signs of protein deficiency such as nutritional oedoma and reduced serum albumin. Data from nutritional surveys in the various states in India collected under the guidance of the Indian Council of Medical Research (ICMR) during the last twenty years give much the same findings. The majority of the subjects covered in these surveys were children of school age. Kwashiorkor was observed in 2–3% of the cases. Other signs associated with states of protein malnutrition were observed in 15% of the children examined, while retardation of growth was more or less universal. The incidence of protein deficiency was relatively low among children of upper income groups.

If protein deficiency does then occur and is as widespread as it appears to be, it must be due either to abnormal losses, such as occur during infections, or to low calorie intake. As Table 2 shows, the calorie supply is in fact short of the need. The deficit is small but its significance in the context of protein malnutrition cannot be overstressed. Unless a diet provides the energy cost of synthesizing and retaining protein, a person must lose protein.

Micro-analysis

Individual Intake Compared with Respective Requirements

Ordinarily in a healthy active population with each person meeting his habitual requirements of protein, most people can be expected to have a higher protein intake per nutrition unit than the critical limit given by the average requirement of the nutritional unit minus twice the standard deviation of the individual requirement (a nutritional unit for protein has the same average daily requirement as that of the adult "reference" man). The coefficient of variation based on intravariability is of the order of 10%, so that the lower critical limit for adults of a reference type can be placed at approximately 20g of egg protein. It follows that in any observed distribution, the proportion of individuals with an intake per nutrition unit below 20g can be taken to provide an estimate of the proportion of individuals with a diet inadequate in protein.

TABLE 3

Distribution of households by protein intake per nutrition unit in Maharashtra (in terms of egg protein grams per day)

Egg protein g/day	1971 Urban %	1971 Rural %
0– 5	–	–
5–10	–	–
10–15	0·8	0·5
15–20	1·6	3·5
20–25	8·0	5·1
25–30	16·0	15·4
30–35	19·6	14·9
35–40	16·2	15·2
40–45	12·0	10·5
45–50	8·4	9·3
50–55	6·2	7·0
55–60	4·6	5·4
60–65	2·6	3·7
65–70	1·8	2·8
70–75	0·8	2·3
75–80	0·4	0·7
80–85	0·2	1·2
85–90	0·4	0·5
90–95	–	–
95–100	0·2	0·2
100 and over	0·2	0·9
	100·0	100·0
N	500	429
u	38·5	41·5
S.D.	14·3	15·8
% C.V.	38	38
% Incidence	5	6

Source: National Sample Survey of India, Round 26, July 71 to June 72.

The method has been applied to the food consumption data collected by the National Sample Survey (NSS) during 1972. By way of an example the results for Maharashtra State are reproduced in Table 3. The results relate to random representative samples of 500 households for urban Maharashtra and 429 for rural Maharashtra. In preparing Table 3 the recorded values of consumption of foodstuffs were converted into protein using the nutritive values tabulated by the National Institute of Nutrition. The number of nutrition units were separately calculated for each household on the basis of age and sex of the members of the family and using the 1971 FAO/WHO scale of requirements. In converting dietary protein into "reference" protein in terms of egg, animal protein was considered to have a net protein utilization of 80 and vegetable protein a NPU of 50. No account was taken of any possible amino acid supplementation nor of the fact that NPU in adults of dietary protein relative to egg is much higher than in children. If anything, therefore, estimates of protein intake are on a conservative side.

It must be noted that Table 3 refers to the intake of egg protein by households of four nutrition units on average and not to individuals. The lower critical limit appropriate for application to such a distribution can therefore be placed at approximately $24 - 2 \times 2{\cdot}4/\sqrt{4}$ or 22g of egg protein, assuming negligible waste of food as would be expected among households at the lower tail of the distribution under conditions of chronic food shortage. It is not implied that a household with an average intake less than 22g per nutrition unit will have all its individuals eating below 22g. Equally all households with an average intake above 22g are not likely to have all their members with an intake per nutrition unit above 22g of egg protein. It will be assumed that these proportions counter-balance one another.

It will be seen from Table 3 that less than 5% of the total number of households in urban as well as rural Maharashtra had a protein intake lower than the critical limit of 22g; in other words less than 5% can be said to have an inadequate amount of protein in the diet. This proportion may be even lower since the intake in all probability has been underestimated. If a NPU of 60 were to be used for vegetable protein in place of 50, in keeping with a value more nearly in line with that observed in adults, and a NPU of 90 for animal protein in place of 80, most of which is known to be derived from milk, it is found that the percentage of households that had an inadequate amount of protein is less than 2%. This is about the proportion expected in a healthy active population with each person meeting his requirements for protein. It must be concluded that it is unlikely that protein deficiency will occur as a result of low protein intake.

Correlation Between Protein and Calorie Intake

In the discussion so far it has been assumed that diets are not limited in calories. In actual fact, as was seen in Table 2, the average calorie supply is

TABLE 4

Daily per capita *calorie and protein supply in terms of expenditure level, Maharashtra State, India, 1971*

Item	Monthly *per capita* expenditure in Rs								
	18	18–24	24–34	34–44	44–54	54–64	64–74	>74	Average
URBAN									
Total calories	1380	1430	1620	1870	2060	2210	2210	2760[a]	2080
Total proteins (g)	42	42	49	56	60	64	66	80	61
Animal proteins (g)	1.3	2·2	5·1	5·5	6·6	8·2	10·4	14·2	7·9
Number of households	11	27	94	90	73	56	38	111	500
RURAL									
Total calories	1360	1530	1850	2330	2480	2890	3060	3490	2160
Total proteins (g)	40	45	56	70	75	87	89	106	65
Animal proteins (g)	3·6	4·0	5·3	7·5	8·8	10·2	10·6	15·4	7·1
Number of households	27	67	126	78	56	24	19	29	426

[a]These values are unduly high partly due to the exclusion from the household size of guests and labourers taking meals

lower than the average calorie requirement by about 10% so that a part of the population must be undernourished. This is shown in Table 4. Rich and privileged people everywhere eat all they need and more, but the poor eat only what they can afford which may not always meet their needs. It is not until the income (expenditure) has reached Rs 54 in the urban area and Rs 34 in the rural area that a person is seen to meet his average calorie needs. By contrast protein needs appear to be met even in the group with an income less than Rs 18. Clearly when the food intake is sufficient in amount to meet the energy needs the protein intake is satisfactory.

TABLE 5

Classification of households in Maharashtra according to whether the diets are deficient (D) or not (N) in calories and protein

	Urban			Rural		
	PD	NPD	Sub-total	PD	NPD	Sub-total
CD	4·8	31·8	36·6	3·5 (5·3)	29·8 (6·4)	33·3
NCD	–	63·4	63·4	0·5 (2·3)	66·2 (5·9)	66·7
Sub-total	4·8	95·2	100·0	4·0	96·0	100·0

Figures in brackets denote protein calorie concentration values (NDpCal%)

That this is so is even better illustrated in Table 5 which shows the results of a bivariate analysis for Maharashtra (urban and rural) according to whether the diet is adequate or inadequate in calories, protein or both. A diet is said to be adequate in protein when the intake is above the lower critical limit for protein. Likewise a diet is said to be adequate in calories when the intake exceeds the corresponding critical limit for calories. This level as has been shown elsewhere comes to approximately 2200 calories for households of 4 nutrition units. The dividing lines in the tables are accordingly based at the critical limits for calories and protein. It will be seen that most of the diets which are inadequate in protein (PD) are also inadequate in calories, that is, they are calorie deficient (CD). In other words when the food intake is sufficient to meet the energy needs, the protein needs are usually met. This is also evident from the values of protein calorie concentrations shown in brackets in Table 5. These exceed 5 in all except one cell namely (PD, NCD). In less than 1% of the cases protein deficiency is seen to occur as a result of low protein calorie concentration in the diet. Considering errors in the data this is most likely ascribed to chance. It is concluded that protein deficiency for the most part is the indirect result of inadequate energy in the diet.

Inter-relationship Between Protein and Calories

But even when the concentration on an energy basis of protein in the diet expressed as egg equivalent is higher than five and the protein intake is above the needs of Man, protein malnutrition can still occur if the food intake is not adequate to meet the energy cost of synthesizing protein in the diet. This is well brought out in Table 6 based on the extensive results of short-term experiments on the nitrogen balance in adults in developed countries. It will be seen that if the calorie intake is limited but the protein is not, there is a loss of body protein. As the calorie intake is increased the loss becomes progressively smaller. The table suggests that on average some 2400–2500 calories are needed to achieve a protein balance in adults. This is approximately the value of the critical limit for calories below which an adult man weighing 65kg can be said to be calorie deficient. This value also accords with the calculations of Payne (1971) who has shown that it is not until the calorie intake exceeds 1·5 × BMR (basic metabolic rate) and is adequate to maintain body content of heat that protein is fully utilized. The result is found to be experimentally valid for all age groups. Clearly protein in the diet is partially diverted to meeting the calorie needs of maintenance when the latter are not satisfied. In any assessment of the incidence of protein deficiency in the population, one cannot therefore be guided by the inadequacy of the protein intake alone, but must also take into account the adequacy of calories. People who take adequate or more than adequate protein, but who are not able to utilize the protein for lack of adequate energy in the diet, obviously form a part of the protein deficient population.

TABLE 6

Estimated protein loss (g/day) by an adult taking a diet restricted in protein or calories, or both

Protein intake (g/day)	Calories per day				
	900	1600	2200	2800	3200
0	45	42	40	40	40
20	30	23	21	20	20
40	30	12	−0	0	0
60	30	12	−0	0	0

These are the people with a dietary pattern represented by the cell (CD, NPD). If the different cells of the 2 × 2 classification are represented as below

		Protein	
		PD	NPD
Calories	CD	A	B
	NCD	E	F

then clearly B must be added to A + E to give I = A + E + B for the total incidence of protein deficiency. Incidentally it is interesting to observe that excess protein over and above body needs does not leave any benefit on the protein balance.

Turning once again to Table 5 it is seen that some 30% of households, although they had adequate protein in the diet, are not able to utilize it fully for lack of energy. Protein in their diet is clearly diverted partially to meet energy needs thereby exposing the individuals to the hazard of protein malnutrition. Adding this proportion to the protein deficient diets, the total incidence becomes:

$$I_{\text{rural}} = A + E + B$$
$$= 3{\cdot}5 + 0{\cdot}5 + 29{\cdot}8$$
$$= 33{\cdot}8$$

$$\text{and } I_{\text{urban}} = 4{\cdot}8 + 31{\cdot}8$$
$$= 36{\cdot}6$$

It is concluded that a third of the households are protein deficient of which almost all are so by virtue of their being short of calories. The role of low calorie intake in the causation of protein deficiency is thus much more pronounced that can be assessed when the protein intake is compared with the corresponding requirements. In fact almost the entire protein deficiency is seen to be the indirect result of low calorie intake.

Data from several other states have been examined and also data from dietary surveys collected by the state nutrition units under the guidance of the ICMR. By way of another example, the results of dietary surveys for Andhra State are reproduced in Table 7. The data relate to 2675 households. They confirm that what Indian diets lack is not protein but energy to allow the body to metabolize the protein actually eaten.

It must be added that in one respect the results reported above are in marked contrast to those reported in earlier papers (Sukhatme, 1970a, 1970b, 1972). Whereas some 5% of the total diets were reported to be deficient in

TABLE 7

A 2 × 2 table showing percentage classification of households in rural areas of Andhra according to whether they are adequate or not in calories and protein

Income Rs month	0–50			50–100			100–200			200 and above			Overall		
	PD	NPD	Total	PD	NPD	Total	PD	NPD	Total	PD	NPD	Total	PD	NPD	Total
CD	4 (4·9)	35 (6·4)	39	3 (4·9)	37 (6·2)	40	2 (4·5)	28 (6·2)	30	2 (4·6)	24 (5·9)	26	3 (4·9)	33 (6·2)	36
NCD	0	61 (6·1)	61	0	60 (6·2)	60	0	70 (6·1)	70	0	74 (6·0)	74	0	64 (6·1)	64
Total	4	96	100	3	97	100	2	98	100	2	98	100	3	97	100

protein *per se* but not in calories in the earlier studies, the % incidence of such diets is now negligible. This is mainly the result of using the 1971 FAO/WHO scale of protein requirements in place of the 1965 scale previously used. In the 1971 scale the recommended level for an adult has been sharply reduced compared to the level recommended in 1965. With adults accounting for about one-half of the total size of a household, the requirement of a household per nutrition unit is smaller than before, with the result that there is hardly any household with a diet which can be classified as deficient in protein *per se* but adequate in energy content. In other words none of the diets actually consumed had a protein/calorie concentration so low that protein needs cannot be met when the diet is adequate to satisfy energy needs.

Protein Malnutrition in Children

Two arguments against these data have been presented. Firstly, they relate to households and not to individuals. Secondly, although a household may have enough protein when it has enough food, this does not necessarily mean that a pre-school child would get enough proteins. Despite the fact that the pre-school child represents a group of prime interest, data on the food intake of young children are scanty. However, Gopalan and his co-workers at the National Institute of Nutrition (NIN) have studied several thousand children of pre-school age in rural areas in South India. Table 8 gives data typical of those reported by him. It will be seen that about 80% of children had diets deficient in calories; by comparison the percentage of children with diets deficient in protein is only about 20. What is of interest is that less than 1% of the children have diets adequate in calories but deficient in protein. Considering the errors to which data are subject this must be considered negligible. The results reported in Tables 5 and 7 are thus in complete accord with those of Gopalan. The high incidence of calorie deficiency in Gopalan's results was probably due to the preponderance of poor children in the community which he surveyed. This in no way detracts from the value of the information the survey provides for assessing the relative importance of a low calorie and a low protein intake in causing protein malnutrition and hence in developing measures to combat it.

The proof of the pudding lies in the eating. It is therefore of interest to determine whether a food supplement in amounts needed to overcome calorie deficiency can help avert protein deficiency. Field studies reported by NIN

TABLE 8

Incidence of protein-calorie deficiency in pre-school children in South India

Age (1–5 years)	PD	NPD	
CD	18	63	81
NCD	1	18	19
	19	81	100

CD, calorie-deficient; NCD, not calorie-deficient; PD, protein-deficient; NPD, not protein-deficient.

indeed show that children receiving such supplements had higher gains in height and weight compared with children who had not received the supplement. The food supplement had the following composition:

Wheat flour	23g
Sugar	35g
Fat	10g

providing approximately 310 calories and 3g of protein. The gains in all age groups were statistically significant and confirm that calories were the primary deficiencies in the diets of pre-school children of the poor socio-economic class (Gopalan *et al.*, 1973).

It does not necessarily follow that supplements alone were effective in raising the height and weight of children. The relatively larger attention which the children in the experimental group received in the course of the year could have brought with it an unconscious attention to hygiene and health, thereby influencing the results. It must be added that while protein deficiency is undoubtedly associated with inadequate diet, it is also associated with other factors, particularly infections. In consequence, intervention at any single level whether of food or control of infection is unlikely to be effective. This is well brought out in the studies in three villages in Guatemala by Scrimshaw and his associates summarized in Table 9. In one village some improvements in environmental sanitation and provision of medical care were made; in another village a complete food supplement was made available six days a week to children under the age of 5 years and to pregnant and nursing women. The control village received no intervention. Data were collected over a five-year period. The findings show that a food supplement was apparently accompanied by a reduction in the amounts of second and third degree malnutrition, but not as much as might have been expected. The amount of first degree malnutrition actually increased but this probably included subjects previously suffering from second and third degree malnutrition.

TABLE 9

Nutrition and infection field study (1959–1964)

	Control village	Sanitation village	Feeding village
Respiratory diseases, cases 100/years	56	127	73
Acute diarrheal disease, cases 100/years	129	241	124
Nutritional state			
% normal	14·8	14·4	17·3
% first degree	37·6	34·9	54·5
% second degree	42·6	46·7	27·3
% third degree	5·0	4·1	0·9
Death rate/100 Age 1–4	5·2	3·4	2·4

Source: Taken from Scrimshaw *et al.,* (1969).

Sanitation alone was not effective either, and it is strange that a village equipped with a good system of sanitation should show more increases of diarrhoea and respiratory diseases than other villages. Against this variation the performance of the feeding village is more likely to be the result of change than of the greater inherent nutritive value of the food supplement. The small overall improvement, as in the NIN studies, could be due to increased, though unconscious, attention to matters of health and hygiene thereby making the programme more effective than it would have been if increased food supply alone had been available.

That inadequate energy rather than the low content of utilizable protein is the principal factor accounting for the major part of protein malnutrition can also be inferred from the protein value of diets. These values are calculated from the index known as NDpCal% which measures the utilizable protein in the diet expressed as a percentage of calories. The assumptions implicit in predicting NPU and NDpCal% are still the subject of controversy but it is agreed that they do not seriously detract from the value of the concept or from its use in predicting the protein value of diets with a degree of accuracy adequate for practical purposes. Table 10 shows that the NDpCal% of cereal-pulse based diets, such as are eaten in rural India, has a value larger than 5. As has been seen already, this is adequate to satisfy protein needs, provided the diet is taken in a quantity adequate to meet the calorie needs. Very young infants need a higher proportion of protein and a higher NDpCal%. This is usually provided in the form of breast milk; if the mother's diet is adequate this will be sufficient for the first 3–6 months of life. After this, however, solid supplements of calories and protein are essential. If these are starchy foods providing calories but little protein, then there is a risk that the NDpCal% of the mixed diet met fall below that needed for adequate growth, and the child may become prone to develop protein deficiency.

TABLE 10

NDpCal% of different foods and food mixtures (mixtures providing 2200 calories)

	Rice	Wheat	Maize
Staple alone	4·9	5·7	4·8
Staple + 30g legume	6·2	7·0	6·3
Staple + 60g legume	6·7	8·3	6·5
Staple + 30g skim milk powder	7·1	8·0	7·0
Staple + 45g legume + 15g skim milk powder	6·8	8·8	6·9

Incidence of primary protein deficiency can thus be expected in areas where the staple food is either a starchy root, like tapioca, cassava or plantain. Where, however, as in most parts of India, the staple food is a cereal, rice, wheat, jowar (sorghum), bajra (millet), etc. subjected to normal processing and accompanied by minimal amounts of pulses and vegetables, the protein value of the diet of the population will be greater than an NDpCal% of 5. The requirements for both protein and calories will be met at this level provided total supplies are adequate. When the amounts of legumes in the diet are negligible and the diet is mostly rice or maize, the NDpCal% may fall slightly below 5. Such a diet can still meet the requirements provided sufficient cereal is consumed to meet the average calorie requirements. The danger does not lie in its low protein value for a child fed in this way can be healthy and active. However, as Payne (1971) puts it,

> "any depression of food intake occasioned by infection, by marginal deficiency of minerals or vitamins or by economic factors would result in a calorie intake less than the minimum requirement and would thus expose the child to the risk of protein deficiency".

This need not however be interpreted to mean that a child's needs for protein should be met from protein-rich foods to prevent protein malnutrition. It means that children are more demanding than adults in their requirements and it is easier to meet these requirements with good foods like eggs and milk if one can afford them. These are questions largely of nutrition education, and need special attention in the nutrition programme.

Erroneous Interpretation of the Concept of Needs as a Factor Contributing to the Protein Myth

It may be asked why the earlier studies by the United Nations and its Agencie- reached different conclusions. The main reason is that whereas here the inters relationship between protein and calories has been taken into account by examining the diets simultaneously for the two variates, this was apparently not done earlier. The other reason that has contributed to creating the protein myth can be traced to the new interpretation placed by the FAO/WHO expert committee on nutrition on the concept of requirements in the study of intake data, namely that as the intake falls below the recommended level $(m + 2\sigma)$, the probability of dietary deficiency increases (FAO/WHO, 1971). In statistical notation, if $F(v)$ denotes the distribution function of requirement v, then $(1 - F(u))$ will denote the probability of requirement v exceeding a given intake u. The interpretation placed by the FAO/WHO expert committee merely states that $(1 - F(u))$ increases as u falls, which of course is true. However, underneath this statement is the implicit assumption that for any given intake u, the corresponding requirement v of an individual is known and can be uniquely determined in the sense that the error of measurement therein is negligible. In practice the requirement is not known. What can be determined for an individual is a regression estimate of his intake on N-balance for expected nitrogen retention in the case of a child and zero N-balance for constant body weight in the case of an adult. But an adult individual is rarely in zero balance except on average, and he cannot be in continuous positive or negative balance either. Experimental evidence shows that although the nitrogen balance in a man living on a protein level close to requirements is cyclic in character, it does not have a fixed amplitude and periodicity. The precise manner in which the requirement is regulated is not known, but for any given period under the circumstances described above, it may be assumed to deviate from the true requirement of an individual by a random variable with zero expected value and sizeable variance. Data available in the literature show that the variance between periods within individuals (i.e. intra-variability

σ_w^2) is comparable in magnitude to the true variance between individuals (i.e. inter-variability σ_b^2) and not zero as implied in the principle stated by the FAO/WHO expert committee. The probability of an individual developing dietary deficiency will therefore be small, unless his habitual intake fell below $(m - 3\sigma_w)$ or approximately below $(m - 2\sigma_w)$, where σ is the standard deviation of individual requirements based on total variation among individuals (Sukhatme 1973, and 1974). It follows that the incidence of protein deficiency would be exaggerated if $(m + 2\sigma)$ were adopted as the cut-off point for considering an individual at risk, in accordance with the interpretation proposed by the FAO/WHO Expert Committee. As an example, if it is assumed that u and v are independently but identically distributed with a frequency function $f(u)$, then for incidence.

$$I = \int (1 - F(u)) \times f(u)\, du$$

over all u

$$= \tfrac{1}{2}.$$

This means that 50% of the population will be considered deficient under the interpretation by the FAO/WHO expert committee, whereas if the intra-variability σ_w^2 is allowed for and assumed, in keeping with the available evidence, to be equal to true inter-variability, no more than 2·5% of the population should be considered to be deficient i.e. below $(m - 2\sigma)$ at 5% level of significance. In practice, the average intake may not be equal to the average requirement. Further, the intake will usually vary much more than the requirement. The magnitude of the correlation between intake and requirement will also influence the amount of incidence. The influence of these factors has been considered elsewhere and it was concluded that the incidence will tend to be grossly exaggerated if intravariability is assumed to be zero.

How gross the overstatement can be is also seen from the calculation of the overall size of the gap reported in the UN studies. As an example it has been shown that protein supplies would have to be increased three to four-fold in Maharashtra in order to limit to 2·5% the proportion of the population eating below $(m + 2\sigma)$. In effect this means that 97·5% of the population would have to eat at levels of over-consumption (or waste) several times greater than the average needs in order to limit the population at so-called risk to 2·5%. If it were not protein but some other nutrient, say Vitamin A, it would be justified to describe these levels of consumption as being in the toxic range. Even in the unlikely event where variability of intake is assumed to be equal to that of requirement, the logic amounts to raising the average protein requirement as determined from N-balance studies from m to $m \times ((m - 2\sigma)/(m + 2\sigma))$ without any physiological basis behind it. Such a step is even less justified when in India calorie and protein intake are correlated at the lower end of the distribution and calories are limiting. It is little wonder that the protein problem has been described as a protein gap problem of crisis proportions with the emphasis on increasing supply rather than demand among the undernourished.

Relevance and Role of Protein-rich Foods

The considerable attention that is being focussed on the production of protein-rich foods arises from the possible link between low protein consumption and Kwashiorkor. The importance of ensuring a smooth transition from breast feeding to an adequate solid diet is therefore evident. Weaning foods will undoubtedly help. It is not clear, however, why such weaning foods need to be protein-rich and why so great an emphasis is placed on the production of protein-rich infant foods. No more than 5–6% of the calories in breast milk are derived from protein and yet is accepted as an ideal infant food. If breast milk fails to meet the nutritional requirements of the infant after the first 6–8 months, it is not because its protein content is low but because it is just not available in adequate amounts to satisfy the appetite of a growing infant. On present evidence, therefore, and in the existing state of knowledge, the utilizable protein in the cereal-pulse diet should be more than adequate to meet infants' needs. Care will need to be exercised however to ensure that it is given in an appropriate form which enables the infant to consume sufficient quantities to meet his energy needs.

It is probable that even if a cereal-pulse based diet has more than enough utilizable protein to meet a child's needs, the bulk involved in meeting the energy needs may be too much for the child to take. Thus, whereas a one-year-old child requiring 1,000 calories can meet its needs with about 1·5 litres of milk containing roughly 180g of solids, the volume of cooked grains of rice or idli can be as high as 0·75kg, the equivalent of 0·25kg of dried cereals and pulses. Many studies in India and abroad have been made to see if a child can be successfully weaned and meet his daily energy needs on cooked meals of different dilutions. They all indicate that a child has little difficulty in consuming the needed quantity of the traditional diet of grain if it is given in an appropriate form and provided the diet is evenly spaced during the day. The latter is not much of a restriction since the toddler rarely eats all at one sitting, moving away the moment his appetite is satisfied. When, however, a diet is monotonous and the protein content is only marginally adequate, as for example when starchy roots are used along with grain, a child may turn away without taking enough to meet its needs. Actually, the criticism of bulk would apply equally to cereals fortified with amino acids. Thus, while fortification with lysine may improve the utilizable protein in bread, it will hardly increase its energy content so that the bulk needed to meet the energy needs even with fortified grains, would be the same. Clearly, what a child of 1–3 years needs most is a supplement of a concentrated source of calories which can also bring vitamins and minerals along with it, such as milk or eggs. If protein-rich weaning foods are advocated it should not be because of their high quality protein alone. In addition they should contain a concentrated source of calories, such as oil or sugar, which would reduce the volume of the meal and could also provide vitamins and minerals. Protein foods which do not bring adequate calories to synthesize protein in the diet clearly cannot be expected to make any significant contribution to the solution of the problem of protein malnutrition.

Why, then are developing countries being urged to produce protein-rich foods and to distribute them through special feeding programmes when there is so little justification to back these efforts? The answer in part may be traced to the recent breakthrough in food technology. The last decade witnessed phenomenal developments in creating new protein foods at a cost which is claimed to be only marginally higher than the cost of the primary product and much lower than that of animal protein products. There is therefore a feeling that it must be possible to use these advances in technology for the benefit of the poor without their having to wait for the time when animal products will be available at a cost within their reach. While appreciating this, the fact remains that inadequate quantities of food and not proteins *per se* is the primary problem in the diet of the poor. To add protein or upgrade its quality would merely provide a costly source of calories in order to make up the calorie deficit.

In criticizing the current policy of promoting lysine-fortified bread and similar products, it is not for a moment suggested that these products are not tasty or good products, but they have nothing in them by way of protein value that cannot be obtained from other locally available protein sources. It is also invidious to compare the cost per unit of protein in the new products with that in animal products in an effort to show how amino acid fortified bread is more economic. Actually, the animal products, and milk in particular, have a lot more to offer by way of nutrition than lysine-fortified bread. Yet, India in common with other countries is being successfully persuaded to expand the production of semi-conventional protein in the name of a commitment to combat malnutrition. It would appear that enthusiasts and entrepreneurs have combined to make such production a *fait accompli* even before the public has access to the true facts.

Conclusions

Protein malnutrition is a fundamental aspect of poverty and will persist as long as the purchasing capacity of the poor does not permit them to buy enough food to meet their energy needs. It is therefore important not to encourage dietary variety more than can be helped. This particularly applies to factory production of semi-conventional fortified protein foods which have little to offer by way of nutritional value over and above the cereal/pulse diets. Far from solving the protein problem, it will lead to a restructuring of the food supply to produce protein foods to satisfy the demand of the well-to-do sections of the population, depriving the poor of their share of the primary calories which they so badly need. The recent breakthrough in agriculture has considerable potential to increase the supply of food to meet the needs of Man for the foreseeable future. But increasing the supply in itself will not be adequate to solve the problem of uneven distribution. It is necessary that the supply should be matched by an effective demand on the part of the undernourished. As long as the poor are undernourished and prone to high rates of morbidity and have little to look forward to in life, it is unlikely that they can be sufficiently strongly motivated into adopting family planning as a way of life.

References

FAO/WHO, (1965). Protein requirements. *In* "Nutrition Meeting Report Series No. 37". FAO, Rome.

FAO/WHO, (1971). "Report of the Joint FAO/WHO Committee on Requirements for Protein and Energy".

Gopalan, C., Swarinathan, M. C., Krishna Kumari, V. K., RaO, D. H. and Vijayaraghavan, K. (1973). *Am. J. Clin. Nutr.* **26**, 563.

Payne, P. R. (1971). *In* "Proceedings of the First Asian Congress of Nutrition", p. 245. National Institute of Nutrition, Hyderabad.

Scrimshaw, N. S., Guzman, M. A., Flores, M. and Gordon, J. E. (1968). *Arch. Environ. Health* **16**, 223.

Sukhatme, P. V. (1970a). *Br. J. Nutr.* **24**, 477.

Sukhatme, P. V. (1970b). *Proc. Nutr. Soc.* **29**, 176.

Sukhatme, P. V. (1972). *Indian J. Agric. Econ.* **27**, 1.

Sukhatme, P. V. (1973). *In* "Resources and Population", Eugenics Society Symposium, p. 25. Academic Press, London.

Sukhatme, P. V. (1974). *J. R. Statist. Soc.* **A. 137**.

Marine Fisheries and World Food Supplies

S. J. HOLT

International Ocean Institute, Royal University of Malta

Summary

The paper reviews, up-dates and comments upon studies made by the Food and Agriculture Organization of the United Nations, mainly in the context of its Indicative World Plan for Agricultural Development (IWP). The living resources of the sea are limited, and do not hold the key to adequate nutrition of a continually growing human population. However, the "conventional" resources can yield more, perhaps twice as much as at present. And "unconventional" ones—animals lower in the food pyramid—could be utilized when technical problems of harvesting and processing them economically have been solved. Meanwhile, the growth rate of the world's fisheries is slowing down, and twice in recent years the catch has actually been lower than in the previous year. Existing fisheries are threatened in the short-term by overfishing, and in the longer term by pollution and by society's thirst for energy. Statistics showing the rapid growth of fisheries in the recent past obscure the continuous decline of "quality", as might be seen from the proportion of the catch which is for direct human consumption, rather than for reduction to fish oils and meals for animal feeds. An attempt is made to analyse this and examine "value" statistics.

Although most of the world's fisheries are over the continental shelves and increasingly coming under national jurisdiction, resources drawing on the productivity of the open ocean are of considerable importance. They could, and need to, be managed under a global ocean regime. But long-term beneficial exploitation of stocks living closer to shore will still in most cases require international management arrangements. An important geographical feature of the growth of world fisheries over the past two decades is the movement of products from the coastal waters of developing countries to the markets of richer ones. A new feature of the international debate is the interest taken by the consuming countries as well as by the producers in the continuity of fish supplies and the well-being of the resources. The source and weight of scientific advice on the implementation of management arrangements are becoming important as tension among nations increases over the apportionment of catches.

One possibility of improving ocean harvests is by the culture of fish and shellfish. How great this possibility is, and what global costs would be, have not yet been soundly estimated; the current fashion for it may be a reflection of the political and ecological difficulties of international management of natural stocks. However the coastal zones where mariculture is feasible are just those areas most affected by urban and industrial development, and the two kinds of development may not be compatible. An era may be approaching in which interactions between various uses of the ocean and its resources become as important as the competition between human groups for a particular resource, such as fish stocks. The most critical and difficult question, in this as in other spheres of human activity, is to weigh the present against the future and leave our successors on this planet a rich and diverse heritage.

Several years have passed since I reviewed the situation of world fisheries for the Jubilee Conference of the British Food Manufacturing Industries Research Association (Holt, 1969a,b). Soon after, FAO released its massive review of knowledge of marine fish resources (Gulland, 1970), compiled with the help of very many scientists as part of the Indicative World Plan (IWP) for Agricultural Development. More recently special supplements to that review have been published on particular resources—such as the cephalopods, octopus, squid and cuttlefish (Voss, 1973). Continuing analysis and evaluation, on a global basis, of industrial information and scientific data have a high priority in FAO's fishery work, and require an organized collaboration among specialists in many disciplines and from all regions of the world. I do no more here than offer personal comments on "official" studies and some observations about recent events.

Although Man's use of the ocean for purposes such as energy extraction, transportation and communication is increasing rather rapidly, fishing remains one of the most valuable ocean-based industries and employs a significant proportion of the world population. Total catches doubled each decade from 1950 to 1970, so that protein supply from the sea can be said to have been increasing much faster than the human population. These increases were achieved, however, mainly by the development of new fisheries on previously unexploited or lightly exploited resources, especially in the southern hemisphere. To a lesser extent some existing fisheries were intensified and gave greater yields but, at the same time, more and more of what had been the world's main fishing areas and resources, in the North Atlantic and North Pacific, became overfished—that is, despite more intensive fishing, catches did not increase, and some even declined. By 1970 it could be said that an end to expansion was in sight, and it was estimated that the total catch of about 60 million metric tons could not be increased to much more than 100 million, with 200 million as an optimistic upper limit. These predictions were based on a number of methods, ranging from rather sophisticated mathematical models of population dynamics to simple comparisons of production from apparently similar areas of the ocean, some of which had been heavily fished for decades and some more lightly and recently.

As it happened, 1969 turned out to be the first year since good statistics became available that the marine catch of fish and shellfish actually declined—from 55·9 million tons in 1968 to 54·3 million in 1969. The catch picked up to 60·7 million in 1970, but then dropped again to 60·3 million in 1971, and further to 56·2 million in 1972. A further decline may be expected in 1973 (see below). This is happening despite continuing growth in the amount of effort put into fishing.

Before looking at the causes and implications of these changes, a word is in order about the general statistics, as published annually by FAO. These are compiled from official national returns but are looked at rather critically by the secretariat. Because the catches of whales have always been reported in numbers, rather than as weights, they have never been included in the FAO totals for marine harvest. Recently, Lockyer, at the Whale Research Unit in London, has been calculating the weights of Antarctic whale catches, and in Malta the author has made similar calculations for the world. These show that at one time (1937) the four species of baleen and the sperm whales together accounted for 16% of marine catches, and probably a bigger proportion by value. Even in 1952 they still contributed 10% by weight, the fish catch meanwhile having increased by one-quarter. With the depletion of these stocks the whales now contribute only 2%, but the annual harvest of one million tons is still not a negligible contribution to world food supplies. If these stocks were really given a chance to recover, they could in future decades contribute perhaps about double this amount on a sustainable basis, and thus maintain their 2% contribution to a continuing ocean yield: that is if the traditional attitude that these creatures are a source of food and other organic products prevails over the newer idea that the Man/Food Equation can—and should—be solved without slaughtering the marine mammals. While several arguments support the latter view, that the whales are negligible as a resource is not a valid one. It should also be remembered that application of a cautious sustained yield policy would involve maintaining the number of whales alive in the sea at any time at perhaps two-thirds or more of the levels they attain when they are not exploited at all.

A further caution should be made regarding the interpretation of the catch statistics. Unit prices vary widely as between species and ocean regions. Thus the Mediterranean Sea, with an annual catch of less than a million tons, is usually reckoned as poor in fishery resources. But this catch is almost all consumed directly and fetches high prices. In terms of its landed value ($500 million), the Mediterranean catch is important, being worth more than, say, the productive fisheries of the North-West Atlantic and even of the famous Peruvian anchovy fishery, before its recent collapse. In addition, of course, some of the Mediterranean countries fish in other areas, especially the Atlantic. Add to this the excess of their fish and fish-product imports over exports, and it is found that the Mediterranean region is rather important—it consumes 10% by weight of world fish production (Holt, 1973).

The commercial marine fish catches include hundreds of different species. For a decade they have been dominated, however, by the anchovy (anchoveta)

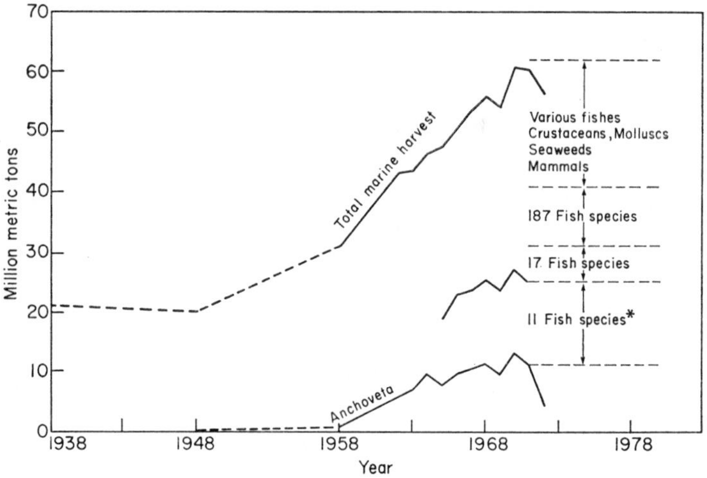

Fig. 1. Species composition of total marine harvest. *Eleven species each of which yielded over half a million tons in 1971, totalled a steady 14 million tons in period 1968–1971. Eight of these were already in the top eleven by 1966; the other three which subsequently declined were South African pilchard *(Sardinops ocellata)*, Japanese horse mackerel *(Trachurus japonicus)* and Pacific herring *(Clupea palassil)*.

of the Peru current, *Engraulis ringens* (Fig. 1). From only 30,000 tons in 1953, the catch of this species grew to 7·2 million tons by 1963. Catches in the period 1966 to 1971 ranged between 10 and 13 million tons annually and accounted for about 20% of the world catches. The recorded catches or landings in Peru of anchoveta are probably about 20% less than the actual catches, for reasons explained by Gulland (1972b). That discrepancy alone is more than the *total* catch of any other species than Alaska pollack or cod! Chile takes some anchoveta, but over 90% is taken by Peru. A further 25% of the total world catches came from the ten or eleven other species whose yields in 1971 each exceeded 500,000 tons. These species are:

	Catch (tons × 10^6)
Alaska pollack (*Theragra chalcogramma*)	3·4
Atlantic cod (*Gadus morhua*)	2·8
Atlantic herring (*Clupea harengus*)	2·1
Chub mackerel (*Scomber colias*)	1·7
Atlantic mackerel (*Scomber scomber*)	0·8
Cape hakes (*Merluccius capensis and M. paradoxus*)	0·8
Gulf menhaden (*Brevoortia patronus*)	0·7
Saithe (*Pollachius virens*)	0·7
Haddock (*Melanogrammus aeglefinus*)	0·5
European pilchard (*Sardina pilchardus*)	0·5

Certain of these—the menhaden, Alaska pollack and chub mackerel are examples—have grown over the last decade. Others—the haddock—have fluctuated widely while the herring has since declined to less than one half of its 1966 peak (see also Table 1).

TABLE 1

Some examples of growth and decline of species fisheries in the past decade

Engraulis ringens (Anchoveta) From nothing in 1948; 30,000 tons in 1958; 7 million tons in 1963; peak at 13 million in 1970, 11 million in 1971, 4·4 million in 1972.
Theragra chalcogramma (Alaska pollack) 350,000 tons in 1958; 700,000 tons in 1963; 3·4 million in 1971, still rising.
Clupea harengus (Atlantic herring) 2·5 millions tons in 1958; 2·9 million in 1963; peak of 4·1 million in 1966; thereafter declining to 2·1 million in 1971.
Scomber colias (Chub mackerel) 700,000 tons in 1964; steady growth to 1·8 million by 1970; may be near peak.

Continued

Scomber scomber (Atlantic mackerel)

200,000 tons in 1964; peak at 1·1 million in 1967; thereafter a slow decline.

Merluccius capensis and *M. paradoxus* (Cape hakes)

80,000 tons in 1958; 140,000 tons in 1964; rising to 700,000 tons 1968 to 1971.

Brevoortia patronus (Gulf menhaden)

Doubled from 360,000 tons in 1966 to 730,000 in 1971.

Sardinops ocellata (South African pilchard)

1 million tons in mid-1960s; peaked at 1·6 million in 1968 but down to 450,000 by 1971 and declining still.

Engraulis capensis (Cape anchovy)

From 180,000 tons in 1965 to 400,000 by 1970, 1971.

Trisopterus esmarkii (Norway pout)

From 80,000 tons in 1965 to 400,000 by 1971.

Boreogadus saida (Polar cod)

From 1,000 tons in 1966 to 350,000 by 1971.

Trachurus japonicus (Japanese horse mackerel)

From an initial 550,000 tons in 1965; halved by 1970–1971.

But

Trachurus trachurus (Atlantic horse mackerel)

Doubled in the same period from an initial 130,000 tons.

The reported total catches of "miscellaneous marine fishes" not identified by species, but certainly including hundreds of species (and probably an increasing number) have grown steadily, from 5·2 million tons in 1958, to 6·6 million in 1965 and 8·6 million in 1971.

These changes more or less cancel out, and it is seen that the year to year movements in total catch have been essentially determined by the varying anchoveta catches. Thus the catastrophic fall in these to only 4·4 million tons in 1972 alone brought the world catch down by 10% in that year. Even less is expected in 1973. The reasons for the fall are not yet clear, but the failure of the recruitment of young fish to the stock seems to be a consequence of over-fishing combined perhaps with unfavourable environmental conditions (Idyll, 1973). This is despite the existence of national controls and the availability of the best advice international groups of scientists have been able to give about a resource which has been the subject of intensive research for several years.

The earliest recognized cases of overfishing, mostly of bottom-living species in the North Sea, North-West Atlantic and North-East Pacific, were of rather long-lived species, individuals of which were being taken too young before their growth potential had been realized. In these cases, the malady was reversible—by fishing less intensively and concentrating on larger individuals the stocks would build up again within a few years—except in the case of long-living and slowly reproducing animals, such as the whales. Other, and several of the more recent cases of overfishing, have concerned shorter living species the reproductive capacity of which, as well as the growth realized, has been affected by fishing. The California sardine, the Hokkaido herring, the Atlantic herring, the South African pilchard (*Sardinops ocellata*) and now the anchoveta declined suddenly, and possibly irreversibly. It seems possible that such declines can be accompanied, or followed by, the rapid increase of another species which has similar food and environmental requirements. Thus, the effects of fishing may be reversible. Further, the catastrophic decline may not occur until there is an unfavourable combination of circumstances—high fishing pressure plus an environmentally adverse year or two.

In the light of these experiences, it may be seriously questioned whether even the lower FAO/IWP estimate of 100 million tons will be reached. It is worth being reminded that to double the present catch will require both large increases and considerable changes in the distribution of the effort put into fishing. On the one hand, more intensive fishing on an *underfished* resource gives increases in yield less than proportionate to the increase in the amount of fishing. On the other hand, in cases of *overfished* stocks, the same or greater catches *could* be taken with less than the present effort—sometimes with very much less. In this latter connection Gulland (1968) has given an example which is worth quoting here in full:

> "The total harvest from the oceans would be increased if some fishing effort could be diverted from the heavily fished but still economically attractive stocks to other less attractive but less heavily fished ones. For instance, off the west coasts of Ireland and Scotland the hake is badly 'overfished' while the blue whiting, which is eaten in some Mediterranean countries and at least could be used for making fishmeal, is not fished at all. If in future half the vessels at present fishing for hake fished for blue whiting, the total catch of hake would almost certainly increase and there would be considerable additional catches of blue whiting. Although such a scheme seems attractive, it is impossible to achieve at present. The ships that continued to fish for hake (with rather more than twice the catch for each ship) would make large profits while the other half would probably be operating at a loss. The problem of deciding who would make the

profit and who would drop out would be difficult enough to solve if only one country rather than three or four were involved."

The data on fishing power and investment necessary to determine how much would be required to take the eventual sustained harvest under conditions of rational management are not available; for future international policy determination such statistics will be as important as the existing data about catches. However, examples of heavily exploited stocks and excessive fishing capacity of fleets can now be found in all parts of the world (Gulland, 1972a). The shore plants of Peru could, if worked to full capacity, process the entire world fish catch; the catching side is also over-expanded and has to be controlled by long closed seasons and other restrictions. The forces leading to increase in numbers, size and efficiency of fishing fleets may continue, but it will soon be even more difficult for over-expansion in one situation to be corrected by diverting efforts to new areas.

Just as the anchoveta determined global trends and obscured smaller

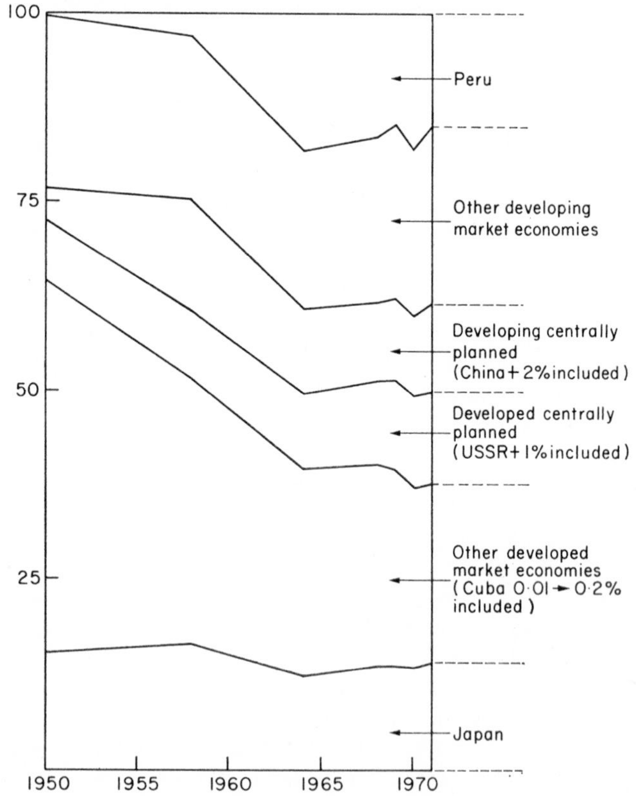

Fig. 2. Trends in marine catches by country groups (percentages of totals).

trends within these, so this domination can lead to other distorted conclusions. Thus, it has been said that in recent years catches by "developing" countries have grown relative to those by the more "developed" countries, to use the UN terminology. This is hardly true if Peru is excluded from the calculation, although a few other "developing" countries such as South Korea, have been able to increase their fisheries substantially. In addition, of course, it is well known that most of the increases by developing countries have found their way to the richer countries, in such forms as fishmeal at one extreme of the price range and frozen shrimp at the other. This process has benefited the entrepreneurs in the producing countries and some of their governments, but not always their people, and certainly not nutritively (Figs 2 and 3 and Table 2).

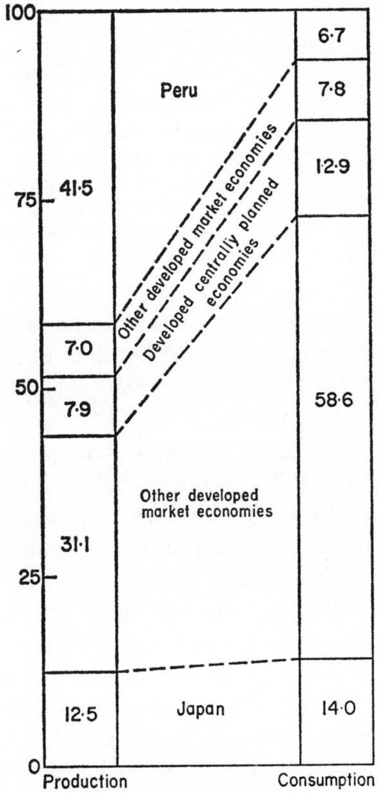

Fig. 3. Percentage of total annual fishmeal production and consumption by country groups: data for 1970 when production was 5·4 million tons. Of this amount 5·0 million tons was derived from "oily" fishes, the proportion (91%) being practically unchanged since the early 1960s.

TABLE 2
Trend in catches by developing countries

Year	Percentage of world catch taken by developing countries		
	All	All except Peru	All except Peru and China
1950	27·3	26·8	22·7
1958	39·4	36·5	24·3
1964	50·5	32·3	23·1
1968	48·6	32·2	23·8
1969	48·4	33·6	25·1
1970	50·6	32·5	23·5
1971	50·0	34·8	24·9

The above figures are derived from combined inland and marine catches, excluding whales. For marine fish alone the performance of developing countries is about the same throughout the period. Most whales were caught by a few of the "developed" countries; they decreased between 1950 and 1958 and thereafter but their contribution to the total was not large enough markedly to affect the trend of figures in this table. Statistics for China were not very good; two-thirds of the Chinese catch is from inland waters.

An important phenomenon of recent years is the shift of fleets of temperate northern hemisphere countries to the exploitation of resources in the tropics and southern hemisphere. This has occurred on both sides of the Atlantic; two examples suffice to illustrate the point. Catches from the Eastern Central Atlantic, between the Straits of Gibraltar and the mouth of the Congo totalled 2·6 million tons in 1971. Of this, 34% was taken by the 22 "developing" countries along that coast—including 28% by five of them: Morocco, Senegal, Ghana, Nigeria and Ivory Coast. The remaining 66% was taken by 19 countries *not* coastal to the region—virtually all "developed" ones, such as USSR, Japan, Spain, Poland, France, Italy and Greece. Furthermore, whereas the rate of increase of catch by the coastal countries averaged 7% annually in the period 1964–1971, that by the non-coastal countries was 18%. The number of "non-coastal" countries participating in the fisheries of this region rose from 14 in 1964 to 20 in 1970, the "newcomers" including Cuba, Norway and East Germany. South Africa came in briefly in 1969 and 1970, but a new phenomenon was the arrival of Bermuda in 1969, increasing to rank as fifth by 1971. The Bermuda registration is a "flag of convenience" for vessels really linked with various maritime powers, including some countries which themselves report catches from the area and others, such as the UK, which do not. There are other flags of convenience among the African coastal states.

South of the Congo, in the South-East Atlantic, the catch grew 4% annually from 1·9 million tons in 1964 to 2·4 million in 1971. This growth is attributed entirely to the increase of catches by vessels from northern hemisphere countries which by 1970–1971 numbered at least 10 countries and accounted for two-fifths of the catch.

The author has tried to calculate approximately the true contribution of marine fisheries to human nutrition. It is well-known that the proportion of the catch which is reduced to meal and oil has been growing steadily since the end of World War II. Some figures are: 13% in 1948, 16% in 1958, 25% in 1961, 35% in 1971 (data actually for marine plus freshwater catches, excluding whales, but this has no effect on the trends. These percentages include 2 or 3% used for miscellaneous purposes, including bait for other fishes.). The fishmeal goes almost entirely to livestock feeding, most of it—80%—to poultry. In fact, fishmeal now provides 11% of the world supply of animal feed protein. The author has calculated, from information provided by colleagues in FAO, by the International Association of Fishmeal Manufacturers, and by producers in Malta, that about 11 tons of fish are required to produce the feed to produce one ton of livestock. Thus one-eleventh of the weight of fish annually turned into meal, the weight of fish going directly to human consumption, and the weight of fish oil produced (most of which also goes directly to human foods, particularly as margarine) have been summed to give the following totals for some recent years (Table 3).

TABLE 3

	Tons $\times 10^{-6}$
1966	32·9
1967	34·2
1968	35·1
1969	34·7
1970	37·5
1971	38·0

The calculation of flesh production is complicated by the fact that the edible portion of livestock ("dressing percentage") differs from that of fish ("fillet yield"). For poultry it is now about 70% and for pigs 76%. Fillet yields vary greatly between types of fishes over a range of 30–70% but are said to average 30–35%. This would mean that to bring fish catches and livestock production to a common unit of flesh weight a reduction factor on the livestock production of five or six should be used, rather than eleven. The author has not done this because to be consistent all the marine catches should not be summed in the first place, but rather appropriate factors should be applied to shrimps, bivalves, squids, seaweeds and so on, and even to different species of fish going to direct human consumption. Furthermore, all units should then be properly reduced to protein yields, and the relation of energy input to the output from the productive system should be looked at; however that must be the subject of a further, and much more difficult, study along the lines discussed by Leach (pp. 139–163). Comments are therefore confined to the above figures for "round fresh weight equivalents", noting that the conclusions do not depend at all critically on the exact factor of 11 for the fish to livestock conversion.

Such calculations rather modify the view of annual progress in obtaining food from the sea. For the above years it is found:

TABLE 4

Mean annual rate of growth (%)	Five-year sliding averages 1966–1970	1967–1971	1968–1972
Marine catches, including whales	5·2	3·2	0·1
Marine catches of fish and shellfish	5·4	3·5	−0·05
Marine catches excluding anchoveta	4·3	3·8	2·8
Catches for direct human consumption[a]	2·6	2·8	3·0
Food entering human food supply directly or indirectly of marine origin	3·4	2·7	2·5

[a]These have maintained a *continuous* growth throughout, averaging 3% annually over the past decade. Fish catches from inland waters have maintained about the same rate of growth; they have constituted, for two decades, 14% of the world aquatic catch.

For comparison it is noted that the estimated current annual rate of increase in human population is 1·8%. So marine production does still have an edge on population growth, but by not nearly so much as the raw statistics would suggest. Any faltering of one or two years in the fishery growth which is not made up immediately afterwards, leads to a fall in per capita production. On the other hand, if an average growth rate of about 4% could still be maintained, fishery production will have doubled and thus reached its estimated maximum in about 17 years—that is by 1990. In fact, recent growth, as is clear from Fig. 4, is more nearly linear than exponential, which would give a few more years to the doubling date.

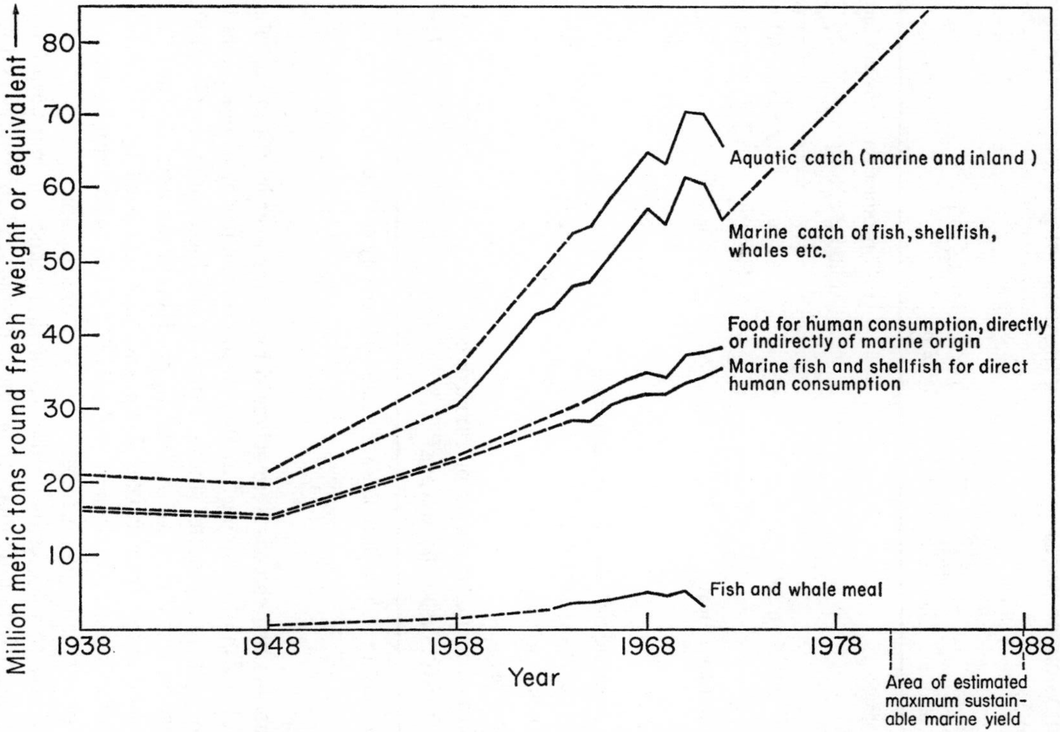

Fig. 4. Growth in supply of food and feed of aquatic origin.

At this point it is worth putting the sea-fisheries into perspective by comparison with production of livestock and dairy products. Blaxter (1968) looked at the growth of animal production in the period 1952–1967. During that period the human population increased by 34%, and production of various commodities as shown below (he does not give a figure for poultry) (Table 5).

TABLE 5

	1967 production millions of tons	15-year increase %
Beef and buffalo meat	278	60
Pork[a]	31	93
Sheep and goat meat	6	50
Milk	373	44
Eggs	9	61
The corresponding values for sea-fish are		
for direct human consumption	31	63
for reduction to meal and oil	21	660
total sea-fish	52	146
sea-fish contribution to human nutrition, direct and indirect via poultry and pigs[a]	33	74

[a] The increase in pork production is attributable only in very small part to the fishmeal contribution to feed.

Increases in fish catches were achieved by taking ever increasing numbers of individual fish of declining "quality"—that is smaller or of less direct use—and by reducing standing stocks. Much of the increase in terrestrial animal production was due to an increase in production per animal. Thus "carcass meat production from cattle, sheep and pigs increased by 73% while the numbers of these animals increased only 41%; egg production increased 61% while poultry numbers increased by 43%; and so on.

It is easy to underestimate the world significance of marine products in human nutrition, quite apart from the fish "hidden" in poultry and pigs. In terms of animal protein production fish now ranks third, after milk and meat. But two-thirds of the milk and meat are consumed by the more affluent countries. The remainder depend largely on aquatic products, mostly marine, for the greater part of their annual intake of animal protein.

It was not the intention of this paper to be pessimistic about the ocean as a future source of food for Man, but rather to lead to an appreciation that success will require more than merely intensifying fishing, going to more new areas (there are fewer and fewer of them left), or improving techniques. Indeed, without control of the total fishing effort and its distribution by region, species, and among countries, improvements in technology simply lead to more expensive and economically less efficient fishing operations. Partial international controls, such as the promulgation of overall catch quotas, actually hasten this process by encouraging a race between operators and between countries to secure greater parts of the quota, always by increasing costs per unit of fishing effort and per unit of yield. If added to this is the fact that controls on one fishery lead to movement of fishing effort into another fishery (for example, a quota on the eastern tropical Pacific tuna fishery has led to periodic movements of US vessels through the Panama Canal to the as yet unregulated Atlantic), and that controls agreed by regional fishery commissions do not apply to vessels of nations which do not choose to join the commission, and are not, in some cases, even binding on the member states (as in the case of the International Whaling Commission), then the growing tendency for states to extend their national jurisdiction over wider areas of adjacent sea, as well as over the sea-bed where oil is the determinant, is understandable.

However, national appropriations will not alone solve overfishing problems, though they may make easier some decisions about who takes the catch. This can be substantiated by many examples; one will suffice here. The fishery for shrimps in the Gulf of California is carried out exclusively by Mexican-flag vessels in waters claimed by Mexico. Some relevant approximate figures are given in Table 6.

TABLE 6

	No. of boats	Catch per boat (tons/year)	Catch (tons)
1950	100	100	10 000
1960	400	50	20 000
1970	800	25	20 000
1973	>800	<20	<20 000

So the same catch could have been taken with half the effort or less, and at even less cost because during this period the efficiency and the cost of a fishing unit—vessel plus fishing gear—have been increasing. The increased costs of fishing are more than balanced by the rise in price of shrimp, so the income to individual fishermen is maintained, or rises, giving continued incentive to expansion and perpetuation of this irrational situation.

If everyone were to appropriate some wide band, such as 200 miles (or up to the median line, if less), then there would still be the problem of the salmon, whales, squid, tuna, and other oceanic animals, and also the movement of fish along coasts from one "national" sea to an adjacent one and across small productive seas such as the North Sea, the Caribbean and the Baltic.

One condition for continued growth—or even maintenance—of the marine fisheries is, then, comprehensive arrangements for their international management, based on sound research. "Comprehensive" includes the effective participation of *all* fishing countries, that is of all coastal countries, and some of the land-locked ones.

At the regional level this aspect of the research and management problem can be seen in areas such as the Eastern Central and South-East Atlantic, referred to earlier, where many fleets are fishing off shores distant from their bases. The FAO Fishery Committee for the Eastern Central Atlantic (CECAF) has met three times—in March 1969, May 1971 and December 1972. Membership has grown but representation by members varies and tends to decline—from 19 attending the first Session out of 23, to 18 out of 28 at the third Session. (Actually 3 members—one African and two "non-coastal" have not attended *any* session—they account for 2% of the catch). Those not regularly attending account for 3 to 5% of catches by Member States. But catches from the area in 1971 by *non*-member states were 40% of the total—30% by the USSR and 10% by a number of others.

South of the Congo the International Commission for the South-East Atlantic Fisheries (ICSEAF) took responsibility at a later date and had its first session in April 1972; the second was in December 1973. Here the situation seems better. There are fewer coastal countries and rather fewer non-coastal fleets operating. Nearly all the catches are taken by the 6 Member States (including, in this case, the USSR) which participated in the first session, or by others which had in October 1969 signed the convention setting up the Commission, had not yet ratified it, but had sent observers to the session.

In these, as in other inter-governmental bodies, some countries do not participate because their statehood or acceptability is disputed by the members, by the UN or by FAO. There is however another rather undesirable aspect of this matter—the extent to which many states are represented at meetings of fishery bodies by staff of a local embassy rather than by the authorities responsible for the conduct of the national fishery in the area, and by the scientists also concerned.

Lastly, in present conditions there is not only the question of bringing all countries which fish in a region into the local management arrangements but also the increasing problem of the "flags of convenience", as mentioned in the example above. Just as some operators of tankers, yachts and other vessels find it advantageous to register their vessels in Liberia, Panama or the Bahamas, although they have little real link with those countries, so, as attempts are made to get more drastic fishery regulations into effect, there is an additional incentive for fishing vessel operators to switch flags. Indeed, with modern fishing operations involving processing at sea, transferred catches, and so on, together with political problems of advanced countries fishing off the coasts of developing countries, it is increasingly difficult to sort out the catch statistics on a national basis. Of course this sort of problem is not unique to fisheries, or even to ocean-based industries—the multi-national corporations have seen to that—but there are special fishery aspects of it.

Some sea areas, such as the Indian Ocean, can certainly yield greater catches through the normal "development" process—exploration to find resources, investment in the appropriate types of vessels and gear, harbour construction, processing and market development. The areas yet to be "developed" in this way lie near to "developing", under-fed countries, and the political problem of their governments and their peoples is how to secure the benefits of these resources. Some are inclined to appropriation, some to the designation of all the offshore resources as a "common heritage of mankind". How this works out will be seen as the UN Conference on the "Law of the Sea" unfolds in 1974–1975.

The weight of living material removed annually from the ocean can undoubtedly be increased enormously as has often been suggested, by exploiting, further down the food chain; by catching smaller species not only of fish but of plankton—especially, perhaps, crustaceans. Instead of catching baleen whales, their food could be caught—the abundant euphausids (krill) and copepods. In some countries, principally Japan and the USSR, the technology for this—both catching and processing—is being actively studied, and so is the relevant science—the biological productivity of this trophic level, and the oceanographic conditions which determine its concentration in time and space. Marketing trials with krill products for human consumption——paste and "cheese"—have already been made. But it is still necessary to look not only for quantities of production, but also for concentrations of biomass, whether fish, whales or euphausids are caught.

It is known that there are considerable, but still unassessed, quantities of squids, and lantern fishes in the open ocean, some in deep water. Voss (1973) thinks that cephalopod catches over the continental shelves could be increased from the present one-and-a-half million tons to a sustainable eight million or so. (There are some discrepancies among published figures for present cephalopod catches. The FAO figure for 1971 was 0·9 million tons as reported; taking into account unreported catches by countries with inadequate statistical systems gives an estimate of a little over 1 million tons.) Oceanic squid potential, estimated mainly on the basis of their predation by sperm whales, might be more than fifty times that amount. But the costs of collecting them, far from land, below the surface and perhaps rather thinly spread over vast areas, may be enormously high whether calculated in terms of money or expenditure of energy. Even normal deep-sea trawling, no "rent" being paid for the sea and the fish there for the taking, turns out to be a highly "expensive" undertaking in terms of energy consumption per kilogram of food produced (Slesser, 1973).

But it is necessary to wait for a more careful analysis of the sense of attacking the next trophic level. For example, a factor commonly assumed in ecological work for the relation between the standing crops of predatory species and their prey is ten. This ratio is of the same order as that describing the efficiency with which anchovetas are now converted into poultry and pigs. If a harvest of planktonic organisms is utilized in this sort of way, with that efficiency, more human food might not be obtained from the sea than by husbanding and harvesting the larger animals which feed on the plankters, and consuming those directly—it depends, among other things, on what proportion of the production at the lower trophic level was in fact being consumed by the particular predators caught. Better calculations than this crude one are needed to develop rational policies in this regard, as well as some consideration of the wider ecological effects of intensive harvesting at trophic levels nearer to primary production. It is also pertinent to ask what special arrangements may be needed to ensure that the people of the world as a whole, especially the under-fed nations, may benefit from any exploitation of these "unconventional" resources, rather than their being effectively "appropriated" by a few powerful nations, as were the whales.

Most attempts at marine fish management have been concerned with a single species or groups of a few preferred species. At that level one can perhaps safely ignore the complex and largely unknown interactions between species, but not when more and more species are exploited more heavily, first mostly those on one or two trophic levels, and then on more trophic levels. Further, fishery management is at present concerned with the resolution of conflict *within* one particular use of the sea—fishing. Attempts are being made to regulate the competition between individuals, between users of different kinds of fishing gear and between national fleets, and to harmonize current use of the resource with its future use. But in the near future another problem may be of as much concern—harmonizing the fishery use of the ocean and sea-bed with other uses, and resolving conflicts between them. Some other uses, such as oil extraction, seem so far to have little effect on the fisheries. But the effects even of the transport, and hence spillage, of oil on living resources are far from well understood. And the effects of the use of the sea as a waste dump, for substances other than oil, on fisheries are seen to be considerable, mainly adverse, and growing. The pace of increase in other marine activities, and the growing diversity of these, must surely soon bring us nearer to a situation where fishery management is recognized as an element of total ocean space management, and where the regulation of interactions *between* uses is as important as the regulation of interactions within a particular use.

A solution to the problem of overall marine management seems to be a necessary condition for a move to the next stage of food extraction from the sea—by culture rather than by hunting. Much has been written in recent years about the possibilities of mariculture—of raising fishes, crustaceans, and molluscs. In some ways this is a refuge from the despair of ever getting effective international action to manage the open sea fisheries; a retreat to sheltered waters already under national jurisdiction and effective control. Earlier attempts to "improve" wild stocks—for example, of plaice in the North Sea, by breeding and transplantation—foundered in the absence of enforceable controls over harvesting. The dangers to significant growth in coastal aquaculture are in the conflict with other uses of the sea—for waste disposal, for tourism and industry and so on. No one can say what is the world potential for mariculture, even using known techniques—or rather, calculation of such a figure is meaningless without reference to decisions about the alternative uses to which coastal waters are to be put. It will be a long time, even in the best conditions, before culture industries could develop to give yields as high as the present larger fisheries. But the products from them *do* go direct to human nutrition, they are usually of high unit value, and the technique often requires considerable labour. The conditions of available labour, relatively unpolluted water and few other uses of the coastal zone are met in several "developing" countries, and with the importation of new techniques developed in Japan and elsewhere, together with appropriate marketing and processing arrangements, a considerable development of various forms of mariculture might be expected in those countries in the next decade.

Finally, to refer to one economic aspect of fishery management for long-term benefits; in the UK at present, and perhaps elsewhere, investment in the public sector is currently measured against a 10% rate of compound interest. It has been pointed out that this in effect rules out any expenditure the benefit from which will not be realized for some decades; the argument has been applied to the slogan "plant a tree in '73", which might make economic sense if the discount were calculated as *simple* interest (Tinker, 1973). It happens that the net growth rate of whale populations is less than 10%—it varies as between whale species, and the average might even be as low as 5%.

Recent studies by Clark (1973a, b) at the University of British Columbia and by others (Crowe, 1969; Fife, 1971; Smith, 1969) have indicated that it may have been fallacious for those who sought rational management of whaling to say that if only whalers could appreciate their long-term self-interest and stop cutting each other's throats, they would keep their activity within reasonable bounds. On the contrary, "rational" economic behaviour would, if the future discount rate is assumed to be higher than the whale stock recovery rate, probably be to exterminate the whales as fast as practicable, or at least to push the stocks down—perhaps irreversibly—to very low levels, and then close down the industry.

The lesson from such bioeconometric modelling, which I would like to see pursued much more, is not that this is indeed how some of the renewable resources of the ocean *should* be treated but that different criteria are needed to guide such long-term activities.

References

Blaxter, K. L. (1968). *Sci. J.* **4,** (5), 53.
Clark, C. W. (1973a) *Science* **181,** (4100), 360.
Clark, C. W. (1973b). *J. Polit. Econ.* **81,** 950.
Crowe, B. L. (1969). *Science* **166,** (3969), 1103: 1107.
Fife, D. (1971). *Environment* **13,** (3), 20.
Gulland, J. A. (1968). *Sci. J.* **4,** (5), 81.
Gulland, J. A. (Compiler) (1970). "The Fish Resources of the Ocean" .FAO Fish. Tech. Pap. (97). Revised edition. Issued 1972 by Fishing News (Books), London.
Gulland, J. A. (1972a). *In* "World Fisheries Policy: Multidisciplinary View" (B. J. Rothschild, ed.) pp. 175–188. University of Washington.
Gulland, J. A. (1972b). "Population Dynamics of World Fisheries". University of Washington, Sea Grant Program.
Holt, S. J. (1969a). "Food from the Sea". Papers of Golden Jubilee Conference of BFMIRA, October 20–21, 1969, No. 10.
Holt, S. J. (1969b). *Scient. Amer.* **221,** (3), 178.
Holt, S. J. (1973). *Opt. Med.* No. 19, 80.
Idyll, C. P. (1973). *Scient. Amer.* **228,** (6), 22.
Slesser, M. (1973). *Ecologist* **3,** 216.
Smith, V. L. (1969). *J. Polit. Econ.* **77,** 181.
Tinker, J. (1973). Review of a paper by W. R. D. Sewell, *New Scient.* **58,** 175.
Voss, G. L. (1973). "Cephalopod Resources of the World". FAO Fish. Circ. (149).
"Yearbooks of Fishery Statistics" published annually by FAO, in two sets of volumes—"Catches and Landings" and "Fishery Commodities". At the time of writing the most recently available were for the year 1971, and provisional catch data for 1972. Special compilations are also issued in the FAO series "Bulletin of Fishery Statistics".

Cultivated Plants—Past, Present and Future

J. T. WILLIAMS

Department of Botany, University of Birmingham

Summary

Some of the most important aspects of the domestication of crop plants are discussed, and the point stressed that the primitive cultivated plants were immensely variable. In the past, Man has dipped into this pool of variability to produce the world's present crops, and plant breeding has become an important modern science. However, the richness of the plant resources is disappearing at an alarming rate from those parts of the world where the diversity is found, and the future of Man will depend heavily on the conservation of the right plant genetic resources.

The dependence of Man on plants relates to his necessity to fulfill diverse needs. Primarily, plants act as a source of food, but their utilization includes their handling in domestic building, clothing, tanning and medicine as well as their utilization for mechanical purposes.

In pre-agricultural times, Man gathered plants from the wild, for instance, the nut of hazel was an important dietary constituent of primitive agricultural Mesolithic Man in Europe (Rankine *et al.*, 1960) as were seeds of many other plants such as dandelions and water lilies (Curwen, 1938). Similarly, in prehistoric times, Man in the Sahara region gathered seeds of wild grasses such as *Panicum turgidum* and even in the agricultural settlements of the present day the seeds are used to supplement the diet, while in subsistence settlements the gathering and utilization of the seeds has persisted unchanged from early days, and long before the introduction of cereals (Williams and Farias, 1972).

Plant domestication began by Man planting what he had collected and domestic races were developed, although this is an over-simplification of the story. Hawkes (1969) pointed out that the domestication process for seed agriculture involved three stages: a) the gathering of plants, and the natural colonization by these plants around dwellings, b) the harvesting of the plants that colonized, and c) intentional sowing of the plants. Furthermore, other plants reproduce vegetatively by roots and tubers, and it has even been postulated that agriculture based on roots and tubers preceded that based on seeds. However, Hawkes considered the stages of domestication to show close chronological similarities. Whatever the form of the actual plant, it is the domestic races that were developed that are considered to be cultivated plants, and the evolution of cultivated races from wild ones is what is understood by the term plant domestication.

Apart from the often obscure details of the evolution of the cultivated races, the domestication process has had profound effects of Man and his environment. Dimbleby (pp. 117–125) has considered the environment and Man's attitude to it through the ages. This paper discusses some of the general aspects of the domestication process which are important when considering the origin and evolution of cultivated plants. Much of the research in this subject tries to reconstitute what has happened in the past, but it must be stressed that the gross dimensions of time and space hide many effective variables, and often, when clusters of characters are analysed, important aspects of historical change, such as cultural significance, cannot be taken into account.

The information about the beginning and development of food production in different parts of the world is provided from direct archaeological evidence when actual plant remains have been found, indirect archaeological evidence which suggests the presence of agriculture, and evidence from ethnology and linguistics, as well as from botany. Most of the botanical work is relatively recent, because cultivated plants have often been taken for granted, origins have been lost and even the wild species from which the cultivated races have been derived have received little uniformity of treatment by taxonomists. This surprising diversity of treatment has been due partly to the fact that these wild species represent widely separated floras that have been treated in different ways without reference to each other, and partly because the dynamic concepts of species themselves had not been rationalized, and evolutionary affinities were masked by descriptions not employing comparable characters.

The types of plants making up the staple diet tended to decrease in variety.

It is a startling fact that of the 350,000 or so species of flowering plants of the world, a minute proportion have been important enough to enter into the world's economy—in fact about 3,000. Manglesdorf (1961) has pointed out that the majority of the people of the world at the present are fed by twelve species only. There are three important cereals—rice, wheat and maize; three root crops—potato, sweet potato and cassava; two legumes—bean and soya bean; two sugar producers—cane and beet; and lastly the coconut and banana. Runners-up would include sorghum and peanuts. These crops are not used equally, and Manglesdorf stressed the fact that at least 30% of all human energy is obtained from the one species of plant, rice. With the rising world population, the problems of food production are immense, and cannot be solved by the wealthy countries capitalizing the poorer ones. Far more fundamental research and effort is required so that the question that this volume poses can be at least partially resolved.

If the vast numbers of non-flowering plants are considered, even fewer have been utilized. The best examples are the lichens, e.g. *Cladonia sp*., the Reindeer moss used by the North American Indians, and *Leonora esculenta,* the manna used by the ancient Israelites; although other plants such as algae and fungi have been gathered for food. In recent years, research has shown that some of these lower plants represent huge untapped reservoirs of potential protein sources for human food.

One of the most significant features of plant domestication is related to settlement patterns. The types of settlement patterns evolved concurrently with diverse civilizations each with its own rationality, logic and reason operating in necessarily narrow thought structures. It must be emphasized that, even in the great civilizations long past, there was nothing to suggest the idea of human evolution and progress, because experience did not encourage the belief in an upward movement, and the relevant mythologies suggested a decline from a primeval golden or heroic age. The hope of earthly social improvement (as a concept of continual progress with no discernible limit: Mazzeo, 1967), had to wait for the Renaissance, although the very long-term socio-economic changes caused by the Agricultural Revolution had paved the way thousands of years before. The long period that Man took to become an agriculturist is about 99·5% of his total period on earth (Hawkes, 1969) and for most of this time period Man had no philosophical concept of progress.

The point has been made that if Man had never developed beyond the hunting and food gathering stage, the maximum population the world could support would only be about one hundredth of what it is today (Dimbleby, 1967). It cannot be said that agriculture caused the increase in population, only that it was one major factor.

The development of cultivated plants, and their utilization in agricultural systems, emphasized the seasonal aspects of plant growth, especially since there was the tendency to limit the diversity of plants utilized. It is necessary to infer strong early selection processes. Vavilov (1926) stressed that the primitive ancestral forms of cultivated plants already possessed properties conducive to cultivation, and Man took what was available, so that part of the domestication process may well have been independent of Man's will. However, in the early centuries of cultivation Man looked for suitable characteristics in the plants, not from the point of view of protein or carbohydrate content, but subjectively from the point of view of taste and desirability. At the same time plants which produced a good stand of seedlings, those that lacked dormancy mechanisms spreading the germination over many months, and those that produced a modicum of yield were all selected for, by the harvesting-planting cycle. In most wild species the seeds are dispersed by the plant, but forms which retained the seed were selected for thus allowing more effective and uniform harvesting.

A corollary of the semi-conscious improvement of the agricultural plants and systems highlights the point made by Vavilov (1926) that a number of crops were not taken into cultivation from the wild but arose later as weeds of cultivation. Of the staple food plants, wheat, barley, rice, maize and potatoes are thus primary crops, taken into cultivation from the wild. Rye and oats are examples of secondary crops, which were originally weeds. As weeds they had been selected unconsciously, as the crop plant was selected, because forms had become adapted to growth as a weed, even in so far as mimicking the crop plant.

Old World

Ethiopia
Mediterranean
Asia Minor, Persia and the Caucasus
Afghanistan, Turkestan and North West India
India and Burma
Far East, Thailand, Malaya and Java
China

New World

Mexico and Guatemala
Bolivia, Peru, Ecuador and Columbia
South Chile
Brazil and Paraguay
United States of America

Fig. 1. Gene centres, or centres of origin and variation (after Vavilov).

Hawkes (1969) has pointed out that the incentive to cultivate the land in the early stages of agriculture arose from the availability of a *surplus* and not from hunger. After the 9,000 years or so since domestication began, the wheel has turned a full circle, and it is now necessary to consider cultivation to stem the tide of hunger.

The idea of food production did not stem from a single origin. There were independent centres of agricultural origins based on many diverse species of plants, and some of them have been well described e.g. that in East Asia (Chang, 1970) or the New World (McNeish, 1965). The botanical evidence concerning centres of domestication of cultivated plants was unified by Vavilov (1926). He described twelve major centres in the world where great variability was apparent in cultivated plants (Fig. 1). These centres, he postulated, were in reality the centres of origin for the crops concerned, or secondary centres of diversity.

Lastly, domestication extending over several thousands of years had its own peculiarities in different areas of the world. These ideas can now be extrapolated directly to Man, and it is understood that the Agricultural Revolution caused a differential increase in some groups of societies. The idea of the agricultural or Neolithic revolution as a concept of diffusion was introduced by Childe in 1958. This certainly explains the spread of intentional food production in the Sahara, Europe and many other areas (Balout, 1955; Clark, 1965, 1969), and in all cases, a cultivated plant, if of economic value, expanded its area to reach its potential agricultural limits. Whether diffusion was due to actual movements of people, or by cultural diffusion or by a mixture of the two, in other words a "cultural ecology" (Flannery, 1965), the Neolithic revolution was a long process that was at least intentional. If superimposed on this hypothesis is the fact that early plant domestication greatly modified the population of Man, and that possible adaptive variation resulted from changes in the economy caused by the Neolithic revolution (even so far as some groups becoming famine-adapted; Brothwell, 1969), then to the intentional aspects must be added a micro-evolutionary result, the evidence of which will be forthcoming from palaeo-histopathological and skeletal studies in relation to disease, stature, age and mortality.

The history of the wheats well illustrates the kind of evolutionary processes that have been elucidated by the work of botanists, plant explorers and plant breeders. In the Neolithic period, the species of wheats that were cultivated are now more or less unknown in modern agriculture, although one is still grown in poor sites in parts of Europe and the Near East as cattle fodder. There were two wheats, Einkorn (*Triticum monococcum*) and Emmer (*T. dioccum*) respectively derived by domestication from the wild forms, *T. boeoticum* and *T. dicoccoides* (Fig. 2). The wild Einkorn has brittle ears, but in the cultivated one the ears remain intact so that reaping and threshing are

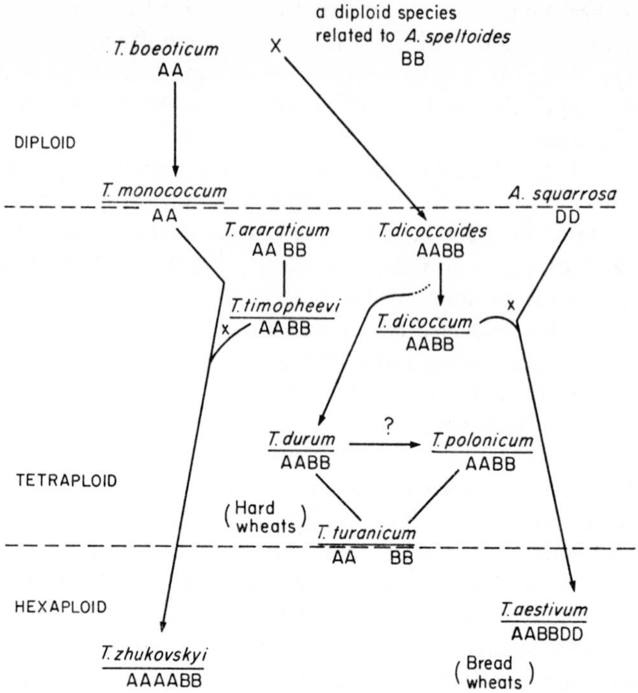

Fig. 2. The evolutionary relationships between species of wheat (those underlined are cultivated, those not, wild).

necessary. Wild Einkorn is found in open woodland and steppe as well as secondarily occuring as a weed, and it shows wide geographical and morphological variation. Similar comparisons differentiate the wild and cultivated Emmers.

The Einkorn wheat was domesticated in South-East Turkey (Harlan and Zohary, 1966) and the Emmer in Upper Jordan. However there are other species closely related to Emmer, e.g. *T. araraticum*, also found in Turkey, and others in neighbouring areas, so that the centre of origin of Emmer may well be further north (Rao and Smith, 1968).

Although Einkorn and Emmer were originally both wild, they differed, because Einkorn was diploid and Emmer was tetraploid. Emmer had arisen by *T. boeoticum* hybridizing with another diploid species, once thought to be *Aegilops speltoides*, but now doubted from protein studies (Johnson and Hall, 1966). These wild ancestors of the wheats were species with quite different ecological requirements, but the hybridization between them had supposedly occurred before cultivation had started, and may have been due to Man upsetting the ecological barriers.

Cultivated Einkorn was carried across Europe from the Near East during the Neolithic period, and there are even archaeological remains from Britain and Ireland. However, Emmer was more widely distributed in the early millenia, and remains have been dated from the Near East and Egypt, India, Ethiopia, though the Mediterranean, and as far north as Britain and Scandinavia, ousting Einkorn in the later centuries of the Neolithic.

Nowadays, the two major wheats are the bread wheat, a hexaploid, *T. aestivum,* and the hard or macaroni wheat, a tetraploid, *T. durum.* These appeared one or two millenia after the start of domestication of Einkorn and Emmer (Helbaek, 1966). Hard wheat arose from the Emmer group of species, and there are some other closely related tetraploid species such as *T. polonicum, T. turanicum* and *T. ispahanicum* found in areas of Transcaucasia and Iran (Kuckuck, 1970). The origin of the hexaploid bread wheat involved another species, *Aegilops squarrosa* which hybridized with Emmer, and it possesses a number of sub species, subsp. *vulgare* being the true bread wheat, *compactum* the club wheat, *spelta* the large spelt or dinkel, *sphaerococcum* the Indian dwarf wheat, and two others, *macha* and *vavilovi* (Mackey, 1954). A study of chromosome structure has helped to elucidate phylogenetic relationships, and a particular chromosomal change called an interchange has helped in sorting out the types of *T. aestivum* first cultivated (Riley *et al.,* 1967). Both subsp. *vulgare* and *spelta* come from the Eastern part of the centre of origin of these wheats, as does *A. squarrosa* and these must have been very early forms (Riley, 1969; Kuckuck, 1959).

The relationships between species are examined nowadays by modern taxonomic and cytogenetic methods, and each case history of the origin and evolution of a cultivated plant points to the overriding importance of the ecological background. It was the plants possessing weedy tendencies that colonized around the settlements, and Hawkes (1969) rightly placed emphasis on the role of weeds in the evolution of cultivated plants, not only in the early stages of domestication but also during later evolution. He posed the interesting question, why were only certain plants with weedy tendencies cultivated? Not only were these tendencies obvious in the primitive cultivars, but also they were apparent in those plants which grew in the field with the crops, and some of them were taken by Man as secondary crops. Weeds have therefore played a continuing role in the evolution of particular cultivated plants, e.g. the hybridization between Emmer and *Aegilops squarrosa* forming the bread wheat.

The role of hybridization in the origin of cultivated plants must be appreciated, because it was not only important in the early stages of domestication and cultivation, but has continued to the present day. In the wheats, hybridization can be observed in Central Turkey between the two diploids, wild *T. boeoticum* and cultivated *T. monococcum,* and in Israel between *T. dicoccoides* the wild Emmer, and *T. durum* the cultivated hard wheat (Zohary, 1969). An interesting point is that if hybridization takes place between two species of different ploidy level e.g. between the diploid progenitors (*T. boeoticum, Aegilops squarrosa*) and the modern tetraploid or hexaploid cultivated wheats, the hybrids are usually mostly sterile. However, plants possess several mechanisms by which this may be overcome, and fertility is thus restored. One method is to double up the number of chromosomes, and this occurred in the origin of *T. aestivum;* and another method is for subsequent introgressive hybridization to take place when there are successive back-crosses to the parental forms, resulting in the flow of genetic material from one species into another, thereby enriching the variation of the cultivated forms. Bread wheats and hard wheats hybridize occasionally with many species of *Aegilops,* e.g. *A. cylindrica, A. variabilis, A. longissima* and other species of *Triticum.* In Sardinia and Sicily, this is even recognized by the farmers, who call the resultant hybrid "dogs tooth" or "bastardo" (Perrino, 1973).

Despite occasional hybridization, the species remain distinct, because of barriers between them. Wheats normally inbreed, but the occasional outbreeding with subsequent introgression has played a major role in their evolution. Frequently there can be observed differences in breeding behaviour between wild and cultivated forms e.g. *Phaseolus* beans where wild species and primitive forms can cross with the cultivated ones, but isolating mechanisms have evolved more strongly between cultivated races. Occasional outbreeding is true for many many other inbreeding crops, e.g. lentils and barley. Other crops such as rye and beet are outbreeders, and despite hybridization and introgression, the species and cultivars have remained distinct due to ecological and other barriers. The diverse forms of beet, such as beetroots, sugar beets, fodder beets can be found growing near together in Asia Minor where their centre of diversity is seen, but in the field the author has observed subtle differences in flowering times, thus acting as a barrier to free hybridization.

The history of wheats, although complicated and only recently largely elucidated, could be sought in the "fertile crescent" of the Near East. Other cultivated plants similarly have been restricted in their origin to particular continents or countries, and the potato is an excellent example from South America, despite later showing secondary diversity when its range was extended by Man to other parts of the world. There are other cultivated plants which arose separately in different continents, the yams being a good example. Yams pose interesting problems since there is a lack of archaeological evidence (in fact, the domesticated forms tend not to flower, so even looking for pollen or seeds is useless; Shaw, 1968), but there is strong botanical and ethnological evidence relating the tubers of these herbaceous vines with wild species in Africa, Asia, Australia and America. They occur especially in the forested tropical regions, and except for Australia, domestication occurred from local forms in the three continents—*Dioscorea trifida* in Brazil and Venezuela; *D. cayenensis, D. rotundata* in Africa, and *D. alata, D. bulbifera,* and *D. esculenta* in South-East Asia (Coursey, 1967). It has been suggested that tuber-growing pre-dated rice growing in South-East Asia (Chang, 1970), but developed after cereal growing in Africa (Alexander and Coursey, 1969); the author's view is that they were more or less contemporary, the centre for yams in South-East Asia being farther south than where rice cultivation started. In West Africa, far more work is needed, because the West African rice (*Oryza glaberrima*), the millets (species of *Sorghum,* and *Pennisetum*), and yams (*Dioscorea*) indigenous to the countries of West Africa, all probably possessed different geographical and local areas of domestication, and hypotheses relating to early agriculture which rely on evidence from Ethiopia, and regions towards Egypt cannot be applied to the West.

The history of the wheats and comments on other cultivated plants have illustrated how the present types of cultivated plants have been obtained. It should be stressed that it is the research into taxonomy and evolutionary relationships of cultivated plants as well as their wild relatives that forms the necessary basis for the work of the plant breeders, in order for them to utilize the material to the best possible advantage. The breeders require information about morphological variation and geographical distributions, so that a wide range of material is available and understood. This approach has certainly been extremely useful in potatoes (Hawkes, 1958; Hawkes and Hjerting, 1969) as well as in all the other major crop plants of the world.

The solution to Man's increasing population lies in an increase in food production and plants are basic in this; but other facts such as control of human fertility must not be put aside, although they are not discussed here. Up to the present day, from the time of the Agricultural Revolution, there has been an improvement in agriculture—and an improvement which, both in quality and quantity, has in general kept pace with the world's expanding population. Despite the efficiency of the present day agricultural systems, however, over 60% of this population suffer from inadequate nutrition, and in this modern age, we can no longer be self-satisfied or admit that there have always been famines in one part of the world or another.

In historical times farmers and agriculturalists selected consciously and unconsciously from what was available i.e. from those forms naturally showing variation, mutations and hybridizations or those that showed desirable characteristics (e.g. high yield, uniformity of growth facilitating harvest, forms adapted to particular areas and climates, and those that were not wholly susceptible to the local pests and disease). At the same time, plants were selected that suited particular agricultural regimes of sowing and harvesting cycles. When disaster struck in the past, even as late as the last century when potato blight (*Phytophthora infestans*) caused famine in Ireland, there was little that could be done immediately. The number of diseases that threaten the few species of major cultivated plants in the world is immense.

The birth of genetics as a science in its own right and advances in plant pathology led to the emergence of plant breeding as an independent discipline, and throughout the world researchers are now working to produce cultivars resistant to diseases, of higher economic yields and quality, higher physiological efficiency and other required traits. The work of the breeders has revolutionized agriculture. It is possible to cite endless examples of breeding work currently in progress, but of particular mention are the ODA supported programme at Cambridge by Dr Alice Evans—linking with the International Institute of Tropical Agriculture at Ibadan in Nigeria—on breeding of large seeded food beans and the small white haricot bean, and the further work on breeding for protein rich varieties of plants for developing countries (especially with reference to the *right* amino acid contents) in cereals and legumes. Rice for India is not desirable if it becomes pasty on cooking, so amylose varieties are required as well as higher protein forms. Similarly in the wheats for bread making, physical dough characteristics are important.

One outcome of recent breeding work has been the so-called Green Revolution as a result of the introduction of the Mexican bread wheat cultivars and new cultivars of rice. Thus whole areas, or even continents, are planted with a few related cultivars that are uniform and highly bred. At the same time, advances in agricultural mechanics and practice have led to uniform methods of cultivation and the elimination of competition from weeds by the use of herbicides. Man has drastically affected his environment, and against this gloomy background of polluted air, land and water, the plant breeders have done many worthwhile things in their efforts to increase yield and to lower malnutrition. It is also important for those breeding for increased productivity to remember that apart from economic considerations, there is a large onus placed on the farmer and his family; and in addition to developing agricultural technology account needs to be taken of enhancing job opportunities and rural incomes.

For a breeder, there are many complex ways in which the genotype of a plant can be manipulated, and referring again to the wheats, it is possible to transfer mildew resistance present in *Triticum carthlicum* to bread wheat producing e.g. cultivar "Gabo" (Kuckuck, 1970); and in the production of hybrid varieties, *T. timopheevi* cytoplasm can be combined with *aestivum* or genotypes and even though male sterility results, fertility restorer genotypes can be combined (Wilson and Ross, 1962).

The use of alien genera for breeding disease resistance in wheat has drawn upon so far *Secale* (rye), *Aegilops, Agropyron* and *Haynaldia*. The techniques of raising pure breeding lines through anther culture of economic plants is being investigated in various laboratories, e.g. in rice a series of plants x, $2x$, $3x$, $4x$ and $5x$ are being used from anther and ovary cultures in the Nippon Shinyaku Institute in Kyoto, Japan. With the availability of a vast range of chemical and physical mutagens mutations of importance can be induced in a variety of crops. The techniques of induced mutations can be used to understand genetic differentiation (e.g. in tetraploid wheats, Rana *et al.*, 1973). The diverse ecological conditions of growth and regional quality preferences have stood in the way of the Green Revolution in rice but attempts in India and Taiwan to use mutation breeding seem promising in overcoming some of these (Mizra *et al.*, 1973; Hu, 1973). All these genetic manipulations in cultivated plants will enable immediate further improvements in agriculture providing the plant improvement goes hand in hand with the improvement of their environment—and this means more widespread use of the technological progress in machinery and fertilizers.

These conditions are a far cry from the situations in the more primitive systems. In such situations there were continual interactions between wild and cultivated races and weeds. The cultivated races that evolved from wild populations were similar genetically, and they were variable, containing genetic resistance factors and adaptation factors for specific environments. These integrated populations of cultivated plants are called land races and the primitive, very variable domestic races are called primitive cultivars. When these forms of cultivated plants were taken by Man to other areas of the world, because of their broad-based variability, they often developed centres of diversity (Vavilov's secondary centres), and so these secondary populations became adapted to new conditions, e.g. maize was taken at an early time from Central America to Northern India, the chickpea was taken there from further west between 300 and 400 BC, lentils and peas developed secondary centres in Ethiopia, potatoes, peppers, tomatoes, green beans and runner beans from the New World have been widely introduced around the world, and there are many other examples.

When Vavilov defined his centres, he based them on field observations of the richness in the genetic variability; and mixtures of genotypes—even species—were grown together in dynamic evolving systems. These areas constitute gene pools with the variation necessary for the plant breeder (Fig. 3). Unfortunately none of the centres are now immune from Man's modern technology, and in them primitive plant material is being replaced at an alarming rate by homogeneous-bred cultivars—thus halting the evolutionary processes that have gone on for thousands of years. The miracle Mexican wheats of the Green Revolution have in a few years swamped whole regions, replacing in one move the richness of local plant material. *Per contra,* this erosion of vital plant resources must be stopped because the germplasm of these primitive cultivars along with their wild and weedy relatives is the material that the breeders will require to stave off further starvation in further generations.

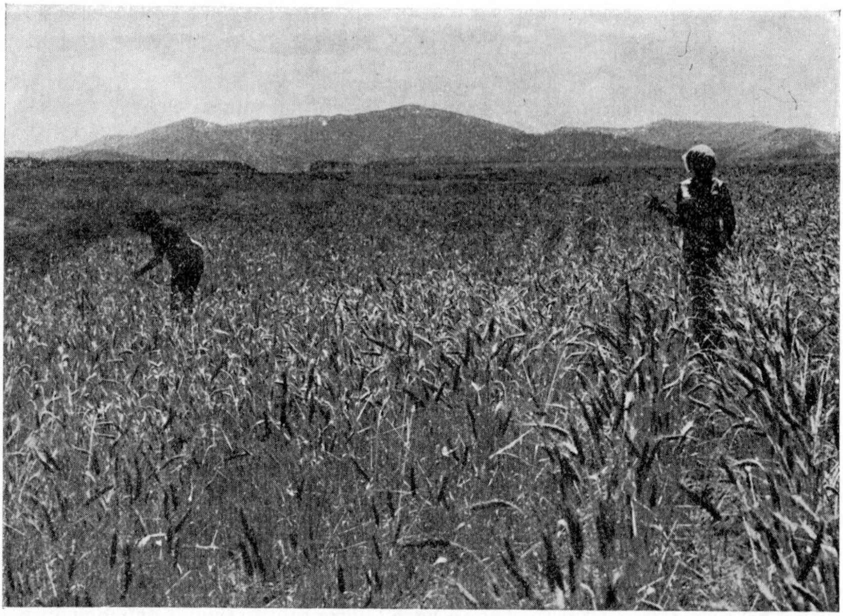

Fig. 3. Variation in a wheat field in Eastern Turkey: collecting for genetic conservation.

Plant breeders have utilized primitive material in recent years and in fact this was what was available to the early breeders. They selected lines from the primitive land races, but as breeding programmes progressed and became more sophisticated, the genetic variability of the crops became narrower and the modern cultivars show only a part of the original germplasm. Recent examples of the use of primitive material include the utilization of wheats from Ethiopia and parts of Asia in European wheat programmes (Weinhus, 1959), and expeditions from most major plant breeding stations have dipped into the variation in the centres of diversity at one time or another for use in their programmes. Examples of typical wheat improvement programmes are given by Quisenberry and Reitz (1967). Table 1 shows the different species currently used by wheat breeders in Britain for their requirements. The actual conservation of genetic resources is another problem, and a few thousand collections in a breeding station is not the answer (for details see Williams, 1974).

TABLE 1
Species of wheat and Aegilops *maintained by wheat breeders in Britain*

Section	Species	Chromosome number
	TRITICUM	
		2*n* =
Monococca	*T. boeoticum*	14
	T. monococcum	14
Dicoccoidea	*T. timopheevi*	28
	T. araraticum	28
	T. turgidum	28
	subsp. *dicoccoides* (= *T. dicoccoides*)	
	subsp. *dicoccum* (= *T. dicoccum*)	
	subsp. *paleocolchicum*	
	subsp. *turgidum*	
	conv. *turgidum*	
	conv. *durum* (= *T. durum*)	
	conv. *turanicum*	
	conv. *polonicum*	
	subsp. *carthlicum*	
Speltoidea	*T. aestivum*	42
	subsp. *spelta*	
	subsp. *vavilovi*	
	subsp. *macha*	
	subsp. *vulgare*	
	subsp. *compactum*	
	subsp. *sphaerococcum*	
	T. zhukovskyi	42
	AEGILOPS	
Polyeides	*A. umbellata*	14
	A. ovata	28
	A. triaristata	28, 42
	A. columnaris	28
	A. biuncialis	28
	A. variabilis	28
	A. triuncialis	28
Cylindropyrum	*A. caudata*	14
	A. cylindrica	28
Comopyrum	*A. comosa*	14
	A. uniaristata	14
Amblyopyrum	*A. mutica*	14
Sitopsis	*A. speltoides*	14
	A. longissima	14
	A. sharonensis	14
	A. bicornis	14
Vertebrata	*A. squarrosa*	14
	A. crassa	28, 42
	A. vavilovii	42
	A. ventricosa	28
	A. juvenalis	42

The inexorability of the present situation has been stressed many times (Bennett, 1968; Frankel and Bennett, 1970; Hawkes, 1971; Harlan, 1971) and the United Nations Food and Agriculture Organization has a unit dealing with genetic resources. The FAO Panel of Experts on Plant Exploration and Introduction has repeatedly emphasized the urgency of the matter and made lists of priorities for action.

Almost 10 years ago FAO established a Genetic Resources Centre at Izmir in Turkey, with funds from the United Nations Development Project, and plans are now in hand for this to act as a centre for exploration and conservation of germplasm for five Middle East countries. This example was an initial step in the establishment of a world network of gene banks. Other Institutes are in operation, notably, those co-ordinated by the European Association of Research in Plant Breeding (Eucarpia), namely, the Germplasm Laboratory at Bari in Southern Italy for Mediterranean crops, Braunschweig-Völkenrode in Germany for German and more northern crops, and one at Stockholm in Sweden for Northern Europe. These are Institutes dealing with many crops, and there are others founded independently, such as the great N. I. Vavilov Institute of Plant Industry at Leningrad where the pioneer work of its founder has continued, and many of his original collections maintained, the Institute for Cultivated Plants at Gatersleben in East Germany, and the Seed Storage Laboratory in the USA Department of Agriculture.

There are other Institutes more limited, in their research or conservation and evaluation of germplasm, to particular crops—the International Potato Centre in Peru, the Commonwealth Potato Collection at the Scottish Plant Breeding Station, the International Maize and Wheat Improvement Centre in Mexico, the International Rice Research Institute in the Philippines, and many other research Institutes. Even so, it will be some time before there is a global network of gene banks in action all using techniques of an international standard for conservation.

When it comes to the actual conservation, the practical perplexities are considerable. The following are some of the major concerns of a gene bank:

1. adequate exploration and collecting, with all the attendant problems of sampling and documentation, and full representation of the gene pools of the species;

2. conservation of the material. The storage of seed of most species can be aided by using controlled cool, dry storage; but seeds of some plants are short-lived and as yet adequate techniques for them have not been advised. Research is advancing in the use of tissue culture for plants that are propagated vegetatively, e.g. fruit trees and root crops such as yams;

3. rejuvenation of material when necessary, either for immediate utilization in breeding programes or for maintaining the stocks in long term storage. The latter should only be necessary at infrequent intervals, and then the rejuvenation should take place in field conditions similar to those where the material was collected;

4. screening and evaluation. It is pointless simply collecting and conserving without some preliminary screening so that information is available about desirable genes or characters for the breeders, and information is available to tell the collector whether or not he has adequately sampled the gene pools;

5. information storage and retrieval using an internationally agreed system.

In order to carry out all these procedures, and to bring grist to the mill, trained staff are necessary with an overall appreciation of the problems and techniques of genetic conservation. To this end, Professor J. G. Hawkes initiated the internationally-orientated postgraduate MSc Course in Conservation and Utilization of Plant Genetic Resources in the University of Birmingham, UK, where students receive a grounding in the essential problems relating to the origins, evolution and exploitation of cultivated plants. Prior to starting the course, students have an opportunity to obtain field collecting experience for a short period at the Centre in Izmir or the Germplasm Laboratory at Bari. The observations made in such a centre of diversity as Turkey, or at the evaluation trials in Southern Italy, of wheats from the Mediterranean, Afghanistan and Ethiopia allow them to appreciate the enormity of the problems of genetic conservation right at the beginning of their training.

The facts that some of the Institutes have been established and others planned, and that a start has been made on the training of specific workers, do not detract from the great urgency for the implementation of active genetic resource conservation on a world scale. This is a problem that politicians must face in order for sufficient international funding to become available. The continued support of the few countries which now provide funds cannot be relied upon, nor the valuable support of organizations such as the Rockefeller Foundation which has taken responsibility for four major world crops. It is not an exaggeration to say that upon the scientific conservation of existing plant resources, and their present and future utilization, rests the future of Mankind. The centres of diversity that Vavilov outlined mostly lie in developing regions of the world, which need the new technologies. At the same time we have a duty to ensure that the rich heritages of plant resources in these regions are not swept away on the tide of progress. They will need to be available for developing cultivated plants of the future. Even with scientific developments in the production of new types of foodstuffs from plants, genetic conservation will be the major integer contributing to a balance of the Man/Food Equation.

References

Alexander, J. and Coursey, D. G. (1969). *In* "The Domestication and Exploitation of Plants and Animals" (P. J. Ucko and G. W. Dimbleby, eds), pp.405–426. Duckworth, London.

Balout, L. (1955). "Préhistoire de l'Afrique du Nord". Arts et Métiers Graphiques, Paris.

Bennett, E. (1968). Record of the FAO/IBP Technical Conference on the Exploration, Utilization and Conservation of Plant Genetic Resources, 1967, Rome.

Brothwell, D. R. (1969). *In* "The Domestication and Exploitation of Plants and Animals" (P. J. Ucko and G. W. Dimbleby, eds), pp.531–545, Duckworth, London.

Chang, K. C. (1970). *Antiquity* **44,** 175.

Childe, V. G. (1958). "The Prehistory of European Society". Pelican, London.

Clark, G. (1965). *Antiquity* **39,** 45.

Clark, G. (1969). "World Prehistory: A New Outline". University Press, Cambridge.

Coursey, D. G. (1967). "Yams". Longman, London.

Curwen, E. C. (1938). *Antiquity* **12,** 135.

Dimbleby, G. W. (1967). "Plants and Archaeology". Baker, London.

Flannery, K. (1965). *Science* **147,** 1247.

Frankel, O. H. and Bennett, E. eds. (1970). "Genetic Resources in Plants—their Exploration and Conservation". IPB Handbook 11. Blackwells, Oxford.

Harlan, J. R. (1972). *J. Environ. Quality* **I,** 212.

Harlan, J. R. and Zohary, D. (1966). *Science* **153,** 1074.

Hawkes, J. G. (1958). *Euphytica* **7,** 257.

Hawkes, J. G. (1969). *In* "The Domestication and Exploitation of Plants and Animals" (P. J. Ucko and G. W. Dimbleby, eds), pp.17–29. Duckworth, London.

Hawkes, J. G. (1971). *Outlook Agric.* **6,** 248.

Hawkes, J. G. and Hjerting, P. (1969). "The Potatoes of Argentina, Brazil, Paraguay and Uruguay". University Press, Oxford.

Helbaek, H. (1966). *Econ. Bot.* **20,** 350.

Hu, C-H (1973). Mutation Breeding for Short Stature in Rice. Paper presented at 2nd. General Congress, SABRAO, India.

Johnson, B. L. and Hall, O. (1966). *Acta Agric. Scand. Suppl.* **16,** 222.

Kuckuck, H. (1959). *Wheat Inform. Service* **9–10,** 1.

Kuckuck, H. (1970). *In* "Genetic Resources in Plants—their Exploration and Conservation" (O. H. Frankel and E. Bennett, eds), IPB Handbook 11, Blackwells, Oxford.

Mackey, J. (1954). *Svensk. bot. Tidskr.* **48,** 579.

Manglesdorf, P. C. (1961). *Econ. Bot.* **15,** 279.

Mazzeo, J. A. (1967). "Renaissance and Revolution: The Remaking of European Thought". Secker and Warburg, London.

McNeish, R. S. (1965). *Antiquity* **39,** 87.

Mizra, R. N., Gangadharan, V. and Sreedharan, P. N. (1973). Problems and Results of Rice Breeding through Induced Mutations. Paper presented at 2nd General Congress, SABRAO, India.

Quisenberg, K. S. and Reitz, L. P. (1967). "Wheat and Wheat Improvement". American Society of Agronomy, Wisconsin.

Rana, R. S., Shinde, Y. M. and Kharkwal, M. C. (1973). Mutagenic Response and Genetic Differentiation among Tetraploid *Triticum* Species. Paper presented at 2nd General Congress, SABRAO, India.

Rankine, W. F., Rankine, W. M. and Dimbleby, G. W. (1960). *Proc. prehist. Soc.* **26,** 246.

Rao, P. S. and Smith, E. L. (1968). *Wheat Inform. Service* **26,** 6.

Riley, R. (1969). *In* "The Domestication and Exploitation of Plants and Animals" (P. J. Ucko and G. W. Dimbleby, eds), pp.173–176. Duckworth, London.

Riley, R., Coucoli, H. and Chapman, V. (1967). *Heredity* **22,** 233.

Shaw, T. (1968). *Current Anthrop.* **9,** 500.

Ucko, P. J. and Dimbleby, G. W. eds. (1969). "The Domestication and Exploitation of Plants and Animals". Duckworth, London.

Vavilov, N. I. (1926). *Bull. Appl. Bot. Pl.-Breed.* **16,** 1.

Weinhus, F. (1959). *Handbuch Pflanzenz.* **2,** 216.

Williams, J. T. (1974). "An Index of the Living Plant Collections in the British Isles". Bentham-Moxon Trust, Kew.

Williams, J. T. and Farias, R. M. (1972). *Econ. Bot.* **35,** 13.

Wilson, I. A. and Ross, W. M. (1962). *Wheat Inform. Service* **14,** 29.

Zohary, D. (1969). *In* "The Domestication and Exploitation of Plants and Animals" (P. J. Ucko and G. W. Dimbleby, eds), pp.47–66. Duckworth, London.

The Cost: Natural and Economic Constraints

Man's Attitude to the Environment Through the Ages

G. W. DIMBLEBY

Department of Human Environment, Institute of Archaelogy, University of London

Summary

Man has inevitably had an impact on his environment. His use of fire gave him a powerful tool even before he practised agriculture. After that, his impact became progressively greater and more deliberate. The ecological balance was often disrupted and there is much evidence of the failure of early agriculture.

Pre-agricultural Man probably recognized his dependence on Nature, but as agriculture developed his dependence seemed less obvious until agriculture and not Nature seemed to be the basis of his livelihood. The extraordinary spread of agriculture took it to regions such as Western Europe where a stable balanced agriculture was probably achieved for the first time. Nevertheless, there were still disaster areas of soil deterioration and erosion.

The age-old practices of manuring and fallow may indicate a recognition of dependence on natural balance, or they may have been obvious expedients. Through historical time the Christian ethic as then taught supported the concept of Man above Nature, which was provided for his delectation and support. This seemed to be confirmed by the apparent successes of the Scientific and Industrial Revolutions and was particularly strengthened by the progress of medical science which so dramatically reduced the debit side of the population equation.

The modern predicament is the fundamental one of human attitudes; on the one hand those who believe that his science and technology have indeed made Man independent of Nature, and on the other those who hold that as long as Man has to eat organic food, drink pure water and breath clear air, he is tied to an ecological system on the health of which his own survival depends.

In talking about the Man/Food Equation we are discussing a situation which is critical now. It may seem irrelevant to be concerned with the distant or even the recent past, yet there are good reasons for doing so. The situation as it is today has not just happened; it has developed, like any other ecological situation, and the relevant time-scale is a very long one. One of the essential components in this equation is Man's attitude to the environment and some believe that unless this is changed the equation will not be balanced. At the very least, entrenched attitudes restrict intellectual manoeuvre and can lead to myths which are perpetuated as self-evident fact.

For instance, agriculture must be depended upon to solve the food problem as it has done in the past. Agriculture has come to be regarded almost by definition as "a good thing", synonymous with civilization, regardless of the fact that throughout the ages agriculture has had its disastrous failures as well as its successes. It is as necessary to question modern agricultural methods just as much as more primitive ones, because their capacity for environmental damage if they are faulty is on a far greater scale than ever before. Another myth which seems to have its origin in ancient tradition is that the remaining areas of forest (mainly in the tropics) can be cleared for agriculture, in just the same way that temperate forest land was cleared in earlier times. This myth should be exploded by a knowledge of tropical forest soils and what happens to them when exposed.

These two myths arise out of beliefs which are widespread and which many would accept as axiomatic. One is that Man has reached his present condition by his own efforts, despite the constraints of the natural world, and consequently his survival must equally depend on his dominance over Nature. The second attitude is that in the world there is always new land (forest) to be tamed or conquered.

The aim of this paper is to trace Man's relationship with his natural environment from prehistoric times to the present day. In the earliest periods this can only be done by inference from the evidence extracted from archaeological sites.

Presumably at some early stage in his history Man was a member of an ecological community in some sort of equilibrium with his habitat, but long before agriculture was instituted he had moved out of this stage. His ability to create fire put a major ecological tool into his hand, all the more effective because there would be no means of stopping a fire once started. If the use of fire became linked to his hunting activities this would combine fire and grazing—a combination that has had formidable effects on the landscape in many parts of the world. It is not possible to judge from the archaeological record alone what the attitude of hunter/gatherers towards the environment would have been, but anthropological studies of modern cultures of a comparable level suggest that fire was started whenever there was something to burn, as often for the fun of it as for necessity (Egler, 1952; Bartlett, 1956). On the other hand, the worship and placating of gods in trees, streams and large animals suggest that other forms of environmental exploitation were not always wanton. Nevertheless, there is evidence that even in pre-agricultural times damage was done from which the environment never recovered. In Britain Mesolithic Man brought about ecological and pedological changes which have determined the landscape ever since (Simmons, 1969).

The reasons for the development of agriculture, some ten to twelve thousand years ago, are unknown, though theories abound. Many of these are ecological, involving such considerations as population growth, soil deterioration, climatic change, and, most recently (Leopold and Ardrey, 1972) the possible influence of fire itself. In this last theory it is suggested that the adoption of cooking made possible the use for food of a wide range of plant products which hitherto had been inedible and this then led to the cultivation of suitable plants as staple foods.

Whatever the causes of domestication of plants and animals, farming, once established, was a system which could not be used without disturbance of the natural ecosystem. This is not to say that an agricultural system cannot be in ecological equilibrium, but that equilibrium cannot be the same one as in the natural ecosystem. In the Old World it seems probable that agriculture was first established in a park-woodland type of landscape, making use of plants and animals from that habitat. The cereals would be present in the open aspects of the ecosystem, being light-demanding species. This fact alone means that agriculture must disturb the natural ecosystem; if it is to be practised in a wooded landscape the trees must be cleared, or if it is carried into more arid areas some form of irrigation will be necessary if these same domesticated crops are to be grown.

In other words, Man must create a new ecosystem to suit the species he wants to grow. However, this new ecosystem is not always ideal; it may be deficient in some of the favourable properties offered by the original ecosystem. For instance, Hole *et al.* (1971) have commented on the fact that the introduction of agriculture into the Khuzistan steppes in the sixth millennium BC effectively eliminated the small legumes which previously had figured in early Man's diet. Agricultural systems tend to carry their weeds with them, often to the detriment of a richer local flora. Floral diversity may also be reduced by concentrated grazing by domestic stock. The introduction of European stock into African savanna has markedly reduced the species present (Hopkins, 1965). The same can be seen in many rough grazing regions of Britain, where the general range has an impoverished flora, but cliffs and places beyond the reach of the animals show remarkable richness.

The earliest forms of agriculture did not attempt to bring about a permanent change in the landscape; rather they were based on a system of shifting cultivation in which crops were gathered until fertility dropped and then the land was allowed to recover under fallow as attention was directed to new areas. Later as the population became more sedentary and nucleated, more permanent usage of the land was practised. In some cases this was achieved satisfactorily but in others the system broke down for one reason or another, depending on circumstances: desiccation, nutrient deficiency, salinity, wind erosion, etc. Though Man had challenged Nature, there were times when the natural factors of the environment thwarted him.

Through the long history of the spread of agriculture, failure was always a possibility. If the ecosystem that was being converted was a fragile one, agriculture soon failed. In Britain, for instance, large tracts of heathland and moorland carry abundant prehistoric remains, a mute pointer to the failure of early agriculture on the poor soils (Dimbleby, 1962). In contrast, it survived and persisted on the richer soils, although even here not without some erosion of the lighter soils (Evans, 1966). It was probably not until historic times that an ecologically balanced agricultural system was achieved, based on mixed farming. It has been suggested that Man can take little credit for this; it was almost fortuitous, arising from the happy combination of a benign climate and young fertile soils in Western Europe (Hyams, 1952). That European systems of agriculture have no absolute virtue is shown by the sad failures which have occurred when they have been exported into other regions, in particular semi-arid and tropical areas.

Whilst it is true that soil dressings of ashes, manure, marl, sand, etc. have a long and honourable history, going back to prehistoric times in some instances, it is to be doubted whether they were seen as a means of redressing soil balance until perhaps the last century. They were probably treatments that were found to increase production and were adopted to an extent that was economic and convenient. In some cases soils were created that were over-rich—there was no absolute standard.

Before going on to consider how agriculture has developed in the last century and a half, let us now look at its development from the earliest times and see how it reflects Man's attitude to Nature. Religious beliefs and teaching were important. The Judaeo-Christian tradition in particular had a major impact on the development of Western culture. The early scriptures reveal an attitude in which there is no doubt in the writers' minds that the fruits of the Earth are provided for Man and that he is expected to exploit them to whatever extent is necessary. The Genesis story of the Creation speaks in terms of tillage and pastoralism, practices already so long-established that even at the date of these writings they were regarded as primeval. Nowhere is there any understanding of a reciprocal interest between Man and wild Nature; it is there to be exploited. On the other hand, the Hebrew laws do show some sense of stewardship in agriculture and though stewardship features even more strongly in the New Testament, it is not there applied specifically to the Earth's resources but rather to human talents and trustworthiness. The medieval church developed a pre-occupation with the God/Man relationship and in general regarded the natural world as unredeemed, for which attitude St Paul had given it ample precedent. The created world was provided by God for Man's use, as was clearly stated in Genesis.

Whilst even human life was held cheaply in medieval times, the natural world of animals and plants had no rights at all, an attitude still to be found in some countries with an ancient Christian tradition. Given this background, it is not surprising that the Scientific (including medical) and Industrial Revolutions, when they came, were only concerned with Man. They rode rough-shod over wild Nature.

The advance of medical science cured men of many of the ills to which they had traditionally been subject. Mortality, especially among children, was drastically reduced. Here the Christian doctrine of healing showed this to be the will of a benevolent God. The development of science, blossoming into the Industrial Revolution in another way demonstrated the dominance of Man over Nature and its complete subjugation to his will. It resulted in the good life for many (not all) and who could deny that this too was divinely ordained? Later, it seems, there grew up a philosophy which saw these achievements as those of Man solely through his own efforts. Why bring God into it? A development that did much to promote this view was the application of Liebig's chemical theories to agriculture. Here life and the inorganic world met. Some decades later Darwin's work was posing similar debates but on a different front. The shock waves of these encounters still reverberate in the minds of men today, sometimes in quite irrational ways.

It is commonly assumed that all processes can be explained in terms of the physical sciences, and those who talk in terms of life processes are accused of clouding the issue with some sort of mystery or magic; a hangover from the days when the theologians used the mysteries of life as their main supporting plank in the argument against the agnostics. Such an argument is, of course, quite indefensible in these days of biochemistry, biophysics and molecular biology, but it is mentioned here because it can still be found among farmers and even among some agricultural scientists. As long as it only applied to the fundamental life processes it could be ignored, because much can be done without knowing the answers at the fundamental level. Unfortunately the same criticism has been levelled against ecology, on the grounds that ecology is dealing with interactions between living organisms and that its results are frequently expressed as relationships (community, competition, etc.) and not in terms of the exact sciences. In the debates on the environmental crisis in recent years there have been many examples of such biased and ill-informed sniping at the subject, particularly by highly qualified specialists in non-biological fields. Plant ecology as a science dates back to the end of the last century but it has had to develop in the strong climate of chemical biology. Many people think it is a new subject, the product (or cause?) of our present obsession with environmental problems. What has in fact happened is that it has been neglected as irrelevant to the production of natural resources, and it is probably true to say that ecologists themselves must share some of the blame—they have so often excluded man-made communities from their attention. However, the enormous strides in agricultural science, particularly in the development of chemicals that have no parallel in natural systems, have shown that ecological relationships are involved, and that these have turned out in many cases to be even more complex in their ramifications than ecologists themselves had imagined.

This development has caught the layman completely unprepared. Ideas penetrate slowly as if by oral tradition, even in this literate age. Many folk will assert that God created the world for Man—the Bible says so—even though they have no other religious belief. Most people accept without question that agriculture is largely a matter of applied chemistry—the more that is added, the larger the yield. There is an underlying feature to these entrenched views—they are all favourable to Man himself. They set Man up as being in control of his own destiny, subject to no other laws than his own well-being. This is part of human folk-lore, going back for thousands of years. In the course of that time many people have thrown out religion, which tied Man to a Being greater than himself—though it must be admitted that God gave Man (or it was thought He did) freedom to use the world as he wanted. But now Man is halted in his tracks by the ecologists who say, in effect, that he cannot do as he pleases with the world, without damaging his civilization. Is this alien creed to be believed or should it be ignored and Man allowed to carry on as before? Why are people taking it seriously now whereas they never did before?

The answer to this probably lies in the nature of ecological change. Ecosystems have a certain resilience, a resilience against change. When they have to change they change slowly; there are, of course, exceptions, especially where the system is precariously poised. Some changes are so slow compared with the human life-span that they are not recognized as changes. Indeed, it was not until the development of pollen analysis, in the second and third decades of this century, that even in Britain a glimpse was caught of the scale of the change. Elgee (1912) assumed without question that the North York Moors had been heather covered since the Ice Age, until Erdtman (1927), the Swedish pollen analyst, showed that they had been covered with forest—until three to four thousand years ago as is now known. They have been used for agriculture, sheep-raising and now grouse, with progressive deterioration of plant cover and soil. This slow change has not only meant that Man did not always recognize that he was degrading his own environment, but also that he had time to adjust to it. Human history contains many examples of Man's way of life being adjusted—nearly always downwards—to the new condition. Where change was recognized as such it was usually attributed to something beyond Man's control such as a deterioration of climate.

Things are different now. The impact of Man is much greater. The means of changing the environment are more effective (e.g. agricultural machinery); the effects of a large and growing population are obvious not only in everyday life, but reason tells us what the effects could be in the future. No longer is only one side seen of the life-death equation that medical science tilted so dangerously. But above all, Man can see change within his own lifetime. The rural haunts of childhood are now obliterated by urban growth. Wind and water erosion of soil are commonplace in many parts of the world, and even though the cause is known, Man is powerless to stop them until he can reduce his pressure on the land. The poisoning of wildlife by the products of his civilization has come to everyone's notice. The environment is at risk because of his own actions. Some now see this, but the age-old philosophy of Man's supremacy blinds others to the facts. Sadly it is often those most devoted to humanity and in a position of power to act who are unable to see the present, let alone the future.

Man has come to realize that the present ecological crisis in the world has arisen through his own failure to recognize that as long as he is dependent on food derived from living organisms, on air of reasonable purity and appropriate composition to breathe, and on potable water, he is dependent upon a complex ecosystem. Ecology has shown that ecosystems have their laws; if these are flouted the system changes or breaks down, with inevitable consequences for those organisms dependent on it. It is remarkable how unwilling we are to accept any constraint in favour of non-human life; it goes against the grain. Yet we are prepared to accept constraints arising from inanimate natural phenomena; we do not willingly put our hands in a flame, or step off a high building—the consequences are immediate and obvious, cause and effect are powerfully associated. The violation of ecological laws does not have an immediate effect, though in the long run the penalties may be even more drastic, because they do not affect just ourselves as individuals but our whole community.

Though in this symposium the prime attention is being paid to feeding the world's population, this is only one aspect of the ecological predicament everyone is in, and it is closely inter-related with other pressures. First and foremost is the problem of stabilizing the world population. Until this is done efforts to balance the Man/Food Equation will be in vain. Further, the environment can be damaged and its capacity for food production reduced, for instance by the extraction of mineral resources or urban expansion. The demands for both food and resources may be so great to meet a steeply rising population that the environment cannot provide enough of either. In other words, it is no use having an ecologically sound policy for one aspect of human life and not for another. As has been indicated, human life as a whole depends on a healthy environment. There is little doubt that technology will have to play a large part if the world population is to be fed. Projects such as the Green Revolution may arise from such technology, but unless they are ecologically acceptable they will not foster the welfare of Man. If the Green Revolution leads to contamination of water supplies from the high levels of fertilizers necessary it may do harm rather than good. Equally it is an unacceptable answer to turn to so far unexploited areas for food production, there are good reasons why they have remained non-productive for so long. Scientific opinion advocates the intensification of food production on existing cultivated land (Penman, 1968). The sea could be exploited more intensively—but only within limits. The present use of marine resources is grossly wasteful and Man seems likely to contaminate the seas before he learns to use them efficiently. Intensified exploitation may have some short-term value but is no answer to the long-term problem. Until this is accepted the attention of research workers and technologists will not be directed where it should be—to the stabilization of population coupled with the development of methods of agriculture which are environmentally harmless. If the same amount of money had been put into bio-ecological research as has been put into agricultural chemistry over recent decades, we might now be in much less difficulty.

Basically it comes down to attitudes. Are we prepared to find out what are the environmental laws and to plan within these limits? Are we prepared to co-operate with natural processes, or do we try to subjugate Nature and assert our own schemes? The latter option has a long history going back to prehistoric times, but it has not yet succeeded—otherwise this symposium would not be held. Does modern Man have to be tied to this formula?

References

Bartlett, H. H. (1956). *In* "Man's Role in Changing the Face of the Earth" (W. L. Thomas, ed.), pp. 692–720. University of Chicago Press, Chicago.

Dimbleby, G. W. (1962). "The Development of British Heathlands and their Soils". Oxford Forestry Memoirs No. 23.

Egler, F. E. (1952). *Vegetatio* **3,** 213.
Elgee, F. (1912). "The Moorlands of North-Eastern Yorkshire". A. Brown and Sons, London.
Erdtman, G. (1927). *Naturalist* (*London*) 1927, 39.
Evans, J. G. (1966). *Proc. Geol. Ass.* **77,** 347.
Hole, F., Flannery, K. V. and Neely, J. A. (1971). *In* "Prehistoric Agriculture" (S. Struever, ed.), pp. 252–311. The Natural History Press, New York.
Hopkins, B. (1965). "Forest and Savanna". Heinemann, London.
Hyams, E. (1952). "Soil and Civilization". Thames and Hudson, London.
Leopold, A. C. and Ardrey, R. (1972). *Science* **176,** 512.
Penman, H. L. (1968). *Science J.* **4,** 43.
Simmons, I. G. (1969). *In* "Domestication and Exploitation of Plants and Animals" (P. J. Ucko and G. W. Dimbleby, eds), pp.111–119. Duckworth, London.

The Man/Food Equation

ARTHUR BOURNE

*Department of Environmental Sciences, University of Lancaster**

Summary

The natural constraints that operate on and work through the biosphere determine the total biomass on the planet's surface. If this is in equilibrium, as it seems to have been over the past millenia, an increase in one species must occur at the expense of the others. Man's phenomenal population growth has been at the cost of other species. He has achieved his dominance by becoming specially adapted to an unstable ecosystem that he cannot allow to mature if his population is to be supported. Already the system can only be maintained artificially through the addition of manufactured nutrients and protective chemicals. Without these the present agricultural system would collapse and the human population would be involuntarily reduced. The constant struggle to keep the system going is costly in energy and materials, and as supplies of both of these are finite, the prospects for Man's future must be questioned. If he were to concentrate on purely technological food production, the latter constraints would apply equally but there would be a further factor, Man's limitations as an animal. Although his technical advances may be exponential, these are not matched by the adaptation of his own physiological and biochemical regime.

The present artificially maintained fragile ecosystem is nearing its limits of development and the prognosis is that food production must decrease with a concomitant reduction in the human biomass. Eventually this will reach a new equilibrium within a self-sustaining ecosystem.

* Now care of Academic Press.

The human population of the planet Earth is presently estimated to be in the region of 4000 million and increasing at an overall rate of 2% per annum; by the end of the century it will reach a staggering 7000 million. As it is seemingly impossible even with modern intensive agricultural methods to meet the nutritional requirements of the existing population, how can we produce the food necessary to meet the increased demand forecast for the next twenty-five years and beyond? It is patently obvious that the human species cannot go on increasing indefinitely. Sooner or later brakes on its growth will be applied—the questions are when and how. In my view they are already being applied, through the natural constraints that limit ecosystem productivity within the biosphere. In this paper these constraints and how they set the limits to the human population will be examined.

The biosphere has been defined (Vernadsky, 1929) as that part of the Earth in which life exists, not, as some would have it, as the film of living organisms. The requirements for life are that there should be an ample supply of energy, sufficient water in its liquid state, and interfaces between the liquid, solid and gaseous states of matter. The first of these, and the one upon which the others depend, is and has been met for millions of years through the energy derived from the fusion reactions proceeding in the Sun's interior. The input of energy from geothermal sources seems to be of little direct account*, though in the long-term cycling of minerals it is an essential component of the biosphere.

The Sun's output of energy has, according to some authorities, remained fairly constant throughout the time that life has existed on the Earth (Brandt and Maran, 1972), while others believe that it has a periodicity, which may be linked with climatic changes such as the onset of glacial periods (Dilke and Douglas, 1972). Whatever the conditions of the Sun, fluctuations in the solar energy available to the biosphere, that is the portion of the energy actually reaching the Earth's surface and not the amount received by the outer layers of the atmosphere, have occurred from time to time. These fluctuations have produced marked variations in the quantity of liquid water available to life; thus, at times, they have restricted the biosphere and at others they have provided the means for its expansion. It is the energy reaching the planetary surface, therefore, that sets the limits to the biosphere.

From the above it appears that the Sun has, over the millenia, provided a steady-state energy regime within which fluctuations have occurred on the planet's surface. If the Sun's output has remained constant then some mechanism must be sought to explain the changes in climate that various regions of the Earth have been subject to and in particular to account for the glacial periods.

* Geothermal energy probably played a more direct role in the origins of living systems.

The last of these periods, the Pleistocene, is of particular interest, as will be seen later, in the development of Man, and in view of the current concern over pollution it is important that the mechanisms that bring about such periods are understood. Increases in the energy reaching the planet's surface could, paradoxically, have been responsible for the Ice Ages, by producing large quantities of water vapour, thus shutting out the incoming radiation; if this were so then the reverse, a reduction in energy coming in, could be the cause of their demise. Cooling would certainly take place if there were to be a substantial opacity to the incoming radiation produced by a build-up of prolonged and thick cloud cover. It has also been suggested that intensive volcanic activity could, through the injection of volcanic dust, gases and water vapour into the atmosphere, have reduced the radiation reaching the Earth's surface. Certainly lower temperatures have been recorded after especially large eruptions and it is known that even comparatively small eruptions can inject hundreds of thousands of tons of dust into the atmosphere (Bourne, 1964).

The retreat of the last of the Pleistocene ice-sheets (*c* 10–20,000 BP) released the water that had been locked up as ice, thus providing an increase in the liquid water and at the same time liberating vast amounts of mineral nutrients and increasing the land and sea surface, thereby augmenting the biosphere. This provided the opportunity for an expansive spread of living organisms. It is significant that the genus *Homo* made great advances in the arts of domestication at about this time and the reason for this may become apparent later.

Given, then, a long-term steady-state energy system, within which short-term fluctuations may occur, the overall view would be that once a system of organisms had been established the total mass of living material (expressed as dry weight or biomass) would respond to and reflect the energy and material flow in the biosphere. If this holds true, it follows that if the biosphere maintains a biomass proportional to the energy flow, then if the latter remains constant so will the former. Therefore, provided that a state of equilibrium is maintained, an increase in the biomass of one species or group of species must occur at the expense of a reduction in the biomass of other species. A similar regime would apply for energy—if one species increases, there will be a corresponding reduction in energy available to the other species. However, although the availability of energy is the overall controlling factor, there must also be a sufficiency of liquid water and mineral nutrients. It is conceivable that these could be exhausted in a system which was continually assimilating them, but as it happens the mineral and gaseous materials of the planet are themselves in slow but continuous circulation, and these cycles take millenia, and even millions of years, to complete. If living organisms had been too closely geared to these slow moving cycles, they could not have evolved in the way they have. Therefore, in order to be freed from this "tyranny" of the geological and geothermal cycles, organisms developed a method by which they could "free-wheel" or disengage directly from the slow moving geological regime. This method was the establishment of systems of organisms in which solar energy was borrowed to drive the system, providing sufficient liquid water and mineral and gaseous nutrients were available. These systems or ecosystems were, and still are, dynamically evolving and responding to conditions on the planetary surface. It is these ecosystems, of which Man is part, that ensure that life continues. However it must not be thought that the ecosystems are completely free of the geological and geothermal cycles—indeed an ecosystem consists of its constituent organisms plus the totality of the physical-chemical factors we call the environment (Tansey, 1935), so although a certain "immediate freedom" from the geological regimes is provided, the ecosystem is ultimately bound to these.

An ecosystem is energized and begins with the fixing of the visible part of the solar spectrum by plants, and the rate at which the energy is fixed sets the limits on its productivity. The light-fixing or photosynthesizing plants are, therefore, the link between the energy source—the Sun—and the plant/animal community or ecosystem, or in other words the plants form the "terminals" between the Sun and the ecosystem. The photosynthesizing plants are the only way in which solar energy can enter into an ecosystem. However, what is of particular importance is the rate at which this energy is fixed and the way it flows through an ecosystem.

The productivity of the photosynthesizing plants, the primary converters, depends on a number of factors such as temperature, number of daylight hours, length of growing seasons etc, and the gross productivity is the rate at which energy is fixed. However a considerable proportion (over half) of the energy so fixed is used in the plant's own respiration. It follows, therefore, that if the energy required for respiration equals that fixed there is nothing left over for the system as a whole. It is only when the energy required for respiration is less than the energy fixed that there is something left over for the plant-eater, or herbivore. This remainder is the net production of the plant. This can be simply expressed as $GP - R = NP$, where GP represents the gross production, R the energy required for respiration and NP the net production. It is the amount of the latter that decides the nature of the ecosystem.

The net production of the plants is the energy base upon which the rest of the ecosystem depends. After fixation the energy has to be distributed throughout the system and this is achieved by a series of steps or food chains. Throughout this simple transference there is a loss of energy to the environment. The greatest loss occurs at the herbivore level, because plant-eaters have to expend a significant proportion of the energy in converting plant tissue into animal tissue. Carnivores are more efficient, the main reason for this being that it is easier to convert one animal's tissue into another's—the biochemistry is not too dissimilar.

The situation, however, is not quite so simple as might be implied from the above. The steps described, although useful for clarity, are misleading in that they leave out the important role of the organisms of decay and those animals, including Man, that extract energy from several different levels in the food chain. The organisms of decay return some of the energy lost in the succession of energy transferences to the plants. Because of the complexity of the ecosystem it is much more useful to think of a web of numerous food chains. However, the steps described above, that is the plant-herbivore-carnivore relationship, do enable the energy flow system to be seen clearly. The feeding or trophic levels of the system provide a means of calculating the biomass or energy transfered at each level and when seen thus, a biomass or energy pyramid becomes discernible. From this it follows that generally speaking the biomass of the producers, that is the plants, must be greater than the biomass of the herbivores and the biomass of the latter greater than that of the carnivores. The same goes, without exception, for the quantity of energy at each level. No matter how much energy is available at the base, the quantity transfered at each trophic level seems to be fixed at around 10% (Lindeman, 1942).

As an ecosystem matures, the consumer population increases adding to the respiration of the plants (R_1) that of the consumer animals (R_2), and therefore the net production of an ecosystem (NPE) equals the gross production (GP) minus $R_1 + R_2$. This represents the energy stored within the system—the standing crop. It is the NPE that decides whether an ecosystem is developing (successional) or mature (climax).

A mature or climax ecosystem is a system where NPE is zero—there is no energy remainder. These mature systems are the most efficient of the ecosystems and they represent stable communities. Such systems require long periods of time to develop. The tropical rain forests are climax ecosystems and as such are the most stable communities on Earth. Other characteristics of climax systems are the extreme complexity of their food webs and the great diversity, though small populations, of the constituent species. The first of these ensures that should an energy chain break, there are numerous alternative routes through which energy can be shunted. The second provides the gene pool or bank from which new species can develop when opportunities arise, an important factor at times of reduced biosphere. In such periods the complex food webs and the wide range of species guarantees survival and repair and the base stock from which new ecosystems can develop as the biosphere once again expands.

A successional ecosystem on the other hand has a relatively uncomplicated system of pathways through which the energy can flow and is as a consequence more sensitive, so much so that the disruption of one of its major pathways may bring about its total collapse. Although unlike a climax ecosystem a successional ecosystem because of its net productivity can support large populations of a small number of species, it is always tending towards stability, in other words it is trying to evolve into a climax ecosystem. This can be summed up in the phrase "Nature achieves stability by investing in diversity and complexity".

The whole community of organisms on the planet lives in one of these two systems, each of which is restricted by the energy fixed by the photosynthesizing plants, which are in turn limited by the solar flux, the availability of nutrients and liquid water. These then are the basic constraints which limit the biomass of living organisms including Man.

The populations of the species *Homo sapiens* occupying a niche in a climax ecosystem, such as a tropical rain forest, are forced by the system to remain small (high species diversity—small population).* If this is the case then it is apparent that modern Man with his vast population could not live in such a system and the origins of Man's success must lie in his utilization of successional ecosystems. This may have first occurred in river valleys, estuarine and coastal zones, where climatic changes and/or seasonal flooding may have made it difficult for the establishment of climax ecosystems. In such areas the NPE would have been greater and Man would have had more opportunity of a larger share of both the producers and the consumers. Other animals (pig, dog) being similar "opportunists" would be found increasingly in association with Man, perhaps even forming temporary symbiotic relationships. The essential criteria would be that the animals should be facultative symbionts (Man, pig, dog) and from such relationships it is not a large step to domestication. However the findings of the palaeoecologists must be awaited before the earliest processes of domestication are understood. Evidence to hand of actual domestication of both animals and plants only dates from about the end of the Pleistocene, *c* 12,000 BP (Ucko and Dimbleby, 1969).

This process would be enhanced and accelerated during the interglacial periods of the Pleistocene when the expansion of the biosphere encouraged the development of new ecosystems. During these periods the opportunist species would increase in number and species development would take place as the ecosystem matured. At times of glacial advances the ecosystems would retreat as the biosphere contracted. Some of the new species would succumb but sufficient would remain at the periphery of the boreal zones.

* This may explain why the fossil evidence suggests that at one time in parts of East Africa several species of man-like primates had been able to exist as contemporaries.

By the time of the last retreat Man had become predominantly a successional ecosystem species. Better equipped to crop the herbivores and to keep off the carnivores, able to extend through cooking his range of plant foods, he was ready to take advantage of the developing ecosystems at the end of the Pleistocene.

The so-called Agricultural Revolution, rather than the beginning of a phase in Man's development, was a climax in itself. A similar developmental phase preceded what is now called the Industrial Revolution in the eighteenth and nineteenth centuries. The real beginnings of agriculture will be found by looking much further than the Middle East and further back in time, to Africa, Asia and possibly other areas and in the interglacial deposits in the higher latitudes.

The significance of this to modern Man is that by becoming a successional ecosystem species Man's population could increase (low species diversity—large population). His especial qualities of being both herbivore and carnivore suited him admirably for the role, it meant he could move and live almost anywhere, for it did not matter too much if he assumed a herbivore or a carnivore role or both. By the use of fire and eventually agriculture Man ensured that the system would never develop. *To maintain a large population it is not in Man's interest to let the ecosystem mature.*

Man's rise in population is a direct result of the post-Pleistocene extension of the biosphere and his method of maintaining a successional ecosystem. If the premise holds good that the energy available at the planet's surface has remained more or less constant during the post-Pleistocene period and that the biosphere and the biomass it contains must reflect that constancy, then the growth in the human population during this period must be at the expense of other species and evidence of this readjustment must be available. Man's effect on the biomass of other species during the Pleistocene and post-Pleistocene has been described (Martin, 1968) and there is no shortage of evidence to show changes in biomass distribution as expressed in terms of reduction in geographical distribution, populations and even in actual extinction of species during historical times. As the human biomass increases still further the readjustment in the biomass distribution will continue and accelerate and this development brings with it the concomitant instability of the successional ecosystem. For a time this was moderated by farming practice, at least in some parts where Man rotated his crops, pasture etc., but modern agricultural practices have increased the instability by reducing still further species diversity, destroying the decay cycles and depleting the soil nutrients. Modern monocultural practices are the ultimate in specialized and inflexible ecosystems. The natural system tries to rebalance the situation, non-agricultural plants (weeds) continually try to establish alternative arrangements, but are, and have to be, destroyed by Man. The monocultural method provides the means for the human population to increase, but it also encourages the increase of Man's competitors—cereal-eating insects, rodents, birds etc.—to combat which Man has to exert increasing ingenuity and amounts of energy. Oddly enough because of the high reproductive rates of these competitors, Man's attempts to combat them encourages their resistance to his arsenal of chemical weapons (Bourne, 1972). The ecosystem thus developing consists of Man, his crop and competitors. If this trend continues the man-made ecosystem will become still further impoverished and the human population dependent on an increasingly vulnerable energy base. This makes almost incomprehensible the efforts being made to accelerate the rate of converting mixed farming to single crop practices, dependent as these are on highly sensitive high-yield plant varieties that are vulnerable to insect herbivores and epidemic diseases. This investment in furthering an unstable ecosystem is not in the long-term interests of Man, especially when it can only be maintained artificially.

Another factor now becomes evident. Man can no longer depend solely on the solar energy being fixed by the producers, he has to supplement this energy by utilizing that "stored" millions of years ago in coal and oil, and without this input modern agriculture would collapse. This reliance on fossil energy increases still further the vulnerability of monoculture, particularly so when it is realized that the stocks of fossil fuels are limited (oil is estimated to run out within 30–40 years and coal within 100–200 years) and taking into account that these form both the material from which agricultural chemicals are made and the fuel for making and transporting them. Additionally the requirement for fossil fuels is shared by many other equally demanding industries. Even the advent of more nuclear and possible fusion power reactors does not necessarily lessen the immediacy of the breakdown, because the problem of thermal pollution causing increased evaporation may accelerate the build-up of atmospheric moisture and precipitation with the eventual cooling of the higher latitudes, thus bringing about those conditions conducive to a reduction in the biosphere.

The dependence on fossil energy was the cause of the failure of the Green Revolution—the concept of developing plants that are more efficient in utilizing solar energy holds true only so long as it is possible to replace the nutrient minerals the new plants remove from the soil. In modern agricultural practice little is returned to the soil because most crops are harvested, removed from the land and transported to urban areas, and human metabolic wastes by and large end up in the sea and not on the land. Consequently it is necessary to use artificial fertilizers and the requirement for these has increased by 125% in less than a decade. Calculations have shown that the investment in energy terms in agriculture is much greater than that produced (Leach, this volume, p.139). In principle this is not a cause for concern, for as has been seen the base of an energy pyramid is always greater than the product at any trophic level, for example the energy input into the so-called primitive "slash and burn" practice was also greater than the product. The principle is universal but the real danger lies in the system's sensitivity to climatic changes, competitors, the availability of fuel and nutrient supplies, and the concomitant dangers from chemical and thermal pollution. These latter in themselves constitute major threats to many ecosystems and could eventually cause a recession in the biosphere. The hazards of pollution and the interference with the Earth's atmospheric envelope and hydrological cycle have been discussed elsewhere (Bourne, 1972) but the continual injection of dust particles, whether they be of fertilizer or pesticide off the land or soil particles taken up during times of drought, is of particular importance in view of the dependence of the biosphere on the solar influx.

To augment the area under cultivation is the only way of increasing agricultural production, but competition for land for housing, industrial plant and other urban infrastructure is already a major problem, and those regions which have not until now known cultivation are mostly unsuitable. The felling of the tropical rain forests only exacerbates the problem, for as it was noted earlier these ecosystems have no NPE, there is little or no energy in the soil, rather most of it is contained in the forest canopy. At best the land cleared could provide a limited harvest for a few years after which it would become wholly dependent on fertilizers and pesticides so thinning out further the share of fossil materials. Additionally the destruction of the canopy may influence the hydrological cycle locally to such an extent that large and expensive irrigation and drainage schemes may have to be introduced. Experience has already shown that disease organisms confined to the upper stories of the forest canopy are brought down on felling and rapidly adapt to the new low level situation, causing loss to crops, domestic animals and suffering to Man. The destruction of those rain forests still standing will deprive the planet of the last stronghold of the oldest, most complex and most stable of all ecosystems with their rich diversity of species of both animals and plants. The felling now underway in West Africa and Brazil is the first step in the creation of the West African and Great Brazilian deserts.

In the search for new exploitable land another possibility is to move closer to the northern ice-sheets, but here an equally delicate ecosystem is already established with an exceedingly low biomass and a short growing period not at all suitable for agriculture. The deliberate melting of the ice-sheets would again only exacerbate the problem by flooding at the same time much of the important growing areas of the world.

Present attempts to bring into cultivation marginal lands and the deserts are energy intensive, requiring fertilizers, pesticides and irrigation, and even if such schemes were to be successful, the increase in food production that they would have provided would soon be outstripped by the growing human population.

With no more new agricultural land left and that remaining being fully utilized, the only alternative is technological food production but this is highly energy intensive and the energy supply risks and environmental dangers described earlier are therefore of serious significance. Another but rather different problem with such proposals is that while it may be said that technological advance develops at an exponential rate, the physical and biochemical behaviour of organisms including Man do not, and biochemical and even structural failures related to modern Western dietary habits are on the increase (see this volume, Burkitt, p. 247; Crawford, p. 235; Feingold, p. 215; Painter, p. 257).

Man is already in a position to make a choice between alternative life systems. He can either stabilize and even reduce his population in order to synchronize it with the natural productivity of the biosphere, or he can opt for a completely technological system of food production. The adoption of the latter holds numerous unknown hazards and requires that Man's technology is sufficiently developed to take over from the "natural" system he would be abandoning. He would have to be in a position to be confident that he would have adequate supplies of materials, water and energy, and that the new ecological regime, for that is what it would be, would not disturb the atmospheric and hydrological cycles of the planet. He would have to be certain that he could become completely dependent on it, otherwise he could be heading for the complete extinction of his species. For once he abandoned the old or "natural" system, he would have no back-up on which to draw if his technological food machine failed.

The question arises, is the Technological Revolution likely to be any more successful than the Green Revolution and is it sufficiently advanced to replace the older system for already the rate of growth of *Homo* is outstripping the rate of growth in food production? The artificially maintained fragile ecosystem is nearing its limits of development and the prognosis is that food production must decrease with a concomitant reduction in the human biomass.

The outcome of this situation is that the biomass of *Homo sapiens* will eventually reach a new equilibrium within a self-sustaining ecosystem. The constraints that are operative in the environment in which Man has evolved and upon which he is still dependent make the final reduction of his biomass inevitable in the long run.

References

Bourne, A. G. (1964). *Science Progrès/La Nature* (3350), 226.
Bourne, A. G. (1972). "Pollute and be Damned". Dent, London.
Bourne, A. G. (1972). *In* "Ecology in Theory and Practice", pp.253–270. Viking, New York.
Brandt, J. C. and Maran, S. P. (1972). "New Horizons in Astronomy". W. H. Freeman and Company, San Francisco.
Dilke, F. and Gough, D. (1972). *New Scientist* **56,** (823), 162.
Lindeman, R. L. (1942). *Ecology* **23,** 399.
Martin, P. S. (1963.) "The Last 10,000 Years". University of Arizona Press, Tucson.
Tansey, A. G. (1935). *Ecology* **16,** 284.
Ucko, P. J. and Dimbleby, G. W. (eds) (1969). "The Domestication and Exploitation of Plants and Animals". Duckworth, London.
Vernadsky, W. (1929). "La Biosphère". Libraire Félix Alcan, Paris.

The Energy Costs of Food Production

GERALD LEACH

Science Policy Research Unit, University of Sussex

Summary

The intensive highly mechanized Western farm is remarkably efficient at growing food on limited acres. But its high yields have been bought at the cost of large inputs of fossil-fuel energy. This energy, which is essentially a substitute for land and labour, is consumed not only on the farm to fuel and power machinery, but also in a myriad of places off the farm; to manufacture fertilizers, tractors and machinery, to transport these goods and the raw materials used to make them, to provide water for irrigation and animals etc. When these energy inputs are traced and totalled up, it often turns out that the Western farmer consumes much more energy as fossil fuel than he produces as food. For a typical gallon of milk in the UK, the ratio of energy input to output is more than 2·5, equivalent to using over two gallons of petrol to produce each pound of milk protein.

For industrial nations this agricultural energy consumption is a minor part of the overall energy demand (about 6% in the UK). It is also minor compared to the energy consumed in the long chain, now typical of urbanized societies, from the farm to the human mouth—a chain that includes extensive food processing and packaging, distribution, advertising, retail shops, transport for the customer to the shops, and last but not least, cooking and refrigeration in the home. Yet it is sufficiently high to raise serious doubts about the wisdom—indeed the possibility—of attempting to feed growing world populations by energy-intensive agricultural methods modelled on those of the West. A preliminary calculation suggests that if the energy-intensive farming typical of the UK was applied world-wide to give the present world population of about 4000 million a high standard of nutrition, energy consumption for agriculture alone would be 40% of total world energy use. Energy considerations alone strongly suggest that alternative strategies of food production must be sought; some of these are discussed.

Introduction

Industrial Man appears to believe that the world runs on money and can best be run as a money system. Isolated in his cities far from the basic realities of the world, he uses money as the universal criterion for judging whether or not something is worth doing and for assigning values and costs to things.

Money has its uses, but when it is the only language spoken Man lives in a world of illusions, possibly dangerous illusions. The true constraints on Man's ability to manipulate the environment for his own ends are ultimately set, not by printed notes, but by physical or "real" resources such as land, minerals, soil nutrients, water, the pollution absorbing capacity of a region, time (that is, labour), skills, and energy. Human ingenuity may mask this fact for a period, but almost invariably it does so merely by relieving pressures on one resource at the expense of increasing pressures on others—as, for example, when extra energy and machinery are used to reduce pollution or to grow more food on the same land area.

Of course, in principle this is all known; yet how little real notice is taken. Ecologists pay very close attention to these physical resources when studying biological systems, the biosphere, but as yet there is virtually no equivalent unified science for the much larger sphere of technical, industrial and commercial activities: the technosphere. Instead there is economics. And usually an economics that is grossly misused by carrying reductionism to absurd lengths. The real resources required for this or that activity may be measured, but almost as soon as this has been done, they are converted into money terms which are brought together into a single sum, and then this is bandied about as if it were the only resource worth discussing. Most people have at least a vague idea of the money cost of Concorde, for example but who can say what this is *for*? How much in terms of labour, fuels, metals, land, etc.?

Now the economist will reply that this simplification does not matter: his sums will reflect faithfully the availability or scarcity of real resources and hence answer the objections raised above. In an ideal world this may be true. But in practice money almost invariably reflects not the true cost of using a resource asset but today's *price* for that asset, while that price may itself be a quite arbitrary valuation. It reflects present day values and not real, long-term costs.

In other words, money and real resource evaluations may not agree and often sharply disagree. A classic instance of the latter situation has occurred recently over the massive plans to develop the vast coal and oil shale reserves of the arid Mid-Western USA. Cash economists have shown that these resources can be developed by spending so many billions here and there, and even that it will be economic to exploit the oil shales when world oil prices reach about six dollars a barrel. Yet an independent study has now shown that both the coal and oil projects may founder, or be severely limited by lack of *water*. A water budget prepared well in advance may have saved much wasted time, prevented much false optimism, and perhaps led to more realistic alternative options—such as reducing energy demand instead of trying to increase energy supplies.

It is for such reasons that I believe that there is an urgent need to extend ecology into an "ecology of the technosphere": to develop a new science that will supplement economics by thorough studies of the inputs, outputs, flows and conversions of physical resources in Man's techno-industrial world. My own work on the energy costs of food production is an attempt to help develop such a science.

But why energy? Energy, along with land, is the most fundamental of the real physical resources. Water *can* be recycled or won from the sea. Most minerals *can* be mined at lower and lower concentrations or recycled or substituted for. Pollution *can* be stopped by various technical corks and filters. Labour is, in theory, plentiful in a world that is even now largely under- or unemployed. Even land is an expandable resource up to a point: it can be built on or farmed more intensively. However, most of these attempts to "save" resources require, in the last analysis, more energy, often much more energy; while energy is the only resource that in the long term runs into final limits—not so much because enough cannot be provided (though that is a problem), but because the resultant waste heat and pollutants cannot be dissipated. Even now there are places on Earth, such as Moscow and Manhattan, where the man-made heat flux sometimes exceeds 10% of the natural solar heat balance; and there is a disturbing suggestion that carbon dioxide and dust from burning fossil fuels, along with a resurgence of volcanic activity, are the prime causes for the recent disastrous shift in latitude of the drought and monsoon belts in the northern sub-tropics (Bryson, 1973).

Man may be nearer the limits of energy consumption than is often supposed. But even if not, there are other reasons for giving energy pride of place as the major "real" resource to consider. Energy prices are bound to rise substantially in the mid-term, and perhaps much more in the long-term as the industrial world is forced to move towards a nuclear economy (see pp. 157–158). By measuring the total energy input to any production process, some idea can be obtained of how dearer energy will affect it and the prices of its products. This is particularly relevant to agriculture in the Third World, where food production is becoming (and may have to become) more energy-intensive with greater use of technical inputs such as fertilizers, machinery, irrigation and sprays. How will these developments fare when the energy inputs on which they are ultimately based cost much more?

Energy can also give a useful measure of the total *scale* of human activity and of economic development: for example, the energy density of a region—the primary energy consumption per unit land area—records population density, material living standards and industrial output combined. More interestingly, energy can also measure the *pace* of activity. This point has been strikingly made by the analysis by Berry and Fels (1972) of the total energy required to make an average American car, including all production processes for all material inputs. They found that of the total 32 million kilocalories* (kcal) required, only 6 million were theoretically necessary: most of the other 80% were due to the need to make cars as rapidly as possible. While industrial activity clearly cannot be slowed down to the exceedingly slow theoretical minimum rates, equally clearly energetics has much to say about the true costs of haste in modern societies and about the intensity of industrialisation. These insights, too, are particularly relevant to global agriculture.

Fortunately, these ideas about the value of energy analysis have caught on rapidly in the past few years, which have seen a small but sudden surge of energy studies for a wide variety of systems, from national economies to the production and re-use of milk bottles. It is worth looking at these briefly before turning to agriculture specifically.

On the national level, Herendeen (1963) and Just (1972) have independently analysed the USA economy and its sub-sectors as an energy flow system using economic input-output tables for 1963. Among their many fascinating revelations is the finding (by Herendeen) that the petrol going into the tanks of American cars accounts for only 57% of the total energy consumption by the automobile, the rest being due to oil production and refining, car manufacture, repairs, parking and garaging, insurance, and road construction. A comparable though cruder analysis for 1968 has been made by Makhijani and Lichtenberg (1972). In the UK, the Systems Analysis Research Unit of the Department of the Environment has begun mapping the flows of several important resources (including metals, fuels, power and water) across the entire economy on the grounds that future planning should be based as much on these realities as on money evaluations (Wright, un-

*960 kcal = 1 kwh; 38,000 kcal = 1 imperial gallon of petrol; 6·4 million kcal = 1 ton coal equivalent (UK); 7·0 million kcal = 1 tonne hard coal equivalent (EEC standard); 10·5 million kcal = 1 ton oil equivalent.

published). To date preliminary studies have been completed for 1963 (breaking the economy down into 70 sub-sectors and commodities) and for 1968 (90 sub-sectors), again using the input-output method. Thus it is found that in the UK in 1968, while most industries consumed, directly or indirectly, from 40–50 kilowatt hours (34,400 to 43,000 kcal) for every £1 of sales, a few consumed less than 20kwh and some more than 200kwh (including fertilizers and cement). Similarly, while a pair of shoes required 32,300 kcal all-told to manufacture, a gallon of paint needed 87,700 kcal—or rather more energy than is contained in two gallons of petrol.

It should be stressed that such input-output studies are able to measure the *total* consumption of energy (or any other commodity) by each industry due to the entire network of supplies feeding it, and not merely the direct purchases by the industry of fuels and power. This total consumption can be called the energy network input, or ENI. However, though they are a valuable, quick guide to total energy costs, they do suffer from several drawbacks. The most serious are that they do not distinguish between different end-products of any one industry, or between home-produced and imported products, even though these may have very different energy costs.

Consequently, a second line of attack has developed, starting from the end-product and tracing its entire network of inputs in energy terms, using production, transport, mining and a host of other relevant data. This "process approach" can be very time-consuming though it does seem to produce more reliable results than the input-output method: at least, in many cases attempts by different people for the same product agree fairly closely with each other, while they all disagree substantially from results using the input-output method. The work on the American automobile by Berry and Fels (1972) is a classic of this kind. Other notable studies are Bravard and Portal (1971) on the mining and recycling of metals; Hirst (1972) on American transport; an Open University study of milk bottles and their delivery; unpublished work by Chapman on metals, water, bricks and other building materials; and a study of fertilizers and other agricultural inputs by Leach and Slesser (1973).

Energy Budgets for Agriculture

Many people have assessed the *natural* energy flows in agricultural and other ecosystems. Many have combined these with *human* energy inputs (i.e. muscle power) for "primitive" agricultural societies such as the hunter-gatherers, swidden and subsistence farmers. Broadly speaking, what is found is that the conversion of natural solar energy to human food energy is extremely low (almost invariably less than 0·1%) but that in terms of food energy produced to human energy put in, yields are usually very high. Black (1971) has reviewed these yields and shown that for subsistence and swidden farming the energy ratio, or E (output of food energy/input of human energy) ranges from 3 to 34, with most crops falling in the range 15 to 20. These high figures say much about the life styles of such people; most "primitive" farmers do not need to work very hard to provide their basic needs. However, they do require considerable areas of land.

Modern intensive farming presents a complete contrast. What it has done is to increase yields per acre and very greatly increase yields per man hour (sometimes more than 100-fold) but at the cost of large inputs of a third form of energy input: *fossil fuel subsidy*. This point has been made most succinctly, and provocatively, by the American ecologist Odum (1971):

> "Much of the power flow that supports modern agriculture is not spent on the farm but is spent in the cities to manufacture chemicals, build tractors, develop varieties, make fertilisers, and provide input and output to marketing systems which in turn maintain mobs of administrators and clerks who hold the system together. As we stand on the edge of the vast fields of grain with tractors and production as far as the eye can see, we are tempted to think that Man has mastered Nature, but the plain truth is that he is overcoming bottlenecks and providing subsidy from fossil fuel".

Now it is only these fossil fuel subsidies that are of concern here; and for a simple reason. Solar energy is a perpetual and plentiful free gift; human energy is in theory plentiful, though not free; but fossil fuel energy is neither perpetual nor plentiful nor free. It is necessary to know how large these fossil fuel subsidies are, and even if they are large, how much they *matter*.

Surprisingly few people have attempted to answer these questions, at least with the care they deserve considering their importance for global survival and planning. Odum (1971), one of the pioneers, has looked at a few food systems, but used rather crude data based on a fixed quantity of energy per dollar spent. Black (1971) has made a cursory study of five crops grown in the UK but took only tractor fuels as his measure of energy subsidy. In a widely quoted article in *Environment,* Perelman (1972) has looked at American agriculture using a figure for tractor fuel consumption that is about three times too high and an energy cost for nitrogen fertilizers that is about 50% too low.

To be of any real value energy budgets must be constructed more carefully than this (though an accuracy of better than ±10% is probably utopian, not least because of the huge variability from farm to farm). Fortunately, a start on such high grade budgets has been made. Pimental *et al.*

(1973) at Cornell University have assessed the energy subsidy for maize growing in the USA from 1945 to 1970, counting up machinery construction, fuels and power used on the farm, fertilizers containing nitrogen, phosphorus and potassium, seeds, irrigation, insecticides, herbicides, transport, and labour (metabolic energy only). The results establish what many have suspected: that while maize yields have increased greatly (by 138% in the period) the energy subsidy has increased much more, from 0·93 to 2·90 million kcal/acre, a 3·1-fold rise. As a result the energy ratio, E, has decreased from 3·7 to 2·8, both figures being far worse than for almost every "primitive" agricultural system based on human energy inputs.

Slesser (1973) has made a much more comprehensive study of 131 food systems, ranging from subsistence growers to the most intensive Western "factory farms," and including true factory methods such as single-cell protein production from carbohydrate wastes or fossil fuel feedstocks. His pioneering results are very interesting since they are the first to show the relationship between food outputs per acre and energy inputs across the whole spectrum of intensification: as might be expected, what is found is a marked tendency to diminishing returns going up the scale towards larger energy subsidies. However, Slesser has so far been unable to incorporate some important energy costs (including machinery, construction and irrigation): his results for animal products such as milk and eggs are consistently lower, sometimes by two to three times, than my own—even though the same figures are used for those inputs that are included.

In deference to Odum, who launched my interest in agricultural energetics with his famous remark that industrial Man "no longer eats potatoes made from solar energy; now he eats potatoes partly made of oil", results will first be quoted for the humble potato.

Table 1 is a somewhat simplified energy budget for an average acre of potatoes in the UK in the crop year 1940–1971 (yields averaged over five years). The main reason for including it is to show what factors are counted in my budgets, and what are excluded; to illustrate the kinds of source that are used; and to give some values for energy costs per £1 or physical quantity for different farm inputs. However, it must be stressed that this is a preliminary budget only, and that it does not include important information on the variations of inputs and yields.

It should be noted that the energy costs shown include a proper allowance for the energy costs of providing energy: in the UK in 1970–1971 it took 1·21 kcal of primary energy to produce one kcal of petroleum fuels (if no credit is given for non-fuel uses of petroleum), 3·49 kcal to provide one kcal of electricity, with equivalent factors for coal of 1·04, and for gas plus all other solid fuels combined, 1·31 (Leach and Slesser, 1973). These factors are very close to those for the USA (Herendeen, 1963). Not included in the budget are

TABLE 1

Energy budget for one acre of maincrop potatoes, UK 1970 to 1971 averages

	kcal/unit	000 kcal	% of total
INPUTS			
Fertilizer:[a] N 151 lb	7350/lb[b]	1110	22·9
P_2O_5 151 lb	900/lb[b]	136	2·8
K_2O 210 lb	1000/lb[b]	210	4·3
		1456	30·0
Tractors: 25 hours,[a] 45–50 h.p.[c]	42000/hr[c]	1050	21·6
Other machinery, fuels, electricity:[d]		1290	26·6
Sprays: £9[a]	36800/£1[e]	331	6·8
Sundries: £9[a]	30000/£1[c]	270	5·6
Irrigation:[f] 2·5 acre-inch= 57,000 gallons (0 in wet year, × 2 in drought year). Includes power for pumping on farm.	8/gal[g]	460	9·4
TOTAL TO FARM GATE		4857	100
ASSUMED TOTAL		4900	
Approx. transport farm gate to city (34 miles)[h]		540	
TOTAL TO CITY		5440	

OUTPUTS	
Yield 10·5 tons[a] less 1·03 tons returned for seed[a]	=21,300 lb
Edible yield after deducting loss from peelings:	
new potatoes (14% peelings)[i]	= 18,300 lb
old potatoes (27% peelings)[i]	= 15,600 lb
Energy content 352 kcal/lb,[i] hence energy yield:	
new potatoes	6440 000 kcal
old potatoes	5490 000 kcal
Energy ratio (output/input) at city	
new potatoes	1·2
old potatoes	1·0
Crude protein content of edible portion 2·1%,[i] hence	
Energy subsidy per lb protein:	
new potatoes	14,200 kcal/lb protein
old potatoes	16,600 kcal/lb protein

[a]Nix, J. "Farm Management Pocketbook", 4th edition (1970–1971 crop year), from Wye College, London University. General recommendation for most soils is rather higher in "Potatoes" (Bulletin 94, Ministry of Agriculture, Fisheries and Food), giving an energy cost of 1640 000 kcal (or +12%), but for Fen soils, on which most potatoes are grown, N need be only 130 to 140 lb, giving an energy cost of 1300 000 kcal (—11%).

[b]See Leach and Slesser (1973). P_2O_5 and K_2O costs include mining ores, beneficiation, and shipping to UK.

energy costs for capital equipment such as farm buildings, or fertilizer and machinery factories, since they are very small compared to the energy flows through the capital plant (less than 1 % with fertilizer factories); transport of materials and equipment to the farm, which is trivial compared to other costs (0·1 % with fertilizers); and the human energy input for farm labour (less than 1 % of other energy inputs). Like Pimental *et al.* (1973), the total support energy needed to maintain the life style of the farmer and his workers is also ignored, on the grounds that what they do off the farm in their free time is irrelevant to the business and energy budgeting of agriculture. Slesser (1973), however, includes this cost, adding 500,000 kcal/hectare (200,000 kcal/acre) for all systems where the energy subsidy exceeds one million kcal/hectare year (400,000 kcal/acre year).

Table 1 reveals that Odum was not exaggerating: with an energy ratio of 1·0 to 1·2, potatoes are made not partly but wholly of oil. In fact the E ratio must be considerably worse than this, for the author has not counted in many of the energy-using steps in the long path from the farm gate to the customer's mouth—including processing, wrapping, canning, wholesaling and retailing, customer transport to the shops, and cooking. To illustrate how large these costs "downstream" of the farm gate may be, consider canning and customer transport. The can for a standard 1lb net weight of food weighs close to 2oz, while the rolled steel of which it is made has a total energy cost

---

[c] MAFF statistics show that the bulk of farm tractors are in this range, while MAFF booklet "Farm as a Business, No. 6: Labour and Machinery" gives 0·7 gals diesel fuel/hr as standard for most field operations. At 50,000 kcal/gal (see Leach and Slesser, 1973) fuel costs/hr = 35,000 kcal. Estimation of machinery manufacture, repairs, tax etc. from many sources including main references Berry and Fels (1972); Herendeen (1963); Makhijani and Lichtenberg (1972); Wright (unpublished); Bravard and Portal (1971); Hirst (1972). All machinery depreciation and repairs taken as 30,000 kcal/£1.

[d] Nix (*a*) gives £8/acre for fuel and repairs; £17/acre for machinery and power costs on intensive arable farms. The proportions of these sums for fuel, electricity and machinery depreciation plus repairs have been deduced from full statistics by different farm types in "Farm Incomes 1972" (HMSO, London) for the 1970–1971 crop year and average farm sizes. Multiplying the results by data for energy/£1 from *c*, gives a total cost for all machinery, fuel and power of 2340 000 kcal/acre. The figure given is this total less the total for tractors.

[e] Cost for insecticides and herbicides 11,500 kcal/lb (Leach and Slesser, 1973). Conversion to cost/£1 for potatoes from analysis of prices of different products and average quantities used (ICI Farm Management Service data – personal communication).

[f] "Potatoes", Bulletin 94, Ministry of Agriculture, Fisheries and Food.

[g] Mean of estimates by Chapman (The Open University); and Smith (1969). This is for mains water delivered to the farm. Figures given in *a* for the cost of impounding water on the farm or pumping it from average wells suggest very similar final energy costs. An additional charge for power used to pump water for gun hoses has been added.

[h] Average haulage for food in UK is 34 miles (unpublished road statistics from Department of the Environment). 10·5 tons potatoes plus 0·5 tons of purchased seed must be hauled; assumed 15 ton lorries, empty return, hence 1440 kcal/ton mile (Leach and Slesser, 1973).

[i] "Manual of Nutrition", HMSO.

of about 800 kcal (14·5 million kcal/long ton) (Berry and Fels, 1972). This is more than twice the nutritive energy value of 1lb of potatoes (352 kcal), and indeed of nearly all vegetables. Shopping by car in the UK carries an average energy cost of about 1700 kcal/mile for petrol consumption alone (average car 27 miles/gallon; ENI for petrol 46,000 kcal/gallon) (Leach and Slesser, 1973).

TABLE 2

Energy budget for standard white loaf (28·25 oz): UK 1970 to 1971 average yields

	kcal	% of total
INPUTS		
For 1·67 lb wheat: fertilizer	380	26
fuels, power, machinery etc.	600	41
sprays	20	1
TOTAL TO FARM GATE	1000	68
Milling to 1·22 lb flour (72% extraction)[a]	176	12
Baking[a]	202	14
Transport (farm-mill;[a] mill-baker;[a] baker-shop)	79	6
ROUNDED TOTAL	1460	100
OUTPUTS		
One loaf: 2030 kcal, 8·3% digestible crude protein[b]		
Energy ratio (output/input):	1·4	
Energy per lb protein:	9,970	

[a]National Farmer's Union and Flour Milling and Baking Research Association (personal communications).
[b]"Manual of Nutrition", HMSO.
No credit given for wheat offals after milling: these make only a small difference to the output when counted as animal feed converted to animal products.

Potatoes rarely incur many of these downstream costs, but much of the food eaten does. Furthermore, these downstream costs are bound to increase on a global scale as populations become increasingly urbanized—a process that is a direct consequence of agricultural change; it is therefore proper to count them into any agricultural energy budget. With crops that *must* be processed to make them edible, it is of course essential to budget at least as far as the factory gate, since stopping at the farm gate can be most misleading. This point is well made by Tables 2 and 3, which give preliminary energy budgets for a standard 28-oz (795-g) white loaf and for sugar from beet in the

UK. With the bread it is found that milling, baking and transport account for about one third of the total energy cost, but with sugar the processing and transport account for some two thirds of the total.

TABLE 3

Energy budget for one ton sugar beet: UK 1970 to 1971 average yields

	000 kcal	% of total
INPUTS		
For 1 ton beet + 0·67 ton tops (of which 0·17 ton grazed, 0·50 ton ploughed in):		
fertilizer	83	7·6
fuels, power, machinery	171	15·7
sprays	39	3·6
TOTAL TO FARM GATE	293	26·9
Sugar factory: fuel, limestone, water only: (output 0·13 ton sugar; 0·07 ton dry pulp; 0·045 ton molasses)[a]	763	70
Transport: (beet to factory; sugar to city; pulp and molasses to farm, where used as animal feed)	35	3·1
ROUNDED TOTAL	1090	100
OUTPUTS		
Sugar direct to Man[b]	521	
Grazed tops, pulp, molasses via animals to Man, assuming mean conversion of 13% for sheep and cattle, edible carcase weight basis	16	
TOTAL	537	
Energy ratio (output/input):	0·49	
Protein:	not applicable	

[a]Kneese *et al.*, (1970).
[b]"Manual of Nutrition", HMSO.

The staples considered so far—maize, potatoes, bread and sugar—turn out to have energy ratios in the range 0·49 (sugar) to 2·8 (USA maize). These low energy efficiencies may surprise many people who are not accustomed to thinking of fossil fuels as a major input to farming. If they are surprised at this they may be astonished by the figures for animal products. Consider, for instance, the egg, which once came at almost zero energy cost from hens scratching around the farmyard living off wastes and low grade grain, but is now produced in the Western world by production line factories at an energy cost that is relatively enormous. Table 4 gives a preliminary budget for an average battery hen system in the UK and shows that the energy ratio is a

TABLE 4

Energy budget for one battery hen, UK 1970 to 1971 average: rear + 52-week laying period + hen carcase

INPUTS[a]	kcal/unit	kcal
Initial egg		560
Hatch chick from egg: 0·095 to 0·365 kwh, assume 0·1 kwh	3000/kwh	300
Rear pullet to 20 weeks:		
electricity: 2·3 kwh	3000/kwh	6900
medicines and vet: 3·9p	30000/£1[b]	1170
tractor hours (carting food etc): 0·01	42000/hr	420
water: 9 gallons	8/gal	70
buildings and equipment: 2·2p	30000/£1[b]	660
food: 22 lb	675/lb[c]	14850
	TOTAL	24930
Adjust total for average 5% mortality	TOTAL	26240
Laying bird (52 weeks):		
electricity: 5·6 kwh	3000/kwh	16800
medicine and vet: 5p	30000/£1	1500
tractor hours: .05	42000/hr	2100
water: 45 gal	8/gal	365
buildings and equipment: 12·5p	30000/£1	3750
food: 104 lb	675/lb[c]	70200
	TOTAL	120955
No adjustment for mortality required[d]	ASSUMED TOTAL	121000

OUTPUTS

216 average size eggs[d] + 3·66 lb cull carcase [d] (dead carcase weight) + manure NPK (ENI equivalent of 11,000 kcal—ignored):[e] 560 kcal/egg

216 eggs = 24·5 lb edible portion = 17640 kcal[f]	2·92 lb protein[f]
Hen carcase = 2·5 lb edible meat = 1640 kcal	0·52 lb protein
TOTALS 19280 kcal	3·44 lb protein

Energy ratio = 0·16 (input/output = 6·3)

Energy subsidy/lb edible protein = 35,000 kcal

[a]Data for unit costs from Nix, J., "Farm Management Pocketbook", 4th ed.; "Intensive Poultry Management for Egg Production" (Bulletin 152, MAFF); "Poultry Housing and Environment" (Bulletin 56, MAFF); "The Farm as a Business: No 5, Poultry" (MAFF); "Business Control in Poultry Keeping" (Bulletin 191, MAFF).

[b]Estimates from main reference Wright.

[c]Food costs estimated as follows: 70% assumed to be barley grown at energy cost of 640 kcal/lb (separate energy budget). The remaining 30%, usually protein concentrates, is also assumed to be barley. Though some of these concentrates will have been grown in the tropics at low energy costs, shipping to the UK makes up much of the difference; other concentrates, such as fish meal, are considerably more energy-intensive, depending on the

mere 0·16 (i.e. over 6 times as much energy is used as is produced) while it takes some 35,000 kcal to produce 1lb of digestible protein (77,000 kcal/kg)—an energy cost of nearly one gallon of petrol equivalent to provide the protein purchased by an average Briton every five days (0·94lb, 430g) (HMSO, 1973).

Nor are such high figures exceptional—except in comparison to the majority of the world's farmers. Table 5 lists a range of food production systems in roughly ascending order of energy cost. In the UK all the animal products listed have energy costs over 25,000 kcal/lb protein (55,000 kcal/kg) while the most costly—USA milk "in the shops"—has an energy input 64 times higher than the best "primitive" system (South Pacific atoll fishermen). The energy ratios tell a similar story, with a *thousand*-fold difference between the best and the worst (Chinese rice paddies and fish from freezer trawlers, in which exactly one ton of fuel oil is consumed for each ton of gutted fish landed).

What is to be made of all this? On their own these figures show only that modern, intensive, mechanized farming is peculiarly energy intensive compared to traditional agriculture. But that should hardly be a blinding revelation. What must be known is whether this fact matters. And to discover that, it is necessary to set energy costs in relation to other factors such as labour use, land use, food and energy prices, the total energy consumption of industrial societies, and the future availability (or otherwise) of energy for the world.

Unfortunately there is insufficient data as yet to make any rigorous or conclusive comparisons along these lines, though there is enough to allow some broad patterns and trends to be sketched in.

Energy Costs and Labour

The major impact of energy subsidies has been to save not land but manpower. Consider a typical subsistence agriculturalist who works his crop with

---

source. This 30% is also charged for preparation and processing at 82 kcal/lb and for transport within the UK at 35 kcal/lb (confidential data from very large animal feed producer).

[d]Flock mortality is normally 10% per year, but the unit costs given take this into account. The output of eggs and cull carcase also takes this into account: normal production for a hen surviving the year is 240 eggs, of which about 5% are substandard rejects (240 × 0·95 for mid-year surviving flock × 0·95 for rejects = 216).

[e]Credit for manure NPK is ignored because energy costs of collection and spreading approximately equal the credit.

[f]Nutritive values from "Manual of Nutrition" (HMSO).

an E of 20. To provide himself with a round million kcal of food energy per year (2740 kcal/day) he needs to work for about 42 days of 8 hours (assuming 150 kcal/hr). In fact he will have to work more than this to support dependents, but this does not alter the argument presented here.

TABLE 5

Food production systems

		000 kcal/ lb digestible protein	000 kcal/ kg digestible protein	E ratio (energy out/ energy in)
BIO-ENERGETIC LEVEL				
Atoll fishermen[a]	South Pacific	0·8	1·8	
Rice paddy[b]	Yunan, China			53
Maize[b]	Yucatan, Mexico			29–13
Taro-yam gardens[c]	Tsembaga, New Guinea			20
Rice paddy[b]	Dayak, Borneo			10
Pigs[c]	Tsembaga	9·9	22	(2)
FOSSIL FUEL LEVEL				
Wheat[d]	UK farm gate	6·5	14	2·2
Oats	UK farm gate	6·7	15	2·0
Barley	UK farm gate	9·0	20	1·8
White bread (if UK wheat)	Bakery UK	10	22	1·4
Potato (old)	UK farm gate	15	33	1·1
Sugar beet	UK city shops	–	–	0·49
Milk (+calves, cull cow)	UK farm gate	25	55	0·33
Broiler hen	UK farm gate	29	64	0·11
Battery egg (+cull)	UK farm gate	35	77	0·16
Fish: freezer trawlers, fuel only	UK dockside	36	79	0·05
All fish[e]	USA 1963, shops	17·7	39·0	
All cheese	USA 1963, shops	18·8	41·4	
All meat	USA 1963, shops	32·6	71·8	
Milk	USA 1963, shops	51·2	113	
	One lb oil equivalent:	4.7 000 kcal		
	One kg oil equivalent:		10·3 000 kcal	

[a]Odum, quoting Alkire (1965).
[b]Harris, M., unpublished, quoted in Rappaport (1968).
[c]Rappaport (1968).
[d]All UK data by Leach.
[e]All US data from Herendeen (1963). Milk is exceptionally high probably because it includes bottling.

Now take a British farmer, who can grow and harvest an acre of cereals for about one man-day per year. The crop will provide about 4×10^6 kcal/acre, hence he need work for only two hours to provide his needs of one million kcal (assuming, rather absurdly, that he lived by bread alone). However, working beside him are a number of "ghosts"; people who are rarely counted in agricultural statistics, but are in fact vital to farming since they *allow* this high productivity—namely, all the workers in the agricultural support industries, the energy industries, the water industry, etc. etc. not forgetting Odum's "mobs of administrators and clerks". It has been variously but roughly estimated that including the whole food processing and delivery network, this support manpower amounts to three to four workers for each person on the farm. If three were concerned, the British farmer plus his "ghosts" would need to work for six hours to provide a million kcal: an improvement over the subsistence level of 56 times.

And the cost of this in energy? For bread ($E = 1{\cdot}4$) it would be about 714,000 kcal. Bearing in mind that the primary energy consumption for all purposes in the UK is now close to 38 million kcal/head/year this seems like a cheap bargain: the "energy ration" for 7 days pays for 41 days of labour saved.

However, it may become much less of a good bargain in future and is even now a highly questionable bargain for developing countries, where mass under-employment and the flight to mushrooming shanty cities are among the most dire consequences of the mechanization of agriculture.

Energy Costs and Land

Energy subsidies also save land. They increase yields by opening up bottlenecks in the optimum flow of solar energy and nutrients into the crop, or support larger flows in improved genetic varieties, or help to smooth out climatic irregularities. Ideally, with sufficient data on the energy costs for many different levels of agricultural mechanization and intensification, it should be possible to plot the relationship between land saved and energy expended in going from any energy-land level to another, and even to say how much energy would be needed to provide a given quality of diet on a given quantity of land per person. Due to the large variations caused by climatic, soil and managerial differences—and, in future, the likelihood of technological changes altering the land/energy relationships—this kind of exercise can give only approximate guides. They may, nevertheless, be of crucial importance to long-range agricultural and energy forecasting and planning.

Slesser (1973) has used his data for 131 food-producing systems in this way and derived a relationship for vegetable and industrially produced protein, such that

$$P = 1{\cdot}415\,(e.s)^{0{\cdot}178}$$

where P is protein yield in kg per hectare year and $e.s$ is the energy subsidy expressed as 10^3 kcal/ha year. Some of my data is shown in this form in Fig. 1. A similar broad pattern is revealed. While natural range systems have very low outputs and inputs, bioenergetic systems are intermediate in yields but can be very high if Man is prepared to work hard enough: Ukara Island, on Lake Victoria, supported 11·6 persons/acre (4·7/ha) with a high quality diet including much animal products, but has now been abandoned because the inhabitants have traded off good eating for more leisure (Clark and Haswell, 1970). What is most striking, however, is the way yields flatten off at higher energy intensities (represented here by the UK), especially with animal products.

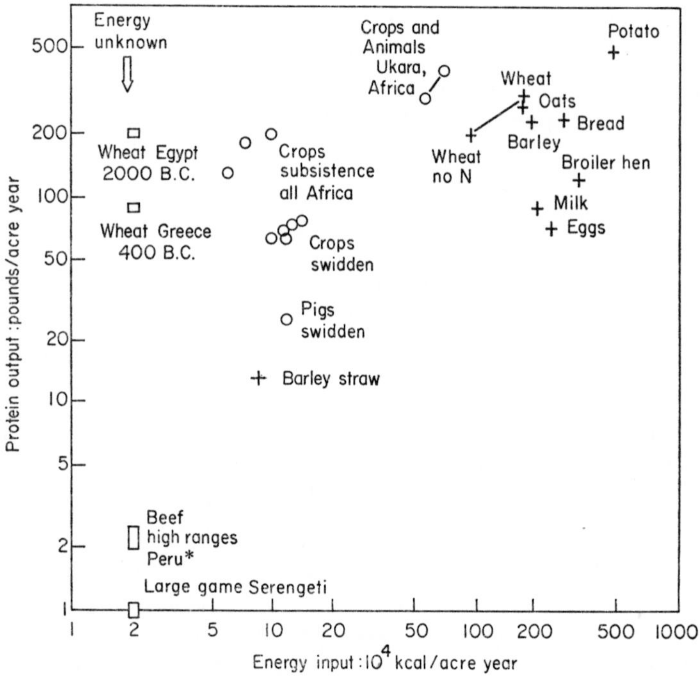

Fig. 1. Relationship between protein yield and energy subsidy. O: Human Energy; +: fossil fuel (all data UK); *data from M. Slesser.

This fact raises the first of several important questions for global planning: how far towards the right hand side of the graph should Western agriculture be *allowed* to go in a world that is short of food and may soon be short of energy?

To dramatize this question, consider Table 6. This shows the *response* in terms of extra protein yield given an extra injection of energy subsidy. Only a few systems have been chosen, deliberately, to emphasize the contrast which can be found between Western and tropical agriculture. The first entry is based on the discovery that by raising the lighting level in a battery hen-house from 0·5 to 2·5 foot candles an extra six eggs can be squeezed from a hen each year. However, the extra lighting consumes 6·63 kwh, giving a response of 247,000 kcal for each extra lb of protein (544,000 kcal/kg)—a phenomenal cost that is, nevertheless, considered "economic". Contrast this with the data for Jamaica and Rhodesia, where sowing indigenous pastures with better grass varieties and with fertilizers produces the same extra yield of animal protein for 1/14 to 1/30 the energy cost.

TABLE 6

Protein yields: response to extra energy subsidies

	Extra energy input (000 kcal) per extra lb protein output		
	vegetable protein		animal protein
Battery eggs UK			
raise lighting levels (+ 6 eggs/yr)			247
Milk UK			
grass response to N fertilizer			82
Wheat UK			
response to N, all farm costs included			
N from 0 to 20 units/acre	4	13% protein conversion	31
N from 60 to 80 units/acre	17		131
Jamaica, cattle on grass			
native grass to pangola grass + 4 cwt fertilizer/acre			8
Rhodesia, cattle on grass			
native grass to improved grass + 80 lb N/acre			18

A rational world would surely see to it that, instead of pumping fossil fuel agriculture to even higher pressures in order (hopefully) to export some of its surpluses to the hungry tropics, the small amount of effort and energy required would instead be spent in the tropics to produce much larger returns.

But, sadly, it does not need energetic arguments to underline the truth that the world does not act rationally.

Energy Costs and Energy Prices

The price of energy is rising rapidly so what impact can the increases be expected to have on the basic question of food prices?

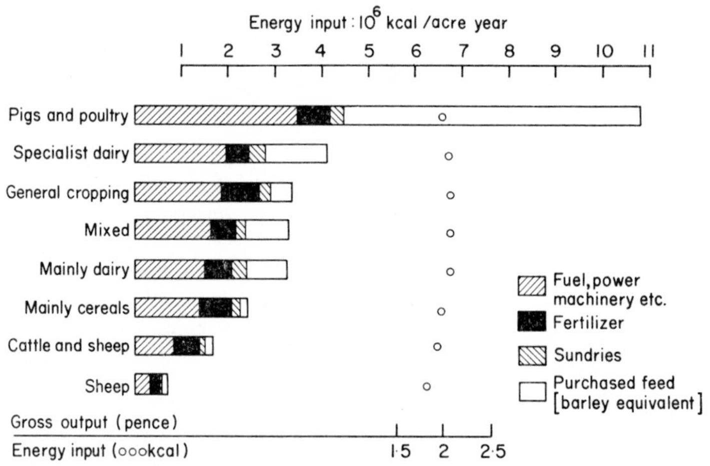

Fig. 2. Energy density for all UK farms (except horticulture).

The best way to approach this question is to consider Fig. 2. This shows the energy density for all UK farms (except horticulture) in 1970–1971: that is, the quantity of primary energy going into each average acre, computed by counting up the energy network inputs for fuels, power, machinery construction, fertilizers, all sundry costs, and purchased feeds (using the approximation that all feeds are barley). It is found that most farms have energy densities in the 2 to 4 million kcal/acre range, with pig and poultry farms scoring much higher and—as would also be expected—sheep farms scoring much lower.

These figures will be discussed again later but for the present argument the point to notice is the series of black squares plotted across the chart. These record the gross output—that is, the farmer's receipts from sales of all his products divided by the energy subsidy required to produce that output. And, rather remarkably, this ratio is practically constant for all farms at very close to 2p/1000 kcal subsidy. (Incidentally, if both the outputs and inputs for purchased feeds are ignored, almost precisely the same figure and narrow spread are obtained for all farms.)

The question now to ask is, what is the price for these kcals of energy subsidy? My estimate is approximately 0·2p/1000 kcal, or 5000 kcal/p. This is close to the price of tractor fuels at the time (5500 kcal/p) and is roughly midway between the cheapest energy then available for large coal, gas or oil consuming industries (8000 to 9000 kcal/p) and the figure for farm electricity (970 kcal/p).

It can now be seen what will happen to food prices if energy prices double (assuming all other factors remain constant). Supposing that the doubling applies to the entire energy network backing the farmer—as seems likely—then the price paid for the energy subsidy on the farm will rise by its present price, i.e. by 0·2p/1000 kcal. To break even, the farmer will therefore have to raise his gross output by the same amount, i.e., from 2p/1000 kcal subsidy to 2·2p/1000 kcal.

This is a rise of 10% which does not seem much. Moreover, the effect on prices in the shops will be very much less in proportion owing to the large price mark-ups between farm and shop. Nor is it found that particularly energy-intensive foods such as animal products and meat fare any worse than the broad averages just cited. Indeed, because they are relatively expensive already, the effect of an energy price doubling is usually to raise their farm gate price by considerably less than 10%: for instance, with eggs under 1970–1971 conditions, by 6%.

However, this does not mean that farming will not be changed, perhaps drastically, by much dearer energy. Nitrogen fertilizer use is one obvious candidate for change, since approximately 15–20% of the purchase price of fertilizer N is represented by the money costs of energy inputs, including feedstock and power (sources listed in Leach and Slesser, 1973). With ammonia synthesis, around 40% of production costs are for natural gas and power (sources listed in Leach and Slesser, 1973). When energy prices double, the prices of these products will rise by roughly these percentages, since there is little scope left for reducing the energy inputs to their manufacture (modern fertilizer plants are working at close to maximum theoretical energy efficiencies).

Nor should it be assumed that a doubling of energy prices is all that is in store. Looking ahead to the twenty-first century, nuclear electricity will have to provide most of the stationary power/energy, and probably at a price at least close to that of today, which ranges from 1000 to 2000 kcal/p. On a useful heat supplied basis, this energy will be about two to three times dearer than the average today, though on a work supplied basis there might be little difference. Liquid fuels, such as hydrogen or methanol derived from nuclear electricity, are bound to be very much dearer than the liquid fuels of today. For instance, estimates by Day (1972) suggest that the cost per therm of energy for synthetic liquid hydrogen and for methanol (made by calcining limestone to carbon dioxide and reacting with electricity-derived hydrogen) will be respectively £0·26–£0·28 and £0·27–£0·33. These figures are about fourteen times those for crude oil at pre-October 1973 prices (£0·021 per therm).

Technological progress may reduce these figures somewhat. Even so, it seems rash to expect that energy prices in the twenty-first century will be less than three times those of today, in real terms. If so, and all other factors being equal, food prices at the farm gate will rise for energy reasons alone by some 20% or more.

Fortunately though, other factors are not likely to remain equal. One major change that seems bound to occur on the farm is a massive effort to reduce energy inputs. Indeed, work in this direction has already begun.

Towards the Zero-Energy Farm

The energy-intensive Western farmer could, with little trouble, reduce his overall energy consumption dramatically—and without any loss of yields or return to labour-intensive methods. Recycling animal wastes partially to replace artificial fertilizers, or using them to generate methane, are two frequently urged solutions since they solve the sometimes critical waste disposal problems too. But by far the largest impact would be made by using sensibly a natural fuel that many farmers now burn wastefully and destructively in their fields—cereal straws.

Most farms grow cereals. An average acre of cereals in the UK yields roughly one ton of straw with a gross energy value of 3 million kcal (2000 kcal/lb, 30% moisture content in the field). This is roughly equal to the *total* ENI/acre for most farms, (Fig. 2) and is more than twice the energy used per acre as fuel and electricity for all farms except pig and poultry enterprises. Preliminary work at Nottingham University (Wilton) shows how this straw might be harvested and turned into a fuel for a very low energy cost. The entire cereal plant is cut with a forage harvester (instead of a combine for the grain plus a tractor and cutter-baler for the straw) and dried. After drying the grain and straw are separated, and the straw could be burned either in a furnace to provide heat for drying, or in an external combustion engine (e.g. Stirling cycle) to provide mechanical power or even electricity. The straw drying would consume about 12 to 15 gallons of fuel (600 000 to 700 000 kcal) under average conditions, giving a net energy yield of 2·3 to 2·4 million kcal. Alternatively, the straw could be fermented (without drying) to a liquid fuel such as alcohol with a net energy yield of around 1·5 million kcal/acre plus by-product material for feeding ruminants. This last figure, equivalent to 36 gallons of diesel fuel, is higher than the liquid fuel consumed/acre for all farms except pig and poultry, and is over 50% higher than the consumption for dairy and cereal farms. With a judicious mixture of fermentation and direct straw-burning, including burning to generate power, and with animal wastes providing methane or nitrogen, phosphorus and potassium, it seems entirely probable that many farms might become self-reliant for all fuels and power, and would need to import energy only in the form of (some) fertilizers, machinery and other technical equipment, and sprays.

Energy Costs in a Global Context

The most important lessons of energy analysis are not for the rich, industrial world, but for the poor world; and, no less important, for the rich world in its dealings with the poor world in a future in which both food and energy supplies may be constantly balanced on a knife edge.

In the industrial world agriculture and food production are relatively minor energy consumers. One way of establishing this point for agriculture alone is to compare the energy densities for farms shown in Fig. 2 with equivalent figures for whole regions and countries. This is done in Table 7. It is found that most farms in the UK have energy densities far lower than even the most rural regions (Scotland, East Anglia, South-West England), about one tenth that of the country as a whole, and 0·5% that of Greater London. If Scotland, with its high proportion of marginal sheep farms, is ignored, the energy density of English farms turns out to be approximately 5% of the energy density for England as a whole. In short, most energy is consumed in towns, factories, transport etc, and not on farms.

Another clue comes from input-output studies. Herendeen's analysis for the USA in 1963 shows that taking food production right through to the shop, the overall energy ratio was 0·22 (4·5 kcal of fossil fuel for each kcal of food produced) and the total energy consumed for agriculture and food manufacturing and distribution was 11·7% of the gross primary energy consumption of the nation. Since the USA was then a net exporter of food, this figure probably overstates the situation. The UK input-output studies for 1968, though very preliminary, give somewhere in the region of 14% as the energy cost of all food production and delivery compared to primary energy consumed. This figure probably understates the real situation because of food imports, but not by all that much: a good deal of that 14% was for processing and distributing *all* food, including imports.

TABLE 7

Energy densities: 10^6 kcal primary energy consumption per acre year

India	1·0
World land area	1·4
Most UK farms	2–4
UK Pig and poultry farms	10·5
USA	7·2
Scotland	9·7
Europe: France, Germany, Belgium, Netherlands, Luxembourg, Italy	20·0
England: East Anglia, South-West regions	20·9
UK	34·9
England	52·7
England: South-East region	79·2
England: North-West region	145
Greater London	592

All UK data are for 1971 from "Digest of UK Energy Statistics 1972" (HMSO): end user consumption converted to primary energy by appropriate factors given in Leach and Slesser (1973) these factors derived in turn from the "Digest". Other data for various years 1968–1971 from national or UN energy statistics.
Note that the primary energy may not be *produced* in the region.

Hence, at a rough guess, something like 12% to 15% of total energy consumed in the industrial world is for food production. In a severe energy crisis food would be only one of our worries, while it would be a trivial problem to divert energy consumption from "luxuries" to food production.

But how would the poor world stand in such a situation? Indeed, how does it stand *now?* Farmers in the developing world are being widely encouraged to apply energy-intensive technical inputs such as fertilizers, machinery and irrigation. Where this process increases yields per acre, or raises the quality of the diet, this is all to the good; and as has been seen, small injections of energy in these forms can produce large extra yields. But all too often these energy-intensive inputs are used primarily to increase yields per *man,* and the pressures to do this are growing—despite the terrible social disruptions so frequently created.

How far can this process go? On energy grounds alone, it appears to be fraught with difficulties. There is, for instance, already a shortage of fertilizers in many developing countries and their price is often prohibitive for poor farmers. Yet, as has been seen, energetic arguments show that these prices are bound to rise very steeply in the long term. It can even be doubted whether sufficient energy will be available for massive intensification across the globe. A very rough sum shows that a world population of 8,000 million (expected in the year 2010) could have about 0·8 acres/head of arable land if a massive effort is made to bring today's range and pasture land under the plough and to win vast areas of now unused land (without this effort there would be 0·44 acres/head of arable land plus 1·4 acres/head of range and pasture). To provide and deliver a European quality of diet with energy subsidies of the order of those now employed in the UK would require some 5 million kcal/head. This figure is nearly twice the *total per capita* energy consumption, for all purposes, of the Third World at present (2·6 million kcal/head) (BP, 1972). When this is multiplied by 8,000 million people, a total energy demand for world food production of 4,000 million tons of oil equivalent is obtained. This is 70% of present world energy demand for all purposes (BP, 1972).

This sum is very approximate, but it does underline two crucial things. First, an energy subsidy for food production that the rich world can call relatively minor—some 12–14% of total energy demand—is enormous from the viewpoint of most of mankind. Second, if 8,000 million people are to be fed a good quality diet, either a great deal more energy in future must be provided *and* much of it diverted to the Third World farmer, or farming must be much more ingenious. Above all, careful thought must be given to *how* and *where* energy subsidy is pumped in to increase yields and save labour.

There is one final consideration. The industrial world is gaining an increasing dominance over the transfer of technology to the Third World, not least to agriculture. It is fostering a massive change from comparatively low yield, high-labour farming to comparatively high-yield low-labour, high-energy farming. Yet is also has an increasing thirst for energy. Could Man be preparing the ground for one of the most appalling tragedies of history?

Odum (1971) has set the scene for this tragedy.

He writes:

"We now have chickens that are little more than standing egg machines, cows that are mainly udders on four stalks, and plants with so few protective and survival mechanisms that they are immediately eliminated when the power-rich management of Man is withdrawn. . . . It is a cruel hoax to send so-called improved varieties which are in reality incomplete parts of the industrialised agriculture to underdeveloped systems" (unless, Odum implies, all the other energy- and skill-intensive parts are sent too). "The man from the poor country, looking at affluence and being told it is due to improved varieties, throws out a workable if low-yield system in exchange for an incomplete part of an agricultural system that cannot operate without the full support of the industrial fossil fuel inputs and management".

The question must be asked whether the rich, industrial world will provide, or allow the poor world to gain for themselves, that full support—when its own fossil fuel inputs are already starting to make it feel anxious? Recent experience gives no grounds for comfort. The rich world's pre-occupation with the gathering energy crisis has been almost exclusively concerned with securing its own energy supplies.

References

Anon. (1973). "Milk Bottle" Pamphlet TS251 13 (An Introduction to Materials, Unit 13), 48, p.48. The Open University, Bletchley, UK.

Alkire, W. H. (1965). Lanotrek Atoll and inter-island socio-economic ties *In* "Studies in Anthropology". University of Illinois, Urbana, USA.

Berry, R. S. and Fels, M. F. (1972). "The Production and Consumption of Automobiles: an energy analysis of the manufacture, discard and re-use of the automobile and its component materials". Report to the Illinois Institute for Environmental Quality.

Black, J. N. (1971). *Proc. Assoc. appl. Biol.* **67,** 272–277.

BP (1972). "BP Statistical Review of the World Oil Industry, 1972". British Petroleum, London. "Third World" taken as World minus N. America, W. Europe, E. Europe, USSR, China, Japan, Australasia.

Bravard, J. C. and Portal, C. (1971). "Energy Expenditure associated with the Production and Recycling of Metals". Report ORNL-MIT-132, Oak Ridge National Laboratory, Oak Ridge, USA.

Bryson, R. A. (1973). *Ecologist* **3,** 366–371.

Chapman, P. The Open University, Bletchley, UK.

Clark, C. and Haswell, M. (1970). "The Economics of Subsistence Agriculture", 4th Edition. Macmillan: St. Martin's Press, London.

Day, G. V. (1972). *Futures* **4,** 331–343.

Herendeen, R. (1963). "An Energy Input-Output Matrix for the US 1963". Report CAC 69, Center for Advanced Computation, University of Illinois, Urbana, USA.

Hirst, E. (1972). "Energy Consumption for Transportation in the US". Report ORNL-NSF-EP-15, Oak Ridge National Laboratory, Oak Ridge, USA.

HMSO (1973). "Household Food Consumption and Expenditure: 1970 and 1971".

Just, J. (1972). "Energy Intensiveness of US Industries". Unpublished report, Department of Electrical Engineering, Massachusetts Institute of Technology, Cambridge, USA.

Kneese, A., Ayres, R. U. and D'Arge, R. C. (1970). "Economics and the Environment: A Materials Balance Approach" (Resources for the Future Inc.), John Hopkins Press, Baltimore.

Leach, G. and Slesser, M. (1973). "Energy Equivalents of Network Inputs to Food Producing Processes". p.38. Obtained from Slesser, M., Department of Pure and Applied Chemistry, University of Strathclyde, Glasgow, UK: or, Leach, G., Science Policy Research Unit, University of Sussex, Brighton, UK.

Makhijani, A. B. and Lichtenberg, A. J. (1972). *Environment* **14,** 10–18.

Odum, H. T. (1971). "Environment, Power and Society". Wiley-Interscience, New York and London.

Perelman, M. J. (1972). *Environment* **14,** 8–13.

Pimental, D., Hurd, L. E., Bellotti, A. C., Forster, M. J., Oka, I. N., Sholes, O. D., Whitman, R. J. (1973). *Science* **182,** 443–449.

Rappaport, R. A. (1968). "Pigs for Ancestors", Yale University Press.

Slesser, M. (1973). *J. Sci. Fd Agric.* **24,** 1193–1207.

Smith, H. (1969). *In* "Transactions of the World Energy Conference" Vol. 18, Section E.

Wright, D. J. Department of the Environment, London. (Unpublished papers.)

The Alternatives

Potential Protein Sources For Human Food

N. W. PIRIE

Biochemistry Department, Rothamsted Experimental Station

Summary

Most of the research on new sources of edible protein is being done in countries where the need for more protein is not, at the moment, acute. It is done to increase the supply of fodder for non-ruminants, to produce cheap substitutes for conventional proteins in human food, to supply products with which the texture of foods can be improved, and as a service to countries that need protein. For a time, protein can be sent to these countries, but research will ultimately be of most use if it leads to methods whereby protein can be made in protein-deficient countries from local products. The countries in most need are not well developed technologically; it is essential, therefore, that the methods of preparation should be simple. There are particular circumstances in which each is pre-eminent:

fish near underexploited water, but not necessarily impalpable fish powders;
soya and cottonseed when they will grow, but possibly fermented to make them palatable instead of being heated and solvent extracted;
groundnuts, if harvested cleanly and processed gently, in wetter regions;
protein extracted from coconuts and leaves in still wetter regions;
micro-organisms grown on agricultural wastes where technology is adequate.
The present and impending need is so great that all these will ultimately have to be used; it would be prudent to get the basic research done now.

People cannot be healthy unless they eat a balanced diet in amounts suited to the work they do and to their individual peculiarities. Regions where there is malnourishment will therefore differ in their most acute nutritional needs. But protein deficiency is the most common dietary fault and it will be the most difficult fault to remedy. Some people suggest that the affluent countries should produce the protein that the others need, but this could not be a permanent arrangement for the protein could not be paid for, and inspite of encouraging instances of personal and national generosity, charity cannot be relied on indefinitely. Not only must protein be produced within a country, it should also be produced near the places where it is needed. It follows, if these propositions are accepted, that methods of production become more useful the less they depend on very sophisticated techniques, and they become most useful when they can be used in a small town or large village. Attention is too often confined to the needs of the city dweller; those who live 50 miles up a dirt track should not be neglected, and even in 50 years time, that group will still be numerous.

There is conflict about how much protein people need. With an arrogant assumption of omniscience some argue that protein needs will be satisfied as soon as the body is not being steadily depleted. This state of "nitrogen balance" is usually reached when 40–50g of protein is eaten each day. Others adduce less quantitative, but no less real, evidence that various aspects of performance improve when more protein than this is eaten (Nutrition Society Symposium, 1969; Pirie 1969a). Even if the figure arrived at from balance studies should prove to be correct, the world shortage of protein in the forms traditionally eaten by people is at present 20 million tons a year. Another 20 million tons would be needed to give everyone a further 15g a day, and the population is expected to double by the end of the century. The need therefore is great and growing and it is very unlikely that it can be met by any single source. The various sources are complementary rather than competitive and all of them, and some more that have not yet been thought of, will probably be needed.

Although nitrogen is the element first thought of in connection with proteins, and is the one on which analytical methods invariably depend, it is not the nitrogen that raises the problems. Nitrogen can be "fixed" where-ever power is available, and legumes can be grown wherever agriculture is possible. It is the availability of reduced forms of carbon that controls the changes undergone by ammonia, nitrate, urea and the other forms of nitrogen that are essential for protein production by every route. Current photosynthesis is the pre-eminent source of reduced carbon and most of the techniques of agriculture are directed at promoting photosynthesis by ensuring that leaves are exposed to light in an undamaged, responsive state, and in a manner adapted to the physiology of the plant and the local climate. Atmospheric carbon dioxide is thus reduced at the expense of light energy. Although there are only about 110mg of carbon in the atmosphere above each square centimetre of the Earth's surface, this carbon dioxide is constantly replenished—there is indeed evidence that the amount is increasing. There are, on average, several grams of reduced carbon in the form of coal, oil, gas etc. beneath each square centimetre of the surface. This is largely the product of past photosynthesis and is probably not being replenished. Estimates of the date by which this carbon store will be exhausted vary, and they contain an element of unreality because exhaustion would involve the replacement of part of the atmospheric oxygen by an equivalent amount of carbon dioxide. A massive increase in carbon dioxide would have dramatic but unpredictable agricultural consequences and might force us to reconsider our fuel policy. The carbonate rocks contain 1 to 2kg of carbon per square centimetre; this is an almost inexhaustable resource if energy is available for the reduction, and the reduction, unlike the burning of fuels, would add to rather than detract from atmospheric oxygen. Approximate figures are set out in Table 1. Clearly, there is no shortage of carbon; but the more abundant the carbon source, the more difficult the process of converting it into food. The immediate problem for those now in need is therefore to ensure that photosynthesis is organized in a manner that will produce the maximum amount of human food.

TABLE 1

The amount of carbon in various forms in the accessible part of the Earth's surface

	Weight per square centimetre of total world surface	Total weight in tons × 10^{10}
Oxidized forms		
Limestone and dolomite	1·8kg	900,000
Oceanic carbon dioxide	7g	3,500
Atmospheric carbon dioxide	110mg	55
Reduced forms		
Kerogen in rock	500g	250,000
Coal, lignite etc.	1g	500
Oceanic water	545mg	270
Soil organic matter	290mg	145
Oceanic sediments	190mg	95
Petroleum	14mg	7
Methane	4mg	2

TABLE 2

Existing and potential methods for producing protein

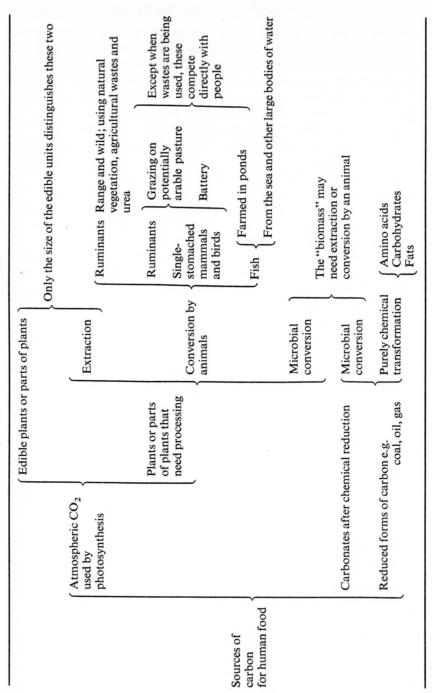

Sources of carbon for human food	Atmospheric CO_2 used by photosynthesis	Edible plants or parts of plants				Only the size of the edible units distinguishes these two
		Plants or parts of plants that need processing	Extraction			Only the size of the edible units distinguishes these two
			Conversion by animals	Ruminants	Range and wild; using natural vegetation, agricultural wastes and urea	
				Ruminants	Grazing on potentially arable pasture	Except when wastes are being used, these compete directly with people
				Single-stomached mammals and birds	Battery	Except when wastes are being used, these compete directly with people
				Fish	Farmed in ponds	Except when wastes are being used, these compete directly with people
				Fish	From the sea and other large bodies of water	
			Microbial conversion	The "biomass" may need extraction or conversion by an animal		
	Carbonates after chemical reduction		Microbial conversion	The "biomass" may need extraction or conversion by an animal		
	Reduced forms of carbon e.g. coal, oil, gas		Purely chemical transformation	Amino acids Carbohydrates Fats		

Table 2 outlines the main existing and potential methods for producing protein. Clearly, the methods differ greatly in complexity. Some are traditional in the regions where protein is most needed, others depend on advanced technology. Some necessitate an inefficient process of conversion by an animal, whereas others could either be used directly by people or could be used after conversion—this introduces flexibility and variety into the system.

By the middle of the seventeenth century—a time usually taken as the beginning of organized scientific research—the basic choices among the edible plants had been made. They had indeed been made some thousands of years earlier when the 100 or so plants on which we depend were chosen. It is possible that primitive people were not invariably the best judges of biological potentialities and it may now be advantageous to enlarge the favoured group. When this is done, special attention should be given to the criteria controlling the choice. Twenty years ago it was hard to persuade anyone of the imminence of the protein shortage of which we are now so conscious; protein content and quality were not therefore prominent among the qualities looked for in a food plant. They now get welcome attention; protein-rich strains of maize that had been under-esteemed for a generation are hailed as "breakthroughs" and protein-rich strains of other cereals are being actively investigated. This is admirable and it raises the hope that, at least in some parts of the world, a cereal-based diet will no longer be protein deficient. The seeds of broad-leaved plants could have a role in world feeding, but thinking still seems to be restricted to plants amenable to the traditional techniques of primitive Man. Consequently, more effort is put into attempts to grow familiar crops in increasingly improbable environments than into attempts to use those species that already grow exuberantly in a region.

Biochemical analysis shows that there are useful components in all plants: the usefulness of a plant species depends on the quantities that are present and the ease with which these components can be extracted and separated. Therefore, alongside the commendable efforts that are being made to increase food supplies by intensifying conventional farming, there is a need for the more radical approach of biochemical engineering. This depends on three propositions:

1. in many parts of the world the plant species used in agriculture are not the ones that give the most abundant growth;
2. in all parts of the world the part of the plant that is normally used is accompanied by straw and other by-products;
3. these plants and materials are unused because they are not amenable to traditional techniques.

For these reasons the physical and biological natures of some of the unused or little-used plants, especially those flourishing in the wet tropics, should be studied. The work could be considered under three headings:

1. how much total growth is there in a year?
2. how much useful protein, fat and carbohydrate is there in this growth?
3. how easily can these substances be extracted for food?

Operations 1 and 2 are extensions of what is already being done and they involve normal analytical procedures. They fit well into the existing research structure and people who could perform them are already trained. It is operation 3 that raises the difficulty and it is because of this difficulty that the 100 favoured species were chosen from among the third of a million plant species. Their cardinal merit is their amenability to handling by primitive techniques.

Knowledge of the composition of plants, and of practical methods for extracting their components, increases steadily, so that hitherto intractable materials can now be handled. As an example, work on the extraction of leaf protein at Rothamsted may be cited. Equipment has been made (Pirie, 1966, 1969b, 1971) in which one ton of fresh crop can be pulped in an hour and the juice pressed out. This brings with it half to three quarters of the protein of the leaf. The protein is then coagulated, filtered off and washed. The alternative of drying the whole juice has been suggested as an "improvement" (e.g. Hartman *et al.*, 1967); this is totally misguided. The protein press-cake contains 60 to 70% water, so that only two tons of water have to be evaporated to get one ton of dry product, whereas the juice contains 90–95% water. Furthermore, the protein in dried juice would be contaminated by about its own weight of material which, according to the leaf species used, is of poor nutritional value, no nutritional value, or harmful in non-ruminants. When properly made, dry leaf protein contains 60–70% protein and 20–30% lipid. The lipid is unsaturated and therefore nutritionally valuable, but in certain conditions, combines with the protein (Buchanan, 1969a,b) during drying or preservation thus diminishing the protein's nutritive value. A stable pale brown product is easily made by solvent extraction, but it is hoped that trustworthy methods of handling can be devised and that the expensive process of solvent extraction will prove unnecessary. Solvent extraction would greatly increase the cost of the product and it would be difficult to organize local production in technically unadvanced regions. At Rothamsted the moist protein has been preserved with salt; in India various methods of pickling have proved successful (Subbarao *et al.*, 1967). Ideally, the protein would be used in the fresh state.

Work will probably continue in such countries as the United Kingdom, New Zealand, Sweden and the USA, but unless there is some drastic change in political and economic circumstances, it is bound to be on only a small scale because the product is not at present needed in these countries. However, research is now starting in several countries where the need for protein is acute.

With support from the International Biological Programme, at Rothamsted a laboratory-scale extraction unit has been made (Davys and Pirie, 1969; Davys *et al.*, 1969) by means of which the yield of extractable protein per hectare and year can be used as one of the criteria by which agronomic experiments can be scored. With little or no growth during the winter, already more than 2 tons (dry weight) of extracted protein per hectare per year have been obtained (Pirie, 1969c); in Mysore the yield is 3 tons (Singh, 1967). These yields of protein greatly exceed those attained by any other system of husbandry.

Stress has been put on the extraction of leaf protein because the yield is large, the methods are sufficiently simple to be used by any community technically competent to handle a tractor, and leaf crops grow well in parts of the tropics where rain is so frequent that it is difficult to ripen a seed crop. It is in these regions that protein shortage tends to be most acute. There is however little advantage in extracting leaf protein in any region where green vegetables are not already prominent in the diet. It is only when a community is already eating vegetables to such an extent that the daily intake of fibre is approaching the maximum set by the physiology of the human gut, that it is worthwhile contemplating the mechanical separation of protein and fibre. There has been surprisingly little research on vegetables for use in the wet tropics and what little there is tends to concentrate on the adaptation of temperate species. This may prove successful but it should be complemented by a detailed study of cultivated tropical plants (e.g. the amaranths) and the various wild species traditionally used as pot herbs. They may not seem very promising now—but neither was the cabbage when selective breeding started on it. With modern methods it will not take 1,000 years to produce from some wild tropical species a diversity of highly productive forms comparable to those to which the cabbage has given rise. Though the yields given by these unimproved plants may be small, the protein content is often good; the immature flowers of *Saccharum edule* (pitpit in New Guinea, duruka in Fiji) contain 40%, and Oke (1966) lists several pot-herbs containing more than 30%. It is unfortunate that the trend is the other way. In developing countries where 30 or 40 indigenous species were regularly eaten a generation ago, all the vegetables may now be introduced species—even the vegetables themselves may be imported. Tropical market gardening deserves more, and more broad-minded, attention from plant breeders.

Although leaf protein would usually be made from a crop grown primarily for this purpose, various waste and by-product leaves would also be used. The various potential sources of leaf are set out in Table 3. The mixed wild

TABLE 3

Sources of leaf for protein production

Crops grown specially because the protein yield per acre-year is exceptionally great.
By-product leaves e.g. cotton, jute, sugar beet, sweet potato and vegetable discards.
Leaves that are not now harvested but that could be e.g. floating or palustrine plants.
Inadequately or incompletely used crops e.g. green manures and cover crops.
Crops from land too briefly moist for normal farming e.g. shores of seasonal lakes and rivers.

growth on unused land is not included. If the land is of such a character that it can be cultivated, fertilized and harvested, it might as well be used for a desirable crop, but if it does not have this character, the yield from it will be negligible after a few crops have been carted away. Areas of water and swamp are exceptions to the generalization that "weeds" are not a promising protein source. They often carry an almost pure stand of one species, and control measures, if weeds interfere with the other uses to which the water is put, are expensive. Furthermore, effluents and drainage water from heavily fertilized farmland increasingly encourage excessive weed and algal growth in many bodies of water. If the weeds are simply killed by herbicides, the essential elements are returned to the water to repeat the cycle, but if the weeds are harvested and processed on land the elements would be removed with a consequent decrease in "eutrophication". When this removal of elements is not required, it would obviously be preferable to mount the processing machinery on a barge. At Rothamsted 30–40% of the protein has been extracted from a few temperate and tropical water weeds, and (Boyd, 1968) has studied a more extensive range; *Justicia americana* and *Nymphaea odorata* are particularly promising. This is a subject well worth intensive investigation. Putting the weeds to use would not only save the costs of other forms of control and purify the water but it could also produce more than half a ton of extracted protein per hectare and year (Boyd, 1968, 1969) if *Justicia* were grown. *Typha* grows even more exuberantly but the extractability of its protein has not yet been measured.

In affluent countries cattle graze on potentially arable land and they are stall-fed on mechanically cultivated and harvested crops. This is a pleasant extravagance that should not be emulated in countries with a food shortage. In those countries ruminants are useful when they graze on non-arable land and when they consume various agricultural by-products. These can, if need be, be fortified with urea and other simple nitrogen compounds. Non-ruminants, such as pigs, chickens and pond fish, need food of a type so similar to that needed by people that it is extravagant to keep more of them than can be maintained on what we discard. Pleasant as the extravagance is, its basic character should be recognized in any discussion on protein sources.

Primitive Man chose an even smaller group of domestic animals than of domestic plants. We are probably unreasonably obsessed with four mammalian species. Even more unreasonable is the herdsman's obsession with keeping species separate. On a wholly artificial sward production may be optimum with one species, but it seems logical to think that a mixture of species, able to graze and browse at all levels, would make fuller use of bush or range land. This has not yet been rigorously demonstrated (Golley and Buechner, 1968) but experiments are being planned.

The fish farm is the equivalent either of a paddock or a pig pen depending on whether the fish must live on the vegetation growing in and around the pond, or whether this is supplemented by offal and other food grown elsewhere. Some of the more ecstatic claims for fish farming disregard that point. Where lakes and ponds already exist, it is obviously wise to farm them, but there is at present no evidence that it would be worthwhile making ponds artificially to rear fish instead of using the land to raise a terrestrial animal. Rivers and the sea are another matter and they could be more fully exploited. FAO estimates that the sea could yield two or three times as much as it now does. That extra protein would be well worth having, but before too much effort is put into reorganizing the fishing industry, it should be borne in mind that one-third of what is now caught is used as fodder rather than human food. Stopping this diversion would have as good an effect as increasing the catch.

The use of micro-organisms is a complement to agriculture and not an alternative to it because, except for the algae and a few photosynthetic bacteria, micro-organisms depend on fermentable material from another source. The physiological peculiarity of micro-organisms is that they can use the soluble constituents of what would otherwise be waste products, e.g. sewage, molasses, woodpulp effluents; they have indeed often been grown in bulk more as a means of disposing of a noxious waste than as a means of getting more food. When chemical and mechanical methods for extracting protein and other valuable components from plants are used on a significant scale, the culture of micro-organisms on the resulting liquors will be an essential part of the process.

The choice of micro-organisms is wide. Most effort has so far been put into the cultivation of yeasts and about half a million tons of dry food and fodder yeast is now being produced. Many yeast species can be used, differing in physical properties, cultural requirements and flavour. The last is important because the lack of enthusiasm so far shown for food yeast has been attributed to its intrinsic flavour; it has also been attributed to the flavour of the anti-foam agent used in making some of the early batches. Several batches have caused digestive disturbances and animals have sometimes not thrived on yeast. Trouble may be caused by microbial contaminants, by intact cell walls, by polyphosphates, by nucleic acid, and in other ways—different methods of handling may be needed to remedy them. All these points need study. There is much less experience with edible moulds, actinomycetes and bacteria, but the prospects for them seem generally good though some people are intolerant of *Hydrogenomonas eutropha* (Waslien *et al.,* 1969).

The idea of growing micro-organisms on certain fractions of crude oil has recently been in the news. There are obvious potentialities here and the initiative of oil companies is to be welcomed very heartily for it is likely to stimulate a general interest in the idea of microbial food. It is important however to keep the project in proper perspective. Oil is simply a carbon source and its value should be assessed in comparison with other possible substrates such as molasses, sulphite liquor, straw, sawdust and so on. In some areas it may well be that oil is the cheapest carbon source, and the fraction used appears to be one that the oil companies are glad to get rid of, but any community that already has waste molasses would be well advised to look into its potentialities before thinking about growing micro-organisms on oil. In a developing country, the process is much more likely to be feasible if based on molasses than if based on oil.

By convention, a preliminary assessment of the value of a proposed protein source is based on its nitrogen (N) content; when criticism is expected, some attempt is made to exclude non-protein N, because even when that is present in the form of amino acids, one or two usually preponderate so that the nutritional value of the product is low. The method used to separate non-protein N (for example by extraction with boiling water or trichloroacetic acid solution) will not usually remove chitin and other N-containing polymers; these substances are such common components of micro-organisms that the assumption that the 6–8% of N the dry organisms generally contain is evidence for the presence of 37–50% of protein, is even more hazardous than with other possible protein sources. The need for thorough biological testing is correspondingly greater.

Finally, instead of using fossil carbon sources as microbial substrates, they, or limestone, could be used as the starting point for complete or partial chemical synthesis. Several amino acids e.g. lysine and methionine, are already being made on a large scale and used to supplement food and fodder in which only these amino acids are deficient. It does not however seem likely that it would be economic to replace protein by synthetic amino acids. When all the essential amino acids are needed at once it will probably be sensible to leave the job of making them to plants and micro-organisms, rather than to a chemical factory.

The food manufacturing industry has vast experience of the difficulties and uncertainties involved in inserting a new form of food into the market. This experience is gained in well-fed communities where a novelty must replace an existing food. It is not therefore strictly relevent in an ill-fed country, where little difficulty is to be expected in increasing the use of a protein-rich food, such as the familiar meats or fish, provided the price is compatible with the local income. Acceptance of unfamiliar meats and fish will be only a little more difficult to gain. Wholly unfamiliar novelties will gain acceptance if they are regularly consumed by a group that carries prestige—as the wide diffusion of "Coca-Cola" shows. Little is as yet known about the forms of advertising, example and propaganda that will be needed to win acceptance for products, such as plant and microbial proteins, that are novel everywhere. Some factors in this problem are discussed elsewhere (Pirie, 1969d, 1972). Here, the most relevant factor is quality.

Before any attempt is made to get a novelty accepted by the public, all rationally based objections must be met. Nothing can be done about irrational objections even when they come from scientists. It is obviously wise to be cautious about admitting newcomers to the table, but caution should not degenerate into fetishism. It is only now that the possibly deleterious components in many traditional foods are beginning to be uncovered (e.g. Synge, 1963); some of them, if their use were now being proposed for the first time, would probably be condemned. The potential hazards in traditional foods arise mainly from water soluble substances such as sulphur compounds and dopa. Substances of that type would be removed from any product subjected to even such minimal treatment as sago and cassava receive traditionally. There is a difficulty here that has to be considered in the light of the present and increasing protein shortage—those who argue that nothing should be used until prolonged tests have demonstrated its safety, overlook the fact that there is no incentive to undertake these tests until use is probable. Furthermore, there is a strong *prima facie* reason for assuming that plant and animal proteins at any rate will be wholesome. The position with food additives is different. They are often added casually for aesthetic reasons or to solve minor technical problems, and companies will spend the $50,000 that an adequate test costs (Morton, 1967) because of the large profits expected from subsequent sales. No-one is likely to make much money out of devising means whereby ill-fed people can produce their own supplies of protein.

References

Boyd, C. E. (1968). *Econ. Bot.* **22,** 359.

Boyd, C. E. (1969). *Arch. f. Hydrobiologie* **66,** 139.

Buchanan, R. A. (1969a). *Br. J. Nutr.* **23,** 533.

Buchanan, R. A. (1969b). *J. Sci. Fd Agric.* **20,** 359.

Davys, M. N. G. and Pirie, N. W. (1969). *Biotech. Biogn.* **11,** 517.

Davys, M. N. G., Pine, N. W. and Street, G. (1969). *Biotech. Biogr.* **11,** 528.

Golley, F. B. and Buechner, H. K. (1968). "A Practical Guide to the Study of the Productivity of Large Herbivores". IBP Handbook No. 7. Blackwell, Oxford and Edinburgh.

Hartman, G. H., Akeson, W. R. and Stahmann, M. A. (1967). *J. Agric. Fd Chem.* **15,** 74.

Morton, R. A. (1967). *In* "Chemistry, Medicine and Nutrition", p.45. Royal Institute of Chemistry, London.

Nutrition Society Symposium, (1969). *Proc. Nutr. Soc.* **28.**

Oke, O. L. (1966). *Trop. Sci.* **8,** 128.

Pirie, N. W. (1966). *Science* **152,** 1701.

Pirie, N. W. (1969a). *Proc. Nutr. Soc.* **28,** 255.

Pirie, N. W. (1969b). *Proc. Nutr. Soc.* **28,** 85.

Pirie, N. W. (ed.) (1969c). "Biochemistry Department: Rothamsted Experimental Station Annual Report for 1968". 112.

Pirie, N. W. (1969d). "Food Resources; Conventional and Novel". Penguin Books, London.

Pirie, N. W. (1971). "Leaf Protein: its Agronomy, Preparation, Quality and Use". IBP Handbook No. 20. Blackwell, Oxford and Edinburgh.

Pirie, N. W. (1972). *Ecol. Fd Nutr.* **1,** 279.

Singh, N. *In* Annual Reports of the Central Food Technological Research Institute (Mysore) in 1967 and later years.

Subbarao, M. S., Singh, N. and Prasanappa G. (1967). *J. Sci. Fd Agric.* **18,** 295.

Synge, R. L. M. (1963). *In* "Progress in Nutrition and Allied Sciences". (D. P. Cuthbertson, ed.), p.31. Oliver and Boyd, London.

Waslien, C. I., Calloway, D. H. and Margen, S. (1969). *Nature* **221,** 184.

Food Production Methods and their Potential For Increasing Food Supplies

J. T. WORGAN

National College of Food Technology, University of Reading

Summary

Agriculture is the main source of Man's supplies of food and in comparison with modern industrial processes appears to be a haphazard, inefficient system of production. Scientifically it is feasible to synthesize all the essential components of the human diet and technological processes have been developed for the production of the fats, vitamins and amino acids. The raw materials required for synthesis consist of water, oxygen, nitrogen, carbon, and to a lesser extent sulphur. A source of energy is also essential. Although in agricultural production the primary source of energy is sunlight via the process of photosynthesis, equivalent inputs of support energy in the form of fertilizers and mechanical aids are required in the agricultural systems of Europe and North America. Energy resources are therefore a critical factor in maintaining sufficient supplies of food from either agricultural or synthetic systems.

The conversion of more complex inedible raw materials to food requires considerably less energy than complete synthesis from simple substances. Adequate quantities of raw materials must be available for conversion and the only potential sources are the hydrocarbons and the carbohydrates. Even the most optimistic forecasts predict that supplies of hydrocarbon will become critical within the next 50 years. However the carbohydrates are a renewable resource which is at present under-utilized. The output of edible carbohydrates from agricultural systems could be increased several-fold by growing crops which give high yields and by reducing in extent the wasteful system of rearing livestock. It is the supplies of protein which would then become critical. Waste carbohydrates can be used as energy sources by micro-organisms to convert inorganic nitrogen into protein. The product is termed single-cell protein and could become a significant contribution to food supplies in the future. Other unconventional sources of protein are the algae, fish protein concentrate, leaf protein, oilseed protein residues and the recovery of protein which is at present wasted. Supplies from these sources are estimated to be sufficient to feed the present world population.

Thus from a combination of agriculture and technology, world supplies of food could be increased several-fold without any appreciable increase in the area of land cultivated and without the need to use excessive quantities of energy.

Unfortunately the urgent problem of inadequate food supplies arises in the developing countries where for a variety of reasons advanced technology is not an immediate solution to their problems. There is therefore a need for the more extensive use of low capital cost, labour-intensive methods to improve the production and utilization of food in these countries.

Introduction

Food, water and in cooler climates adequate clothing are the only essential requirements for the survival of the human race. The current interest in the survival of mankind is therefore primarily concerned with the problem of supporting a large population, whose impact on the world's resources is inflated by the demands of the more advanced technological societies of Europe and North America. Table 1 illustrates the increase in population and

TABLE 1

World population and energy consumption

Historical phase	Population (millions)[a]	Energy used *per capita*[b] kcal/day
Primitive	1	2,000
Hunting	3	4,000
Agricultural	5	12,000
Industrial	1,200	70,000
Technological	3,500[c]	230,000[d]

[a]Deevey (1960).
[b]Cook (1971).
[c]World Population (1970).
[d]USA (1970).

energy consumption throughout the period of Man's history. The energy consumption of primitive Man represents Man's net food nergy need and is only approximately 1% of the total energy consumption of technological Man. The bulk of the 875 million tons of food required in 1970 to supply the population of 3,500 million people was produced by agricultural methods. Smaller quantities of other foods such as fish were harvested from the wild. Although sunlight, via the process of photosynthesis, was the primary source of energy for the production of this huge quantity of food, additional inputs of support energy in the form of weedkillers, insecticides, fertilizers and mechanical aids were extensively used to maintain sufficient output. In the intensive agricultural system of the United States it is estimated that this input of support energy is at least equal to the energy value of the food crop produced (Odum, 1971). The distribution of the gross food energy of harvested crops in the USA is illustrated in Table 2. The proportion, approximately two-thirds, used for animal feed is significant and illustrates

TABLE 2

Distribution of gross per capita *food production of 10,000 kcal/day (USA) (Cook, 1971)*

	kcal
Handling and processing waste	1,500
Animal food—converted to 900 kcal human food	6,300
Human food	
from plant sources	2,200
from animal sources	900
Total consumed as food	3,100

why food from animal sources is more expensive. The 3,100 kcal consumed directly by human beings as food is less than one third of the gross food energy production of 10,000 kcal *per capita*/day. The energy input to an intensive agricultural system can therefore be assessed at three times the energy value of the food produced, i.e. the support energy input = 3 *Ef* where *Ef* signifies the energy value of the food produced. This method of assessing energy inputs is used in the remainder of this paper to compare the energy requirements of potential methods of food production. The 10,000 kcal of support energy *per capita*/day required to provide the diet of the average American is approximately 5% of total energy consumption.

Fertile land and a suitable climate are the other essential requirements for the production of food by agricultural methods. In spite of the energy inputs referred to above it is estimated that half the world's resource of arable land was in use in 1970. The extent of the problem of producing the additional food required to keep pace with the increasing population can be illustrated by reference to the United Kingdom, which, with an intensive agricultural system, produces sufficient food for approximately half the population. Since world population increased by more than 70 million in 1970 the annual increase in world food production needed was three times greater than that of the total production of UK agriculture.

In areas where energy inputs in the form of fertilizers are minimal food output can probably be increased by a significant amount without increasing the area of land cultivated. In other areas where more intensive agriculture is already established it is doubtful whether extensive increases in output can be achieved without endangering the stability of the soil and introducing serious pollution problems. It is probable therefore that considerable additional areas of arable land will need to be brought under cultivation to keep pace with the increasing world demand for food. The world's resource of unused arable land is located in more remote areas where it is more difficult to undertake rapid development. Roads, power supplies, housing and other facilities have to be provided in addition to the land clearance which must take place before cultivation can begin. It is probably the inability to keep pace with the development of new areas of arable land which has caused the recent lag in world food production and has led to the increase in world food prices.

By comparison with modern industrial processes agriculture appears to be a haphazard, inefficient system of production. Output is dependent on local weather conditions and only a partial system of control is possible over the pests and diseases which may ruin both crop and livestock yields. On ecological grounds there are doubts whether intensive agricultural systems can be sustained indefinitely and a breakdown in these systems could cause drastic reductions in yields. Alternative systems of food production, which would be independent of climate or the use of arable land, are therefore worth serious consideration. The main function of these systems would be to supplement agricultural production. They could help to overcome food shortages which may occur because new areas of arable land cannot be developed rapidly enough to keep pace with the demand for food by the increasing population. Their use could also help to stabilize supplies by providing a buffer stock of food which would be independent of weather conditions or the ravages of pests and diseases.

No potential method of food production will be of practical significance unless the resources are available to maintain the output of significant quantities for a considerable period of time. The possible systems of food production and the resources required to maintain them will be discussed in this paper. No new sources of food will be acceptable unless they are safe to eat, are equivalent nutritionally to established food sources, and are palatable products which make a positive appeal to the consumer.

Nutritional, Toxicological and Palatability Aspects of New Food Sources

Foods in the diet of modern Man have been selected by a process of trial and error which has continued throughout the history of mankind. New foods have evolved in recent times which have become the staple diet of a majority of the world population. Wheat, rice and maize for example, as they are known today, were not part of the diet of early Man. Although methods have been developed for testing for any potentially harmful effects of new components in the diet, these methods are not at the stage where a rapid, reliable assessment can be made of the safety of a new food product. A period of thorough testing followed by a gradual introduction of new foods in the diet is therefore advisable. Methods are available for assessing the main nutritional function of dietary components. Since, for many years to come, new food sources will only be used to supplement agricultural supplies of food, the lack of any minor nutritional components will not be significant. However, in the context of providing sufficient food for the world population of the future new food sources may become essential.

The aspects relating to safety and nutritional value are not absolute barriers to the possibilities of producing and using new sources of food. Any limitation by these aspects is due to a lack of sufficient knowledge at the present time and is not due to a deficiency of any finite resource. From both the nutritional and the safety point of view the synthesis of individual components of the diet presents the least problems. Synthetic Vitamin C, for example, is identical with the compound which occurs in plant sources and similar considerations apply to the synthesis of other dietary components referred to below. Other methods of food production which yield complex mixtures involve more intensive studies of their safety aspects and nutritional value.

Man's likes and dislikes as they relate to food are mainly conditioned during the early stages of life and new foods are more likely to be accepted if they conform to the characteristics of traditional items in the diet. Flavour and texture are the two most important properties and the ability to reproduce these characteristics has improved considerably within the last few years.

Characteristic flavours usually consist of a complex mixture of trace amounts of a large number of different compounds, the detection of which has recently improved due to the development of new analytical techniques. The reproduction of natural flavours in their entirety has therefore become a possibility. The amount of material involved in imparting flavour is insignificant in comparison to the bulk of food and the synthesis of flavour compounds would not be limited by lack of any resource.

Texture is another important property which contributes to the palatability of foods. Foods consisting primarily of fats, carbohydrates or proteins can all be given characteristic textures. Margarine is an example of the process of texturing fats, textured vegetable protein has a fibrous structure similar to that of meat products and the recently marketed reformed fruits are examples of the texturing of carbohydrate foods.

Methods and Resources Available for Food Production

Food consists of the essential nutritional components, proteins, energy sources (fats and carbohydrates) and the vitamins. Vitamins are required in very small quantities relative to the main bulk of food. They can all be manufactured by industrial processes and, in relation to the total quantities required, significant amounts of several of the vitamins are currently being produced. In 1970, for example, sufficient synthetic Vitamin D was synthesized in the USA to provide for the requirement of one-third of the world population. Most of this vitamin production was used in animal feed (McPherson, 1972). Neither raw materials, manufacturing capacity nor energy resources are liable to be limiting factors in the production of sufficient vitamins to supplement foods from either agricultural or alternative systems of production.

When the problem of food production is considered on the massive scale required to provide for the human population, there are four possible types of system which can be applied to the only sources of raw materials that are available on Earth. These systems are:

1. total synthesis from water, carbon dioxide and nitrogen from the air;
2. conversion to food of the Earth's store of organic raw materials i.e. the fossil fuels;
3. conversion of organic materials which are continuously being re-

plenished by the growth of plants. In practice this implies the conversion of inedible or waste carbohydrates to human food;

4. the separation of nutrients from indigestible plant material.

The first two methods are independent of the use of arable land. Methods 3 and 4 either depend upon agricultural output or compete with agriculture for land.

The term synthesis in its literal sense implies a build up of complex substances from simple elements or compounds. Since the term is often applied to manufactured, as opposed to natural, products the term "total synthesis" is used in this paper to indicate that the raw materials inputs are simple elements or compounds. This distinction does have practical significance since the main raw materials for total synthesis, carbon dioxide, water and nitrogen are available in abundance. All of the essential nutrients required in the diet have been synthesized and human beings have survived without ill effects for 4 to 5 months on an entirely synthetic diet (Pyke, 1970). Most of the chemical reactions involved in total synthesis are established industrial processes, the efficiency of which has increased in recent times due to the development of more effective catalysts. From a manufacturing point of view the production of food by total synthesis is a feasible possibility. However, since no energy for synthesis is derived from sunlight, the energy stored in the synthesized food compounds has to be provided from an external source. The estimation of this energy input is discussed on pp.188–190.

As an alternative to total synthesis more complex raw materials can, by chemical reactions, be converted to nutrients. The only raw materials available, other than those produced by current photosynthetic activity, are the fossil fuel sources, coal, natural gas and petroleum. These raw materials contain more stored chemical energy than the nutrients which are prepared from them and there is therefore no requirement for an external source of energy for the actual formation of the nutrient compounds. Energy inputs are however required to activate chemical compounds involved in the reactions and to provide the environment for the reactions to take place. Methods of chemical conversion and the energy inputs involved are described on pp. 191–192.

Biological methods for the production of food can be adapted as manufacturing processes. Since the enzymes of biological systems are more effective as catalysts and since the energy for synthesis can be derived from sunlight, biological methods of food production should be more efficient than chemical methods. Their efficiency is assessed on p.190. A disadvantage of biological methods is that there is less control over the type and the relative proportions of the nutrients which are produced. Part of the product, for example, may have no nutritional value and can interfere with the digestion of the remainder of the food product. A possible method of overcoming this problem is to separate the enzyme systems responsible for nutrient synthesis. This method has been found difficult to establish in practice, although recent developments in the application of immobilized enzymes have increased the possibility of establishing a practical process by the use of biochemical reactors. Biological conversion of the fossil fuels to nutrients is feasible and, because of the greater effectiveness of the enzymes as catalysts, should be more efficient than the chemical conversion mentioned above. This process is assessed on p.192. The products of biological synthesis by algae and of conversion by other micro-organisms have been termed single-cell protein (SCP).

All other methods of food production depend upon the raw materials produced by the growth of plants. The total output of biological energy from agricultural systems can be increased several-fold by concentrating on the growth of crops which give high yields. The disadvantage of such systems is that they yield mainly carbohydrate and insufficient quantities of protein are produced to provide a balanced diet. By the microbiological conversion of part of the biological energy output to protein the total yield of nutritious food from agricultural systems can be increased several-fold. Examples and the energy inputs involved in conversion are discussed on p.195. As an alternative to conversion of the surplus carbohydrate any of the other methods of food production described in this paper could be adjusted to yield a high proportion of protein. Supplies of fats, if these should be deficient, can also be increased by synthetic processes or by the biological conversion of surplus carbohydrate. Only a small proportion of the plant material produced from conventional agricultural systems is used as human food. The bulk of the inedible by-products consist of carbohydrates some of which could be converted, by chemical or biochemical methods, to glucose as a source of dietary energy. An alternative use of these by-products is to convert them by biological methods to products containing a high proportion of protein or fat.

The output of protein from agricultural systems can be increased by the growth and frequent harvesting of leafy crops from which a protein concentrate is isolated. This possibility is briefly discussed on p.196, but is referred to in more detail in the paper presented by Pirie (pp.167–178). Protein can also be extracted from the by-products of conventional crops.

The possible methods of food production are outlined in more detail in the sections which follow and approximate estimates are made of the energy inputs required for each method. Land use and raw material requirements are also taken into consideration. Fuller details of the estimates of energy inputs are published elsewhere (Worgan, 1973a). For the purposes of comparison the energy inputs are expressed in terms of the *Ef* values i.e. the number of times the energy inputs are greater than the energy value of the food produced. Where the product consists entirely of nutrients it is assumed that its composition would be adjusted to contain 10% fat, 10% protein and 80% carbohydrate. The energy value of this product would be 4,620 kcal/kg. Microbiological products (SCP) are assumed to contain 50% protein, 40% carbohydrate, 5% fat and 5% inorganic compounds. The energy value of these products is calculated to be 4,150 kcal/kg. The energy inputs required for the various methods of food production described are summarized in Table 3.

TABLE 3

Methods and energy inputs for food protection

Method	Page reference	Energy input	Comments
Methods that do not require arable land			
Total synthesis			
Chemical	188	33 *Ef*	Fossil fuels not required
Chemical and biological (methanol and yeast)	193	14 *Ef*	Fossil fuels not required
Biological (algae)	190	2·8*Ef*	Fossil fuels not required
Biochemical	191	<2·8*Ef*	Fossil fuels not required
Conversion of the fossil fuels			
Chemical	191	6·5*Ef*	Fossil fuels essential
Biological (yeast)	192	3·1*Ef*	Fossil fuels essential
Methods that depend upon or compete with agriculture for land			
Conversion of carbohydrates			
Chemical	194	0·5*Ef*	Fibrous to edible carbohydrates
Biological (fungi)	195	1·7*Ef*	From waste starch and sugars
Chemical and biological (fungi and yeast)	196	2·7*Ef*	From fibrous by-products
Leaf protein extraction	196	1 *Ef*	
Intensive agriculture		3 *Ef*	

Ef Energy value of food produced.

Methods of Food Production which do not Involve the Use of Arable Land

Total Synthesis by Chemical Methods

The stages in the total synthesis of food by chemical methods are illustrated in Fig. 1. The sequence of reactions has been compiled from data presented

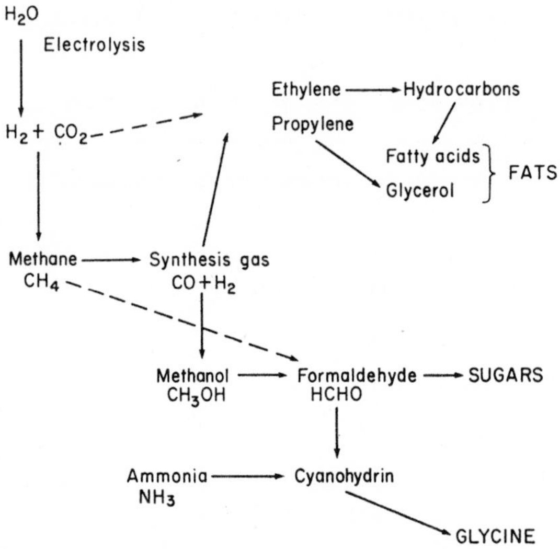

Fig. 1. Chemical synthesis of food.

by Shapira (1968, 1970 and 1971). Hydrogen is produced from water by electrolysis and in the presence of a catalyst combines with carbon dioxide to form methane. Water reacted with methane forms the mixture of carbon monoxide and hydrogen known as "synthesis gas" from which the various intermediate compounds such as methanol, ethylene and propylene, which are required for the synthesis of fats, carbohydrates and amino acids, can be prepared. Nitrogen is introduced into the amino acids by the use of synthetic ammonia, the manufacture of which is already undertaken on a large scale for the preparation of nitrogen fertilizers. The main raw material inputs to the system are water, carbon dioxide and nitrogen. Sulphur is required in comparatively small quantities for the synthesis of the amino acids cystine and methionine. Although the essential amino acids require more energy for their synthesis than glycine, they only need to be provided as 4% of total food intake.

When foods are completely metabolized to carbon dioxide and water the energy released can be determined by burning the food in oxygen and measuring the heat given out. The energy released is known as the heat of combustion and for the fats for example is 9,300 kcal/kg. In the synthesis of foods by plants this energy is derived from sunlight via the process of photosynthesis. When foods are prepared by chemical synthesis from carbon dioxide and water the same amount of energy must be provided from an alternative external source. Since no system of energy conversion is 100% efficient additional quantities of energy to those eventually stored in the synthesized food compounds have to be introduced into the system. An indication of these additional energy inputs can be assessed from the following considerations. The maximum theoretical yield from a chemical reaction can be calculated from the chemical equation. The actual yield of the product from known quantities of the raw material input can be measured. The proportion of the actual yield to that of the theoretical maximum is used to express the efficiency of the process and is also a measure of the efficiency of energy conversion. Most of the reactions illustrated in Fig. 1 can be carried out on an industrial scale with efficiencies of 30–90%. The conversion of methanol to formaldehyde for example can be carried out in the laboratory with an efficiency of 96% and on a large scale with an efficiency of 85%.

In the synthetic sequence illustrated in Fig. 1 methane is an intermediate compound. Its energy value is approximately three times that of the food synthesized. The theoretical quantity of reaction energy as methane required for food synthesis is therefore 3 *Ef*. If each of the four stages involved in the conversion of methane to food are assumed to be 80% efficient the overall efficiency will be 40%. The energy value of the methane required will therefore be $3 \times 100/40 = 7{\cdot}5$ *Ef*. To form this methane one chemical reaction and the electrolysis of water are involved. Assuming an efficiency of 80% for the chemical reaction and 30% for the conversion of energy to electrical energy the overall efficiency of these two stages will be 24%. The total reaction energy required will therefore be approximately $7{\cdot}5 \times 4 = 30$ *Ef*. Additional energy will also be needed to activate the compounds taking part in the reactions and to provide the ancillary energy for operating the chemical processes. The activation energy lost from the system is estimated at 10% of the reaction energy and the ancillary energy input required at 20%. For the five chemical reactions following electrolysis the activation energy will be 10% of $(7{\cdot}5/80) \times 100 =$ approximately 1 *Ef* and the ancillary energy input will be approximately 2 *Ef*. The total energy required for the synthesis of food is therefore estimated at 33 *Ef*. To provide the diet in the USA this energy input would be more than 100,000 kcal *per capita*/day or nearly 50% of the total energy requirement of an advanced technological society.

The Production of Food by Biological Synthesis

In plants the energy required for the synthesis of food compounds is obtained from sunlight via the process of photosynthesis. The only input needed is therefore the ancillary energy required to maintain the environment for plant growth. The single-celled algae are the simplest form of plant life and the equipment required for an algal production system is less complex than that required for a system of crop production. A further advantage of algal culture over a system of culturing plants in a controlled environment is the higher proportion of the algal biomass which can be used as food. Algal production systems will therefore probably be more efficient than the culture of crop plants. For the culture of algae, inputs of ancillary energy are needed to control the temperature, to agitate the culture and to provide additional carbon dioxide to that which is available from a static atmosphere. Because of the small size of the cells simple filtration methods are not suitable for harvesting and energy has to be expended on harvesting the cells by centrifugation. From data presented by Thacker and Babcock (1957) the ancillary energy inputs for algal culture can be assessed at 9,900 kcal/kg of dry algal cells produced. For a cell concentration of 2g/litre a further 1,880 kcal/kg will be needed for harvesting. The total energy input can therefore be assessed at 2·8 *Ef*. This value could probably be reduced by improvements in the method of culture.

The cells of the blue/green algal species *Spirulina maxima* can be separated from the culture by simple filtration. This is partly because of the larger size of the cells and partly because the cells tend to aglomerate because of their shape. Spirulina grows at a high pH value (9·5–10·0) and this increases the efficiency of the absorption of carbon dioxide and reduces problems of contamination of the culture. This algal species was discovered growing in the waters of Lake Chad and for centuries has been one of the main foods of the local people. Pilot plants for its production are established in Mexico and the South of France. Yields of 40–45 ton/hectare/year containing 62% protein are reported (Clement *et al.*, 1967).

Because of the inefficiency of the conversion of energy to electrical energy and of electrical energy to light, systems of algal culture using artificial light have high energy inputs estimated at 138 *Ef* (Worgan, 1973a).

The Production of Food by Biochemical Synthesis

In laboratory studies the enzymes involved in photosynthesis have been isolated and identified. In practice it has proved difficult to establish a production system which would reproduce the overall process for the synthesis of nutrients by photosynthesis. Some of the intermediate compounds are unstable and tend to decompose before the next step in the synthetic sequence can occur. Enzyme reagents are soluble in the reaction mixtures and are not therefore recovered after they have once been used for a reaction. In a production system this means that they would have to be continually replenished. Both these disadvantages may be overcome by the application of the recently developed immobilized enzymes. Both synthetic and natural polymers can be used as supports on which to attach enzyme molecules. The insoluble stable reagents formed can be used continuously in the same way as chemical catalysts. Sequences of enzymes can also be attached to the same support and their use could overcome the problem of the decomposition of unstable intermediate compounds. Biochemical reactors, in which immobilized enzyme systems can be used in industrial processes, are in the early stages of development and are potentially the most efficient method of food production. By the use of sunlight as the primary energy input a system could be devised to yield all the essential nutrients in the proportions specified to provide a nutritionally balanced diet. The amino acid composition of the output could also be controlled to specification. Since no energy is diverted to the synthesis of substances which do not have any nutritional value this method will be more efficient than biological synthesis and will require a smaller area for the same food output.

Chemical Methods of Converting Non-renewable Resources to Food

The fossil fuels are the only feasible source of raw materials. Coal, natural gas and petroleum can all be used to produce the same intermediate compounds which are formed during the series of chemical reactions involved in total synthesis (see Fig. 1). Synthesis gas for example can be prepared from natural gas, coke or petroleum, and ethylene and propylene can be manufactured directly from petroleum by the "cracking" process. The energy value of the raw materials is greater than that of the nutrients manufactured and no external energy input is necessary for the formation of chemical compounds. However the raw materials used do involve inputs of energy. The energy value of petroleum for example is approximately twice that of the energy value of food. The theoretical transformation of petroleum to food in a single stage would therefore require a quantity of petroleum which had twice the energy value of the food produced i.e. = 2 *Ef*. Assuming that there are four stages in the conversion and that each stage has an efficiency of 80% then the overall efficiency of the process will be 40%. The input of raw material energy as petroleum will therefore be 2 × 100/40 = 5 *Ef*. If the activation energy input is assessed at 10% (0·5 *Ef*) of this and the ancillary energy input at 20% (1·0 *Ef*) then the total energy input for the chemical conversion of petroleum to food will be 6·5 *Ef*.

Biological Methods of Converting Non-renewable Resources to Food

The hydrocarbons of petroleum can be used as sources of energy and of carbon compounds for the synthesis of cell biomass by bacteria, yeast and fungi. Nitrogen for protein synthesis can be provided in the form of fertilizer compounds such as ammonium salts or urea. Much smaller quantities of other inorganic compounds containing potassium, sulphur, magnesium and phosphorus are also required. Processes using yeasts have been developed most extensively and manufacturing plants are being constructed. British Petroleum for example are building a plant in Italy to produce 100,000 tons of yeast protein per year. The energy input to the process can be assessed from the following considerations. The yield of yeast by weight is the same as that of the hydrocarbon input. Since the energy value of the hydrocarbon is approximately twice that of the yeast the raw material energy input will be 2 *Ef*. From data published of the relative costs of the various inputs to the process, it can be estimated that the ancillary energy required to provide the environment for growth is approximately half that of the petroleum feedstock and is therefore = 1 *Ef*. Allowing 0·1 *Ef* of energy to harvest the cells then the total input of energy for producing yeast from hydrocarbons is 3·1 *Ef*. Methane, the main constituent of natural gas, is only utilized by bacteria and although processes using methane have some advantages they have not been developed to the same extent as the the growth of yeast in liquid hydrocarbons. The energy input to a methane system will probably be similar to that of the yeast system referred to above.

Coal cannot be used directly by any of the micro-organisms, and biological processes in which coal would be used as raw material would involve an initial stage of converting the coal to liquid hydrocarbons. The overall process of converting coal to food will therefore be less efficient than the conversion of petroleum.

The Production of Food by Combined Methods of Synthesis

The energy input required for a system of total food synthesis can be reduced, compared with chemical alone, by combining chemical and biological methods. Methane or preferably methanol, which is miscible with water, can be synthesized by the chemical reactions illustrated in Fig. 1. The methanol produced can then be used as a substrate for conversion by bacteria or yeast. A bacterial process for the conversion of methanol is being investigated by ICI Limited. A yield of yeast from methanol of 57·5% has been obtained in laboratory culture (Asthana *et al.*, 1971) and on a large scale this would probably be a practical yield of 50%. The energy as methanol required for yeast conversion will therefore be 2 *Ef*. To produce this methanol the electrolysis of water and three chemical reactions are involved. Assuming efficiences of 80% in the chemical reactions and 30% in the conversion of energy to electrical energy, the reaction energy input for the synthesis of methanol and its conversion to yeast will be $2 \times (100/51) \times 3 =$ 12 *Ef*. Further energy inputs for chemical activation (0·3 *Ef*), chemical ancillary (0·6 *Ef*) and ancillary energy for microbiological conversion (1 *Ef*) will be needed. The total energy input to the system will therefore be approximately 14 *Ef* which is less than half the energy input to an entirely chemical synthetic system.

Methods of Food Production which Depend upon Agricultural Outputs or Compete with Agriculture for Land

Only a small fraction of the total organic matter synthesized on Earth by plants is used for human food. Apart from forestry by-products and the possibility of harvesting aquatic plants, the production of regular supplies of other plant raw materials for conversion to food would involve some form of cultivation, and this in turn implies an agricultural production system. That the output of biological energy from agriculture could be increased by the growth of plants which give high yields has been mentioned on pp.184–188. Cassava, for example, yields more than four times as much edible dry matter than maize, from the same area of land. The supplementation of the high yields of carbohydrate with protein from other sources was also discussed on pp.184–188.

One of the most inefficient aspects of agricultural production is the small proportion of the total output which is used. It is probable that less than one quarter of crop plant material is consumed as human food. Additional outputs from conventional agricultural systems could be obtained by the conversion of inedible by-products to food. Most of the crop residues occur on or near the site where they are harvested, while the remaining by-products are produced during subsequent food processing operations. Estimated quantities of some agricultural forestry and food industry by-products are given in Table 4. The carbohydrates in these by-products and in other

TABLE 4

Annual world production of agricultural and forestry by-products and their potential conversion to protein (from Worgan, 1973b)

Source	Quantity of carbohydrate ($\times$ 10^3 ton)	Estimated conversion to yeast or fungal protein $\times$ 10^3 ton
Wheat straw	286,580	57,000
Wheat bran	57,320	11,460
Maize stover	120,040	24,000
Maize cobs	30,070	6,000
Sugar cane bagasse	83,000	16,600
Molasses	9,300	2,300
Sulphite liquor (from wood pulp, USA)	2,040	510

unused plant material are the largest replenishable resource on Earth. A large proportion of the by-products containing them are either dumped or burnt. The examples given are sufficient to indicate that significant quantities are available for conversion to food products. The bulk of these materials consist of cellulose, hemicelluloses and lignin. Lignin is not easily converted to a food product and would probably be most effectively used by returning it to the land to maintain the soil structure. Quantities of starch and sugars occur in liquid wastes from industrial processes. Most of the sugars are pentoses and are not suitable as sources of energy in the human diet.

Chemical and Biochemical Methods of Converting Renewable Resources to Food

Cellulose is the most abundant chemical compound on Earth and the annual quantity synthesized is estimated to be 10^{11} tons. Like starch it is a polymer of glucose although, because human beings do not have suitable enzyme systems, it cannot be digested. It is the main component of fibrous residues, such as cereal straws, which occur as by-products from agriculture. Chemically it can be converted to glucose by acid hydrolysis. This process is carried out on an industrial scale although its main application is to prepare suitable culture media for the growth of micro-organisms. From data presented by Meller (1969) the energy input required for the hydrolysis of cellulose has been estimated at approximately one half that of the energy value of the glucose produced i.e. the input energy = 0·5 *Ef* (Worgan, 1973a). In addition to cellulose nearly all agricultural and forestry by-products contain hemicelluloses. When the hemicellulose polymers are hydrolysed they yield mainly pentose sugars which are not suitable as sources of dietary energy.

The biochemical hydrolysis of cellulose by enzyme preparations has proved difficult to establish as an industrial process. Although active enzymes can be isolated, neither the rate nor the extent of cellulose hydrolysis achieved by their use are sufficient for practical purposes. After a preliminary treatment by mechanical milling, Katz and Reese (1968) obtained rapid and extensive cellulose hydrolysis with an enzyme preparation from the fungal species *Trichoderma viride.* A high energy input is however required for the preliminary milling and this process would not be as efficient as acid hydrolysis.

Biological Methods of Converting Renewable Resources to Food

Waste products containing sugars are suitable as substrates for most species of micro-organisms. Yeasts and fungi may be used for the production of biomass containing a high proportion of fat or protein. Bacteria can also be considered for protein production. Wastes containing starch can be converted by most fungi but not by food yeast (*Candida utilis*). Although several species of fungi will utilize fibrous wastes containing cellulose and hemicelluloses, the process is not rapid enough for it to be considered as a production method. From carbohydrate substrates the practical yield from industrial scale processes of microbial biomass is approximately 50% (Worgan, 1973c). From data presented by Meller (1969) the ancillary energy input for the production of yeast, using glucose as the substrate, has been estimated at 1·7 *Ef* (Worgan, 1973a). If the carbohydrate is not a waste product then the raw material energy input, assessed at 2 *Ef*, must also be taken into account and the total energy input will be 3·7 *Ef*.

Food yeast is the main example of this method of food production which is beginning to make some contribution to food supplies. Waste sulphite liquor (from paper pulp manufacture) is used as the substrate in Russia, Canada and the USA; molasses are used in Taiwan, South Africa, Cuba and the Philippines.

The Extraction of Nutrients from Inedible Plant Material

Carbohydrates, fats, proteins and vitamins occur in a number of plant products which are not suitable as human food because the nutrients are embedded in a protective matrix of indigestible fibre. The separation of these nutrients can provide a substantial alternative source of food. The extraction of vegetable oils from oilseeds and sugar from cane, are examples of methods which are already well established. The oilseeds also contain appreciable quantities of nutritionally valuable protein most of which is wasted by the current methods in use for oil extraction. Alternative processes are being developed which, in addition to the vegetable oil, will yield palatable protein foods. Protein concentrates containing 60% protein in addition to fat and digestible carbohydrate can be extracted from leafy crops. Higher yields than those from conventional crops are obtained if a system of frequent harvesting of the leaves is adopted. This method does compete with agriculture for land. Leaf protein can also be extracted from agricultural by-products and is then supplementary to agricultural production. Both leaf protein and oilseed protein residues are discussed in more detail in the paper by Pirie.

From data presented by Hollo and Koch (1971) the energy expended on extracting protein from leafy plant tissue can be estimated at approximately 1 *Ef*. The separation of oilseed proteins may not involve significantly more energy input than the processes currently in use for oil extraction.

Combined Methods of Converting Renewable Resources to Food

Cellulose and hemicelluloses in fibrous products, when chemically hydrolysed to sugars, are readily converted by micro-organisms to cell biomass. Fungi and food yeast grow rapidly and extensively in culture media prepared from these hydrolysates. Cereal straws and wood waste hydrolysates were used for yeast production in Germany in World War II and are currently produced for the same purpose in Russia. An output of one million tons of yeast per year is eventually envisaged (Bunker, 1968). The energy required as sugars by the micro-organisms will be 2 *Ef* and the ancillary energy for conversion

1·7 *Ef* (pp.195–196). To produce the sugar by hydrolysis will require $2 \times 0{\cdot}5 = 1$ *Ef* of energy (pp.194–195). Since the raw material energy is a waste product originally synthesized by the energy from sunlight, only the hydrolysis and ancillary energy need to be considered as external energy inputs. The total input energy is therefore 2·7 *Ef*.

TABLE 5

Comparison of yields from a maize crop, a cassava/fungal protein system and a cassava/leaf protein system (Worgan, 1973b)

	Yield (kg/hectare)			
	Carbohydrate	Protein	Total food output	Approximate protein/carbohydrate ratio
MAIZE	2000	300	2300	1:7
CASSAVA	8650			
Less 3150 kg carbohydrate	5500		6287	1:7
Conversion of 3150 kg carbohydrate to protein		787		
	From 0·8 hectare	From 0·2 hectare		
CASSAVA	6920		7920	1:7
Leaf protein (separate crop)		1000		

In Table 5 the yield from a conventional crop (maize) is compared with the yield obtained by growing cassava and converting part of the crop energy to protein. The protein: carbohydrate ratio (1:7) is approximately the same for each cropping system although the total yield from the cassava/mycelial protein system is nearly three times that of the maize. If required the microbiological conversion of some of the carbohydrate could be diverted to fat production. A leaf protein cropping system does require agricultural land. However as illustrated in Table 5, if the protein is combined with the carbohydrate yield from a crop such as cassava, the total output of food with a protein: carbohydrate ratio of 1:7 is more than three times that of maize, grown on the same area of land.

Table 6 illustrates the possibilities if the by-products from conventional agricultural crops are fully utilized, by extracting protein from the leaves and converting the residual leaf juices and fibre to protein by microbiological conversion. For both the cereal crop (maize) and the legume (peas) the yield of protein from the same area of land is six times greater from the combined system than from the conventional crop. Assessments made indicate that the

TABLE 6

Comparison of protein yields from conventional crops and food production systems (Worgan, 1973 b,d)

	Yield of protein kg/hectare					
			Fungal protein from			
	Seed	Leaf protein	Leaf juice	Leaf fibre	Maize cobs	Total
MAIZE						
Conventional crop	352	–	–	–	–	352
Combined system	352	300	110	1290	80	2132
PEAS						
Conventional crop	400	–	–	–	–	400
Combined system	400	625	125	1366	–	2546

nutritional values of the combined proteins are better than those of either of the conventional crops. The energy inputs are low for both leaf protein extraction (p.196) and microbiological conversion (pp.195–196). Willcox (1959) has estimated that the total carbohydrate from one hectare produced by the growth of sugar cane could be converted to 11,500 kg of yeast protein. This is almost thirty times the yield obtained from the legume crop given in Table 6.

Although it is not a primary method of production the conversion of plant products to more palatable foods could make a significant contribution towards reducing world food shortages. Individually plant sources of protein are not equivalent nutritionally to animal sources, but by preparing appropriate mixtures of plant proteins an essential amino acid balance can be achieved which is equivalent nutritionally to that of animal proteins. The conversion of these mixtures to palatable foods in the form of textured vegetable proteins or other food products could reduce the consumption of animal sources of protein in the more advanced technological societies. The energy inputs required for conversion are small. The effect of this change can be illustrated by reference to the quantities given in Table 2, from which it can be deduced that twice as much food is fed to livestock in the USA than is consumed by the human population. If the USA were to change to a vegetarian diet this could release sufficient food for approximately 400 million people. It is not suggested that this is a realistic possibility, nevertheless it does illustrate the effect that a reduction in the consumption of animal sources of protein in the developed countries would have on the world supplies of food available for direct human consumption.

Summary of Methods and their Significance in the Man/Food Equation

The chemical synthesis of food requires a negligible area of land, is independent of a source of fossil fuel and could be controlled to yield a diet based on nutritional specifications. The energy input required is however far greater than that of any other method of food production. The estimated energy input of 33 *Ef* would be nearly half the current rate of total energy consumption in the USA. The chemical conversion of the fossil fuels to food has the same advantages as chemical synthesis and requires only one fifth of the energy input. Most of this energy must be in the form of fossil fuel raw materials the future supplies of which are, at the present rate of consumption, liable to become critical in 20–30 years time. Biological conversion of the fossil fuels to food requires a low energy input and if the product is used directly as human food the energy consumption is comparable with that of an intensive agricultural system. The method yields a product with a high protein content and, although the amino acid composition of this protein cannot be adjusted to exact specifications, there are micro-organisms which produce protein which has a high nutritional value.

Biological synthesis has a low energy input that need not be in the form of a fossil fuel source. The estimated value of 2·8 *Ef* could probably be reduced by technical improvements in the methods of production. Because the system has to be exposed to sunlight the land area required is greater than that for chemical synthesis or conversion methods. The type of land surface is however immaterial and production units need not be sited on arable land. The composition of the product can be controlled to contain a high proportion of fat or protein and the same comments apply to the nutritional value of the protein, as those discussed above for the biological conversion of the fossil fuels. Biochemical processes for food synthesis are potentially the most efficient method of food production. Energy inputs would be lower than those for biological synthesis and the system could be controlled to produce the whole range of nutrients in appropriate proportions determined by the nutritional specifications of a perfect diet. Of all the methods of food production described this system is the least developed and its feasibility has still to be established on a laboratory scale.

All other possible methods of food production are either dependent on agricultural by-products for their raw materials or compete with agriculture for the use of arable land. The quantities of by-products which are available for conversion to food are sufficient to make a significant contribution to world food supplies since less than one quarter of agricultural output is consumed as human food. The extraction of unused protein from agricultural by-products and the conversion of cellulose to glucose require energy inputs which are comparable with those of agricultural production systems. The microbiological conversion of agricultural waste products to protein has a low energy input and sufficient quantities of wastes are available to more than double the present world production of protein foods. Any increase in agricultural output will be accompanied by a corresponding increase in agricultural by-products. Where the waste products are from industrial processes their disposal is often a pollution hazard; methods which dispose of these wastes and at the same time produce a useful food product have an obvious advantage.

In some areas of the world, where inefficient methods of agriculture are still common practice, food output could be increased without inputs of significant amounts of support energy. In the main food producing areas it is doubtful whether the present level of food output could be sustained if support energy inputs were reduced. All of the alternative methods of food production, which could be put into production in the immediate future, require energy inputs which are at least equivalent to or, in most cases, greater than intensive agricultural systems. Energy supplies are therefore a critical resource for the production of sufficient food to maintain a large world population. Although, in an advanced technological society, the proportion of energy devoted to food production is small and was estimated at the beginning of this chapter to be less than 5% of total energy consumption, the competing demands for energy may use up the world's resources of fossil fuels within a 20 to 30-year period. If the present world population 3,500 million, were to attempt to attain the current standard of living in the USA, for example, it can be estimated, from the figures at the base of the columns in Table 1, that 25,000 million tons of petroleum equivalents would be required each year. This quantity is ten times world production in 1970 and is more than one quarter of known petroleum reserves. Although alternative sources of energy to the fossil fuels are known to be available on Earth, the harnessing of these alternative sources by safe reliable methods, on the scale required, has still to be established. Thus in terms of energy resources and food production the Man/Food Equation can be expressed as follows:

$$S = \frac{X}{P \times Y} + A$$

where

S = the probability of the survival of a large world population

X = the ability to harness alternative sources of energy to the fossil fuels
P = world population
Y = the expenditure of energy on activities other than food production
A = the possibility of increasing agricultural production without increasing the input of support energy.

If world population approaches a total of 7000 million then the availability of arable land is liable to become a critical limit to sufficient food production. The systems of food production which have been described either do not depend upon the output from arable land or they bring about significant increases in the output of food from a given area. Several methods which do not compete with agriculture for the use of land also have low energy inputs.

In the methods of food production that have been discussed, nitrogen for protein or amino acid synthesis is introduced via the same compounds which are used as nitrogen fertilizers, namely ammonium or nitrate salts and urea. The fixation of one ton of atmospheric nitrogen in these compounds requires $1\frac{1}{2}$ tons of fuel oil (Fleck, 1961). When used as fertilizer allowance must be made for losses due to leaching from the soil and the diversion of nitrogen into weed plants. Of the nitrogen taken up by the plant only part is converted to edible protein. The overall efficiency of the conversion of nitrogen in fertilizer to nitrogen in the food from crop plants is estimated to be no greater than 15% (McPherson, 1972). For the production of food containing 20% protein by intensive agricultural methods the energy input due to fertilizer nitrogen is estimated to be 0·8 *Ef* (Worgan, 1973a). Lower efficiencies will apply if the nitrogen goes through a further conversion process via the animal food chain. In all of the alternative methods of food production considered, the efficiency of the conversion of inorganic nitrogen to protein or amino acids is of the order of 70–80%, or approximately five times greater than that in agricultural systems.

Priorities for Solving the Man/Food Equation

The immediate problem of lack of sufficient food occurs in the developing countries. It is in these areas that the most rapid increases in population are taking place and where food shortages are liable to become more critical in the future. The technological systems of food production that have been discussed above are not an immediate solution to their problems. Lack of capital, trained personnel and an infrastructure of service facilities, including those of transport and power supplies, preclude the introduction of these methods on the extensive scale that would be required. For most of the developing countries methods that involve larger imports of energy sources are liable to aggravate their economic problems. Because the efficiences of the agricultural systems in most of these countries are low there is scope for improvement in food output without the need for large inputs of support energy. However, these improvements in agricultural production may be wasted if the food which is produced is not fully utilized due to poor storage conditions, inefficient methods of processing or failure to make the maximum dietary use of food which is available.

The knowledge required to improve agricultural output and to maximize the utilization of food is available in the developed countries. The transfer of this knowledge and its adaptation to the local culture and environmental conditions in the developing countries would go a long way towards solving the more immediate and critical aspects of the Man/Food Equation. Unfortunately unspectacular solutions, whose primary aim is the modest one of raising the standard of people above subsistence level, do not appeal to governments or other agencies involved in the allocation of aid funds and prestige projects are preferred which create the illusion of progress.

The immediate efforts to solve the Man/Food Equation should therefore be directed towards the spread of knowledge and its adaptation to conditions in those areas of the world where food shortages are most critical. In the developed countries fossil fuel energy and arable land should be conserved, to ensure that sufficient of these resources will be available until alternative solutions to their use are well established practical possibilities. Research into methods of food production which could supplement agricultural output should be intensified and the safety of the products in the human diet thoroughly tested. In the not too distant future every feasible method of increasing food supplies may be needed if the world population continues to increase at the present rate.

References

Asthana, H., Humphrey, A. E. and Moritz, V. (1971). *Biotech. Bioeng.* **13,** 923.
Bunker, H. J. (1968). *In* "Single-Cell Protein". (R. I. Mateles and S. R. Tannenbaum, eds), pp. 229–242. MIT Press, Cambridge, Massachusetts.

Clement, G., Giddey, C. and Menzi, R. (1967). *J. Sci. Fd. Agric.* **18,** 497.

Cook, E. (1971). *Scient. Am.* **224,** (3), 135.

Deevey, E. S. (1960) *Scient. Am.* **203,** (3), 194.

Fleck, Lord (1961). *In* "Hunger Can it be Averted?" (E. J. Russell and N. C. Wright, eds), pp. 40–48. British Association for the Advancement of Science, London.

Hollo, J. and Koch, L. (1971). *In* "Leaf Protein", IBP Handbook No. 20 (N. W. Pirie, ed.), pp. 63–68. Blackwell Scientific Publications, Oxford.

Katz, M. and Reese, E. T. (1968). *Appl. Microbiol.* **16,** 419.

McPherson, A. T. (1972). *Indian J. Nutr. Diet.* **9,** 285.

Meller, F. H. (1969). *In* "Conversion of Organic Solid Wastes into Yeast", Public Health Service Publication, No. 1909 pp 61, 113. US Government Printing Office, Washington, D.C.

Odum, E. P. (1971). "Fundamentals of Ecology". pp. 54–55. W. B. Saunders, London.

Pyke, M. (1970). "Synthetic Food". p. 1. John Murray, London.

Shapira, J. (1968). *Cereal Sci. Today* **13,** 58.

Shapira, J. (1970). *J. Agric, Fd. Chem.* **18,** 992.

Shapira, J. (1971). *Environ. Biol. Med.* **1,** 243.

Thacker, D. R. and Babcock, N. Y. (1957). *J. Sol. Energy Sci. Eng.* **1,** 37.

Willcox, O. W. (1959). *J. Agric. Fd. Chem.* **7,** 813.

Worgan, J. T. (1973a). *In* "Human Food Chains and Nutrient Cycles". (J. G. W. Jones and A. N. Duckham, eds), North-Holland Publishing Company, Amsterdam.

Worgan, J. T. (1973b). *In* "Proteins in Human Nutrition". (J. W. G. Porter and B. A. Rolls, eds), pp. 47–74. Academic Press, London.

Worgan, J. T. (1973c). *In* "The Biological Efficiency of Protein Production". (J. G. W. Jones, ed.), pp. 339–361. Cambridge University Press, Cambridge, UK.

Worgan, J. T. (1973d). *In* "By-products of the Food Industry", Symposium Proceedings No. 16, pp. 11–26. The British Food Manufacturing Industries Research Association, Leatherhead, UK.

The Cost:
Health

Nutrient Requirements

ERICA F. WHEELER

Human Nutrition Department, London School of Hygiene and Tropical Medicine

Summary

Strenuous efforts have been made, especially under the auspices of the UN Agencies, to define the least amounts of energy and nutrients which are needed by normal people in order to grow, reproduce, work and maintain health. These "nutrient requirements" differ for individuals according to their age, size, sex, activity and physiological state, so that the estimates of requirements given in published tables necessarily represent the central values of sometimes ill-defined distributions.

The main function of requirements is to serve as standard values with which individuals' real intakes can be compared. Inevitable errors in the measurement of intakes, however, as well as the between-individual variations in requirements necessitate care when such comparisons are to be made. Methods for estimating requirements differ considerably from one nutrient to another, and thus comparisons of the extent to which the requirements for different nutrients are met in the same diet are not necessarily justified.

These errors and sources of variation, however, can be allowed for in assessing dietary intakes, and it is generally possible to make some judgements about the adequacy of individuals' diets. Such information is needed when national health, agriculture and nutrition policies are under review. It is important to make the distinction between "requirement" (the least amount needed) and "recommended allowance" (the amount which a group of experts has fixed upon as a desirable intake).

In the same way, as an individual's intake can be measured and compared with requirement, the amount of food available in a country can be estimated, divided by the number of inhabitants, and compared with requirements. The errors involved in this "national balance sheet" approach are, however, enormous. The most useful application of requirements is to individuals' food intakes.

In a book dealing with food supplies, the question must be considered "Can we manage to produce enough food for ourselves?", a question which is often asked with regard both to the near and the more distant future. The implication is that if more than a certain minimum amount of food can be made available for a nation, a household or an individual, then their requirements will have been met, and malnutrition and food shortage prevented. Experience shows, however, that even though food may be available it is not always consumed, and that malnutrition may exist in a country which has ample food supplies. One of our main objectives, before the remedy of "increasing food production" is prescribed for the world's nutrition problems, should be to try and diagnose those problems correctly, in the sense that persons or groups of people who are short of food can be identified and an explanation given of why they are in this position.

Statements about food and nutrient supplies abound, and sometimes conflict. For instance:

> "The Advisory Committee has not tried to calculate the size of the protein gap. Various methods have been devised for attempting to do so. Although there may be wide differences in the resulting figures, they indicate that such a gap exists, and the experts are unanimous in emphasising that the gap is undeniable and increasing" (United Nations, 1968);

and

> "At least one in four of the Indian population does not get enough calories, and . . . possibly as much as half of the population do not have enough proteins of the requisite quality" (Quiogue, 1972).

On the other hand

> "Is there a protein gap? If one looks at the figures for world and *per capita* availability of protein the answer is *no*" (PAG, 1973).

These statements are nearly always based on some preconceptions about the quantity of nutrients which people need; that is, on their nutrient requirements. In this paper the ways in which these requirement figures are obtained will first be discussed and then the ways in which they can be used.

The United Nations agencies have produced a number of recommendations as to the amounts of energy (calories or joules) and nutrients needed by normal healthy people. These are defined in varying ways. In the case of energy, the requirement is "the amount adequate to meet the needs of the average healthy person" in a given age/sex/activity group (WHO, 1973), and is obtained by measuring the intakes of healthy subjects. The precision with which nitrogen requirements have been estimated reflects the overwhelming importance which has been attached to protein as a nutrient. Careful measurements have been made of nitrogen losses by all routes from the body; the sum of these plus an allowance of 10% for individual variation, constitutes the adult requirement. Additional allowances for pregnancy, growth and lactation are based on balance studies and analyses (WHO, 1973). Human requirements for other nutrients are much less accurately known, especially in the case of nutrients which are stored in the body in relatively large amounts. Vitamin requirements, for example, are sometimes based on observations of the amount needed to reverse the clinical signs of deficiency, plus variable and arbitrary amounts intended to allow for individual variation (e.g. ascorbic acid, vitamin B_{12}); sometimes on measurements of urinary losses of the vitamin and its metabolites as well (e.g. thiamine); and sometimes, in the absence of any other information, on the amounts needed to prevent deficiency in healthy children (e.g. vitamin D) (WHO, 1967, 1970). When statements about nutrient intakes are made, such as Guzman and Tantengco (1972) for example,

> "Intakes of all nutrients fall short of the recommended level in all age groups, particularly in vitamin A, calories, protein and iron"

it is worth recalling that the definitions of requirements for these different nutrients were reached by different routes and with very different levels of precision.

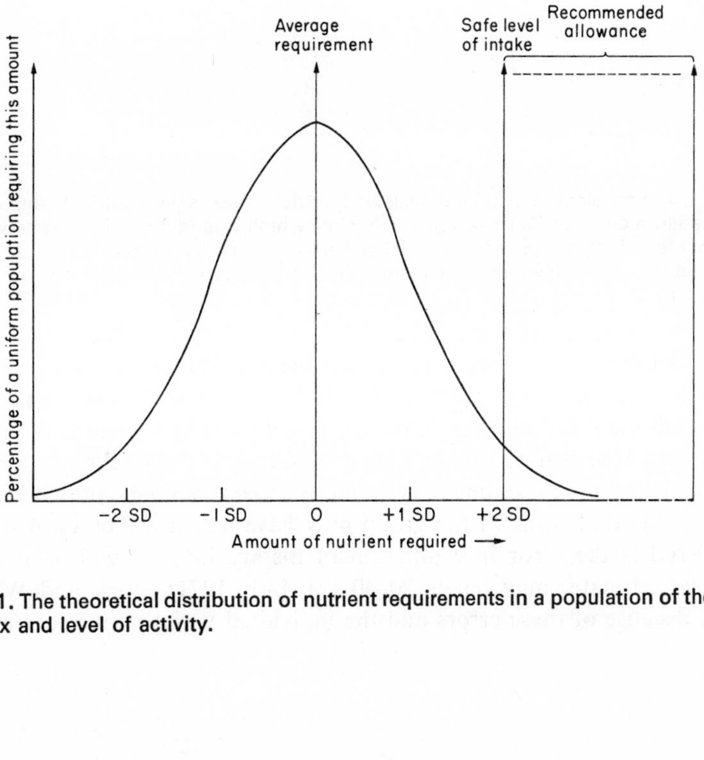

Fig. 1. The theoretical distribution of nutrient requirements in a population of the same age, sex and level of activity.

The situation may also be complicated by terminology. If the "requirement" for a nutrient is to be estimated, then it is assumed that this is the amount which would be required by the average individual in a group matched for age, sex and activity (Fig. 1). However, there will be a range of requirements for this group, because of individual variation, so the "safe level of intake" may be defined as the average requirement plus two standard deviations. In addition, for a number of nutrients, a quantity known as the "recommended allowance" has been defined. This may be the safe level plus a further increment to allow for stress, illness or climatic differences; or it may be an arbitrary "normal intake" figure based on dietary surveys, and believed by some to be an ideal or optimal intake, as opposed to a minimum requirement. Again, the question of maintaining body stores is involved.

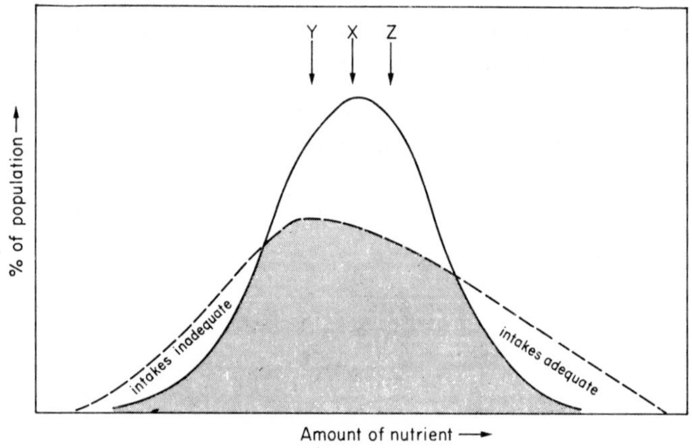

Fig. 2. The problem of matching measured nutrient intakes with nutrient requirements. The shaded area is an "area of uncertainty" in which it is impossible to state whether intakes are adequate or not. —— Distribution of requirements for a nutrient in a population. — — Hypothetical distribution of intakes of the same nutrient in that population.

The fact that a requirement represents the average need for a hypothetical population is important when diets are being assessed. The intake of an individual might fall at point X on Fig 2, but there is no means of knowing whether his true requirement is Y or Z. Similarly if the intake of a group is measured, and the mean intake is found to exceed average requirements, it is still possible that some of the group may have deficient intakes. Also to be considered is the error in estimation of dietary intakes, which, at a conservative estimate, may be ± 20–30% (Marr, 1971; Stock and Wheeler, 1972). Because of these errors and the individual variation in requirements, it may well be that a definite statement cannot be made to the effect that an individual's diet is adequate or inadequate, or that a certain percentage of a group is malnourished. The shaded area in Fig. 2 represents an "area of uncertainty" where it is not possible to be sure if diets are adequate or not. Thus while requirements may be used to indicate the likelihood that a diet is satisfactory, they cannot always provide complete and precise information. Statistical methods for matching distributions of intake with those of requirements are bedevilled by the non-normal nature of intake distributions, which are usually positively skewed (Fryer *et al.,* 1971). One of the weaknesses of the "food balance sheet" approach to assessing national nutrition problems (FAO, 1971) is that account cannot be, and is not, taken of these considerations.

Nutrient requirement estimates, then, can be used to evaluate the dietary intakes of groups and individuals if the error of estimation and the range of individual variation are taken into account. This approach to the diagnosis of nutrition problems is of value, as it not only helps to indicate who in the population may be at risk from malnutrition, but also indicates what factors in the diet may be limiting. However, although it helps to answer the question "Who is malnourished and why?" a weakness in this method of measuring diets and applying requirement figures is that it leads too often to the assumption that inadequate diets can be improved simply by increasing the quantity of certain foods that are available to people. Thus the observation that 40% of West Pakistan households consume diets deficient in protein and energy, was met by a call for increased food production: this was seen as the single answer to the problem (Hussain, 1973). What is missing in this diagnosis and suggested cure for a national nutrition problem, is consideration of the variety of reasons why inadequate diets are eaten. This may be due not only to insufficient food production, but to social and economic circumstances which have nothing to do with national food supplies. It is clear from many surveys that the families who suffer from malnutrition are generally deprived in other ways: they are poor, or they have experienced social deprivation. It is the children of the unemployed, the poorly-paid labourer, the unmarried and unsupported mother, or the farmer at the margin of subsistence, who become malnourished (Oomen *et al.,* 1964; Schneidemann *et al.,* 1971). Although dietary surveys are useful in identifying these groups of people and their dietary problems, yet there is a sense in which the survey is superfluous, for it is already known where malnutrition can be expected to occur. This is extremely relevant to the problems of food supply which are being considered in this volume. If surveys show that poor diets and food shortages are closely associated with poverty and social problems, then it is also necessary to consider whether existing food supplies are really insufficient or whether they are simply not well distributed among the population. Tanzania, for example, had ample food supplies in 1965 (as shown by national food supply figures), yet 5% of children under five years of age were malnourished in some areas of the country (Burgess and Burgess, 1965). This was not a problem of national food production, but of certain families being unable to grow or buy enough food for themselves. The supply of food may be sufficient, but the demand (i.e. the amount which people can and do buy) may be less. The question asked should not be "Can we manage to produce enough food?" but "Can everyone afford to take up their share of what is being produced?".

World food production per head has in fact been rising steadily since the 1950s, when the FAO first began to monitor it. Cereal production, in particular, has increased markedly as a result of new varieties, such that rice production in South-East Asia has increased by 22% over the five-year period 1965–1970, and the Philippines, centre of the new technology, has become self-sufficient in rice production in spite of rising population. It is significant that the increase in food production generally keeps in step with increases in *per capita* income: as the demand for food rises, so the agricultural industries of the world produce what is required (Willett, 1973). This is true on an individual level also. It is well known that as a family becomes more affluent they spend more money on food; conversely, a poor family will not benefit from increased supplies which they cannot afford. In India and Pakistan, the increases in cereal production (the Green Revolution) have greatly benefited the farmers who have sufficient acreage and capital to cultivate new varieties successfully. Those who have become poorer as a result are the small-scale farmers and agricultural labourers, who have suffered from increasing food prices and from the social and cultural upheavals consequent on changes in the pattern of agriculture. It seems unlikely that the diets of these people have improved, even though their country is producing more wheat than ever before (Frankel, 1973). In order to improve the nutritional state of these people, some way of increasing their income is needed, and the problem becomes one of economics, not of agriculture or nutrition alone.

In summary, some concept of nutrient requirements is needed in order to assess diets and identify sections of the population who may be malnourished or bordering on malnutrition. But this should be only one part of the approach to national problems of food supply and nutrition. Careful study of these problems will inevitably reveal the association between malnutrition, food shortage and poverty; consequently to be effective measures cannot just deal with food supply and food technology alone. Policies which will increase the incomes of poor people are difficult both to devise and to carry out (Joy, 1973) but the option is either to attempt them or to choose the easier, but really ineffective, approach of producing more food ostensibly for the benefit of those who cannot afford it.

References

Burgess, H. J. L. and Burgess, A. P. (1965). *E. Afr. med. J.* **42,** 3.
FAO (1971). "Food Balance Sheets, 1964–1966". FAO, Rome.
Frankel, F. R. (1973). *In* "Food, Population and Employment" (T. T. Poleman and D. K. Freebairn, eds), pp. 120–151. Praeger, New York.
Fryer, B. A., Lamkin, G. H., Vivian, V. M., Eppright, E. S. and Fox, H. M (1971). *J. Am. Diet. Assn* **59,** 228.
Guzman, V. B. and Tantengco, V. O. (1972). *Acta Med. Philipp.* **8,** 22.
Hussain, M. A. (1973). *Br. J. Nutr.* **29,** 211.
Joy, L. (1973). *J. Agric. Econ.* **24,** 1.
Marr, J. W. (1971). *Wld Rev. Nutr. Diet* **13,** 105.
Oomen, H. A. P. C., McLaren, D. S. and Escapini, H. (1964). *Trop. Geogr. Med.* **4,** 271.
PAG, (1973). *Pag Bulletin,* **3,** 4.
Quiogue, E. S. (1972). *In* "Proceedings of the First Asian Congress on Nutrition" (P. G. Tulpale and K. S. Jaya Rao, eds), pp. 214–239 Nutrition Society of India, Hyderabad.
Schneidemann, I., Bennett, F. J., and Rutishauser, I. H. E. (1971). *J. Trop. Pediatr. Monogr.* **13,** 25.
Stock, A. L. and Wheeler, E. F. (1972). *Br. J. Nutr.* **27,** 439.
United Nations, (1968). "International Action to Avert the Impending Protein Crisis". UN, New York.
Willett, J. W. (1973). *In* "Food, Population and Employment" (T. T. Poleman and D. K. Freebairn, eds), pp. 44–52. Praeger, New York.
WHO, (1967). "Requirements of Vitamin A, Thiamine, Riboflavin and Niacin". Tech. Rep. Ser. No. 362, Geneva.
WHO, (1970). "Requirements of Ascorbic Acid, Vitamin D, Vitamin B_{12}, Folate and Iron". Tech. Rep. Ser. No. 452, Geneva.
WHO, (1973). "Energy and Protein Requirements". Tech. Rep. Ser. No. 522, Geneva.

Adverse Reactions to Food Additives with Special Reference to Hyperkinesis and Learning Difficulty (H–LD)

BEN F. FEINGOLD

Kaiser Permanente Medical Centre, San Francisco

Summary

After presenting a definition and classification of food chemicals and considering the general classification of food additives based on American experience, the paper lists the clinical patterns of disease attributed to food additives. The theories concerning the mechanisms involved in aspirin sensitivity as well as the relationship of this intolerance to the adverse reaction of food chemicals are discussed, and the inter-relationship of the pharmacological activities of aspirin, indomethacin and tartrazine (FD and C yellow: 11:5) indicated. On the basis of this pharmacological inter-relationship, a hypothesis is evolved which implicates food additives other than tartrazine as etiologic agents of disease.

The role of artificial flavours and colours as a possible cause of behavioural disturbances in Man is indicated, and particular emphasis is placed upon the relationship of artificial flavours and colours to hyperkinesis and learning difficulty (H-LD) in children, and their possible role in the increasing incidence of H-LD among the school children of the USA. The features of the chemical patterns encountered are noted and the management of H-LD in children with the so-called salicylate-free diet discussed.

It is considered that the pharmacological effects of foods and food chemicals should be considered as an additional dimension in the evaluation of factors influencing the health and behaviour of Man as related to the Man/Food Equation.

Foods are mixtures of chemicals, the bulk of which are proteins, fats and carbohydrates. In addition to these basic substances, numerous accessory chemicals occur in foods in varying concentrations. Some of these substances are natural constitutents of the food product, while others known as food additives are incorporated either directly or indirectly during various stages of production, storage and processing. Those substances, except for chance contaminants that accidentally have become a part of food, are known as non-intentional food additives, while those that are purposely incorporated are called intentional food additives.

While both the naturally occurring chemicals and food additives may be involved in the health and behaviour of Man, the scope of this discussion is limited to observations attributed chiefly to artificial flavours and colours (Table 1).

TABLE 1

Classification of intentional additives

1. Preservatives	33
2. Antioxidants	28
3. Sequestrants	45
4. Surface active agents	111
5. Stabilizers, thickeners	39
6. Bleaching and maturing agents	24
7. Buffers, acids, alkalies	60
8. Food colours	34
9. Non-nutritive and special dietary sweeteners	4
10. Nutritive supplement	117
11. Flavourings–synthetic	1610
12. Flavourings—natural	502
13. Miscellaneous: yeast foods, texturizers, firming agents, binders, anti-caking agents, enzymes	157
Total number of additives	2764

The flavours and colours represent three out of fourteen categories that constitute a list of intentional food additives compiled by the Food Protection Committee of the USA National Science Foundation and the National Research Council (NRC, 1965). It is important to note that of the 2,764 chemicals listed in this report, the flavours and colours constitute over 80% of the total.

Colours and flavours make no contribution to the nutritional value of food. However, since both flavour and colour are very important determining factors in consumer acceptance, they are frequently interlinked. As a result, they play identical and important roles in determining the economic success experienced in marketing food products, which in turn may subtly, yet at times very importantly, influence the health and behaviour of Man.

Prior to 1856 when dyes were originally developed from coal tar derivatives, practically all colours added to foods were of natural origin. (Furia, 1968). However, following the development of synthetic colours, there has been a constant increase in the utilization of the synthetic products by the food, drug and beverage industries, so that over one million kg of synthetic colouring materials are added to our food supply annually. This represents over 90% of all the food colouring used, leaving 10% from natural sources.

The various synthetic dyes are derived from four basic coal tar derivatives (ISFP, 1962; AAAS, 1970) (Table 2).

TABLE 2

Basic coal tar derivatives

Triphenylmethane
Azo
Xanthene
Sulphonated indigo

Test samples from each class have from time to time exhibited adverse effects. Derivatives of triphenylmethane, the azo dyes and indigo have known carcinogenic properties, while xanthene products manifest mutagenic potentialities.

By 1900, in the absence of regulations, there were approximately 80 dyes used in the USA for food colouring (FDA, 1973). In many instances dyes from a batch used for dyeing cloth were used for food. By 1906, when the first regulations were instituted in the USA the list was reduced to seven products, which were considered to be of known composition and studied physiologically.

The short term evaluation initially applied to the certification of dyes has proved unreliable with the result that the approved list of colours is constantly undergoing change. With long term usage of dye, toxicity and carcinogenicity frequently become manifest, which leads to either exclusion or provisional listing. Again, on the basis of short term evaluation a new product is substituted. This constant practice of deletion and substitution merely reflects the inherent potential of coal tar dyes to produce adverse effects—a situation that will no doubt persist so long as coal tar derivatives are used for food processing.

The deficiencies of short term evaluation are well expressed in a report on food colours issued in the UK as early as 1954. To quote,

> "We cannot accept the contention that, because coal tar colours have been used in foods for many years without giving rise to complaint of illness, they are, therefore, harmless substances. Such negative evidence in our view merely illustrates that in the amounts customarily used in foods, the colours are not acutely toxic but it gives no certain indication of any possible chronic (long term, continuing) effects. Any chronic effects would be insidious and it would be difficult if not impossible to attribute them with certainty to the consumption of food containing colouring matter".

TABLE 3

Synthetic food colours permitted in several different countries

DYE	UK	Australia	Canada	Denmark	Finland	West Germany	India	Norway	Spain	Sweden	Switzerland	South Africa
Ponceau 4R	+	+		+	+	+	+	+	+	+	+	
Carmoisine	+	+		+	+	+	+	+	+	+	+	+
Amaranth	+	+	+	+	+	+	+	+	+	+	+	+
Red 10B	+			+								
Erythrosine BS	+	+	+	+	+	+[a]	+	+	+	+	+[a]	+
Red 2G	+			+								+
Red 6B	+			+			+					
Fast red E	+	+		+	+		+	+	+	+	+	
Red FB	+	+					+					
Orange G	+			+								+
Orange RN	+			+								+
Oil yellow GG	+											+
Tartrazine	+	+	+	+	+	+	+	+	+	+	+	+
Yellow 2G	+	+		+								
Sunset yellow FCF	+	+	+	+	+	+	+	+	+	+	+	+
Oil yellow XP	+		+									
Green S	+	+		+								+
Indigo carmine	+	+	+	+	+	+	+	+	+	+	+	+
Violet BNP	+	+		+								
Brown FK	+	+		+								
Chocolate	+	+		+								
Chocolate brown FB	+	+		+								
Chocolate brown HT	+	+		+								
Black PN	+	+		+	+	+	+	+		+	+	
Black 7984	+					+						

[a]For colouring whole, halved or stoned fruit only.

The situation with regard to the reliability of colours as expressed in this statement explains in great measure the difficulty various public health authorities are having in arriving at mutual agreement for the authorization of colours to be incorporated into food products. Table 3 which lists the synthetic colours permitted in several countries illustrates this situation (Pyke, 1970a).

Table 4 lists the USA certified colours.

TABLE 4

Coal tar dyes
USA FD and C colours

Trimethylmethane dyes
Blue No 1 (Brilliant blue)
Green No 3 (Fast green FCF)
Violet No 1 (Benzyl violet 4B)
Azo Dyes
Red No 4 (Ponceau SX)
Red No 40 (Allura red AC)
Citrus red No 2
Orange B
Yellow No 5 (Tartrazine)
Yellow No 6 (Sunset yellow FCF)
Xanthene
Red No 3 (Erythrosine)
Sulphonated Indigo
Blue No 2 (Indigo blue)

The necessity to restrict to a rather limited number the chemicals used for colour is aided by the fortuitous circumstance that colour perception functions through a single organ—the eye, which makes the chemistry and measurement straightforward, although the psychology and acceptance of colour may be complex. As a result, the demands of the food processing industry for a great variety of hues, tints and quality can be met by blending a small number of chemicals.

On the other hand, flavour represents a composite sensation consisting of the concurrent reactions of the taste and olfactory receptors to the chemical stimuli, and in many cases in addition there is the reaction to tactile, temperature and pain receptors as well. In other words, flavour of a food or beverage represents the composite impression gained through taste, odour, texture and a group of feeling factors. For this reason flavour is complex from every standpoint—chemistry, measurement, psychology and acceptance.

Table 5, which lists the various chemicals contained in artificial pineapple flavour, illustrates the complexity of the problem in attempting to reproduce what is found in nature, and even this mixture is not absolutely true to nature (Pyke, 1970b).

TABLE 5

Artificial pineapple flavour

Pure Compounds	%
1. Allyl caproate	5·0
2. Isopentyl acetate	3·0
3. Isopentyl isovalerate	3·0
4. Ethyl acetate	15·0
5. Ethyl butyrate	22·0
6. Terpinyl propionate	2·5
7. Ethyl crotonate	5·0
8. Caproic acid	8·0
9. Butyric acid	12·0
10. Acetic acid	5·0
Essences, oils, etc	**%**
11. Oil of sweet birch	1·0
12. Oil of spruce	2·0
13. Balsam Peru	4·0
14. Volatile mustard oil	1·5
15. Oil cognac	5·0
16. Concentrated orange oil	4·0
17. Distilled oil of lime	2·0

The complex character of flavour explains the great difficulty in reproducing the various flavours occurring in nature. In many instances, the ingenuity of the chemists has approached the natural, but there is no synthetic product that cannot be detected by an individual with a very acute sense of taste. Nature, abetted by both public demands and those of the food processors, has been a constant challenge to the food chemists, who have reacted with the development of thousands of chemicals which are being constantly introduced into our food supply as flavours. The search continues. Although several thousand chemicals are now available for food flavouring, the list continues to increase. The precise number of these chemicals in use is not known, since a number of secret formulae are protected by legislation. The UK (personal communication, Ministry of Agriculture, Fisheries and Food, 1973) as well as several other countries have no regulations controlling the use of flavourings.

Recognizing that convenience foods are one of the richest sources of artificial flavours and colours, a recent report of the USA Department of Agriculture points up the widespread use of these chemicals. The report states that more than half of the foods purchased in the USA are ready to cook. Most of the remainder are ready to eat, which leaves only 3·3% that are prepared by the consumer from basic ingredients, e.g. flour, shortening, eggs, milk, etc. This reflects the radical change in life style that has evolved over the past several generations which has emancipated women from many kitchen chores. Through the encouragement and promotion of the food processors, people have become more and more dependent upon convenience foods of every variety.

The literature on flavourings as well as other aspects of food additives is quite prolific. However, the reports on clinical patterns representing adverse reactions to food chemicals are extremely limited and do not reflect the incidence of this problem that would be anticipated in view of the very wide distribution of these chemicals in our food supply. An important factor contributing to the paucity of clinical reports is the lack of recognition that food additives are a relatively common cause of adverse clinical patterns.

Initially, it was believed that food additives served as haptens (i.e. incomplete antigens) to conjugate with body proteins to form complete antigens which have the capacity to evoke allergic tissue responses. However, studies on aspirin in the USA (Farr, 1970; Samter, 1969; Samter and Beers, 1968) supported not only the non-immunological nature of aspirin sensitivity, but emphasized the relationship observed clinically between aspirin intolerance and adverse reactions to tartrazine (FD and C yellow: 11:5), a widely distributed azo food colouring. The observations of the British pharmacologist, Vane, strengthened this concept (Vane, 1971, 1972; Ferreira and Vane, 1971). Vane reported that aspirin and indomethacin, although structurally unrelated, inhibit prostoglandins, which influence the cascading activities of a number of body substances. These observations suggest that the adverse response to these drugs could be pharmacological rather than immunological in nature. Tartrazine (FD and C yellow: 11:5), although structurally unrelated to aspirin can induce identical adverse clinical patterns in aspirin-sensitive subjects; the converse is also observed. This clinical inter-relationship in the absence of a chemical structural relationship is important in interpreting the clinical response and in programming the management of adverse reactions to artificial flavours and colours based on a salicylate-free diet.

The salicylate-free diet was originally designed for the management of aspirin-sensitive patients who failed to respond following the elimination of the drug, but did show a favourable response when all foods with a natural salicylate radical were excluded. As designed initially, the diet listed only foods with a natural salicylate radical (Feingold, 1973) (Table 6).

TABLE 6

Foods containing natural salicylates

Apricots
Berries—blackberries, strawberries, raspberries, gooseberries
Cherries
Currants
Grapes—raisins, wines, wine vinegar
Nectarines
Peaches
Plums
Prunes
Almonds
Apples
Oranges
Cucumbers and pickles
Tomatoes

In some patients even this exclusion failed to control symptoms until it was recognized that tartrazine (FD and C yellow: 11:5), although unrelated by chemical structure, may induce adverse reactions in aspirin-sensitive patients. Following the exclusion of tartrazine, some of the failures, but not all, responded. Accordingly, on the basis of the clinical relationship between aspirin and tartrazine (FD and C yellow: 11:5), it was hypothesized that among the thousands of food colours and flavours incorporated into our food supply, there may be other additives, although unrelated chemically, which may induce adverse clinical responses. On the basis of this premise, the so-called salicylate-free diet was expanded to include not only all foods containing natural salicylates, but also all sources of artificial flavours and colours with and without a salicylate radical. Since flavours and colours constitute approximately 80% of all food additives, strict adherence to the diet will exclude the majority of them. In view of the complexity of the formulae for flavours, the necessity for the empirical exclusion of all artificial flavours can be readily appreciated. The conditions successfully treated with the salicylate-free diet are indicated in Table 7.

TABLE 7

Adverse reactions induced by flavours

Respiratory
allergic rhinitis
nasal polyps
cough
laryngeal oedema
asthma
Skin
pruritus
dermatographia
localized skin lesions
urticaria
angio-oedema
Gastro-intestinal
macroglossia
flatulence and pyrosis
constipation
buccal chancres
Neurological symptoms
headaches
behavioural disturbances
Skeletal system
arthralgia with oedema

It is important to note that practically every body-system is susceptible to involvement by adverse reactions to food additives. Usually only a single region is affected, but it is not uncommon for a mixture of these patterns to occur (Feingold, 1968).

Of the various clinical patterns induced by the adverse reactions to artificial colours and flavours, perhaps the most important and also the most dramatic are the behavioural disturbances in children. The exact incidence of this problem is not known, but figures vary from a conservative 5% of all pupils in the south San Francisco, California school system to 25% in Munroe County in upstate New York. The California Association for the Neurologically Handicapped estimates that in the past ten to twelve years the incidence of H-LD among the school children of California has risen from 2% to an average of 20 to 25%, and in some cases 40% of the entire school population. These figures bear no relation to socio-economic background. The great variation can no doubt be attributed to the definition of hyperkinesis, minimal brain dysfunction (MBD) and minimal neurological damage (MND), as these children are frequently labelled (Bannatyne, 1971). Another factor that influences the statistics on incidence is the failure to recognize that hyperkinesis and learning difficulty are commonly interlinked and are actually different aspects of an identical problem. This is particularly true of dyslexia, a generic term applied to a whole category of reading and spelling disabilities.

Since reading disabilities among children are frequently an expression of the behavioural disturbances induced by hyperkinesis, it is interesting to refer to some figures on reading difficulty in the USA. On March 22, 1973, in a presentation before the USA Senate by Senator Beall from the State of Maryland the following statistics were reported:

> "It is estimated that some 18½ million adults are functional illiterates; that some 7 million elementary and secondary school children are in severe need of special reading assistance; that in large urban areas 40 to 50% of the children are reading below grade level; that 90% of the 700,000 students who drop out of school annually are classified as poor readers."

The massive reading difficulties revealed in these statistics have been compiled by surveys of teachers and principals alike.

An additional alarming statistic was recently released from the Dallas, Texas school system. At graduation ceremonies throughout the city of Dallas in June 1973, anywhere from 500 to 1000 of Dallas' 9000 graduating seniors walked across the stage to be handed diplomas they could not read.

Although statistics outside the USA are presently not available to the author, the overwhelming response from many countries to a recent presentation on H-LD would suggest that similar problems exist in countries throughout the world.

It is interesting to note that a graph projected for the increase in dollar value for the production of artificial flavours and soft drink beverages of various types, parallels a graph for the increased incidence of H-LD among the school children of the USA for the past ten years. The clinical pattern of the behavioural disturbance is chiefly that of hyperkinesis which can range from simple restlessness to extreme hyperactivity, which, interfering with the child's attention span, is reflected in complete disruption both at home and at school.

At home they are less than dutiful children whose willfulness and stubbornness leads to hostility in the parents, to which the response is rebelliousness in the child.

At school they are disruptive and in conflict with their schoolmates. Their impaired attention span leads to learning difficulties in spite of a normal or high IQ. It is these children who are taxing the facilities for special classes for learning difficulties in all school systems. They are challenging the ingenuity of teachers who are constantly seeking techniques to cope with this ever increasing problem. These patients are baffling pediatricians, pediatric neurologists, psychologists, psychiatrists, and educators in the field of hyperkinesis and learning difficulties. A large number of these children are being treated with either methylphenidate (Ritalin), amphetamines, and tranquillizers.

In our experience we have successfully treated some of these children with the salicylate-free diet which eliminates the artificial flavours and colours.

Case 1

A seven-year-old boy presenting a history of extreme hyperkinesis of several years duration. When at home, he was aggressive, slamming the doors and kicking the walls and even charging oncoming cars with his bicycle. At school his hyperactive behaviour was disruptive resulting in his inability to learn. Numerous pediatricians were consulted as well as neurologists, psychiatrists and psychologists, including a complete medical and neurological survey at a teaching medical centre. Nothing succeeded until the child was placed on a salicylate-free diet. After a few weeks of dietary control, the child became well adjusted both at home and at school. Lapses in the dietary programme led almost immediately to a recurrence of the hyperkinetic behavioural patterns.

Case 2

A seven-year-old boy who because of hyperkinesis and learning difficulty, was treated with 40 mg of Ritalin daily from August 2, 1971 to June 2, 1972. The drug was interrupted for about 6 weeks because of intense drowsiness, but in August 1972 it was resumed at a dose of 20 mg daily.

Although the boy attended a special learning class, his hyperkinesis was not controlled, and his scholastic achievement was poor.

Reports from his school indicated:

January 17, 1973: excessive fidgetiness, extreme distractability, inability to adjust to new situations, and irritability. The child talked constantly when he should have been listening. The child was receiving 20 mg of Ritalin daily at this time.

April 3, 1973: the child was placed on a salicylate-free diet, but Ritalin 10 mg b.i.d. (i.e. twice a day) was continued.

April 17, 1973: the mother reported a marked improvement in the child's behaviour with a report from school that he had improved greatly in his reading. Ritalin was reduced to 5 mg b.i.d.

May 11, 1973: the mother reported that the boy was doing very well both at home and at school. Ritalin was discontinued.

June 6, 1973: continued improvement at home. His teacher reported great improvement at school. He advanced in his studies so that he became the best reader. He also showed a remarkable change in his writing ability. The child was promoted to a higher grade.

Case 3

On May 30, 1973 a seven-year-old boy presenting a history of hyperactivity dating to early infancy. Before the age of three the child was described as unhappy, extremely hyperactive and uncontrollable. He was unable to focus his attention on any project for more than 2 to 3 seconds.

At 3½ years the child was placed on Ritalin following which he seemed less active, less distractable, exhibited a degree of "self control" and seemed better able to cope with routine demands.

At 5 years of age the child started school. He exhibited great learning difficulty involving the alphabet and numbers. His classroom behaviour was disruptive, and he had great difficulty socializing with his peers.

At 7½ years Stelazine (tranquillizer) was added to his therapy in order to control to a greater degree his daytime behaviour, particularly at school, when Ritalin was not effective. Stelazine also aided in improving the sleep pattern as well as the constant minor movements of the child.

May 30 to July 2, 1973: the child was given allergy skin tests which proved negative.

July 2, 1973: the child was still receiving Ritalin 10 mg four times daily, or 40 mg per day, and Stelazine 2 mg twice a day, or 5 mg daily.

A salicylate-free diet was ordered for the child.

July 8, 1973: six days after starting the diet, the mother reported "a changed child"—more self control. He was able to reason with his parents and peers. He was less distractable. The Ritalin was reduced to a single dose at 7 p.m. and Stelazine 2 mg at bedtime only.

July 15, 1973: at 7 a.m. the child ate a bakery doughnut which was not permitted on his diet. By 10 a.m. the child became hyperactive, argumentative and unable to exercise self control.

July 16, 1973 (a.m.): the child returned to his "new normal" established by the diet.

July 17, 1973: Stelazine was discontinued. A single dose of Ritalin, 5 mg, at 7 a.m. was continued.

July 23, 1973: 21 days after starting the diet, all medication was stopped.

July 27, 1973: he attended a party at school; ate some candy at 10 a.m. At 12 noon the hyperactive behaviour returned and persisted until July 29, about 48 hours.

August 13, 1973: the child was doing extremely well.

The descriptive characteristics of the clinical pattern are as follows:

1. marked hyperactivity;
2. short attention span—jumps from one activity to another;
3. fidgetiness;
4. irritable—overly sensitive;
5. unpredictable and unmanageable;
6. quick tempered, explosive and panics easily;
7. tolerance for failure and frustration is low;
8. exceptionally clumsy—poor coordination; eyes and hands do not seem to function together; has trouble buttoning;
9. has difficulty drawing and writing;
10. cannot seem to keep from touching everything and everyone in the vicinity;
11. normal or high IQ but fails at school.

In addition it is important to note that the involvement affects boys almost exclusively and that rarely more than one child in a family is affected.

The cardinal features observed following management with the salicylate-free diet include:

1. the rapid, dramatic change in behaviour. Although the history of hyperkinesis with associated disturbances is usually of many years duration (3 to 4 years) and at times dating back to infancy, a favourable response is observed within days after instituting the dietary control. The child loses his hyperkinesis, his motor incoordination, and becomes well adjusted to his environment. The sleep pattern improves;
2. drugs which have been administered for several years can usually be discontinued after about 2 to 3 weeks of management and rarely beyond one month;
3. improved scholastic achievement is also dramatic. Within a single quarter at school the child may show much improvement in his reading and writing abilities as well as with numbers. This is consistent with the observation that these children have either a normal or a high IQ.

Since the incidence of an allergic diathesis among the human population is estimated to be approximately 25%, it is not surprising that allergy is not an uncommon concomitant of H-LD. Although adverse behavioural responses attributed to allergy without apparent involvement of additives have been reported, allergy does not seem to be a frequent primary cause of hyperkinesis. When allergic disease does accompany H-LD, in some cases it may be necessary to institute management for the allergy in order for the salicylate-free diet to be effective.

The ability to "turn on" and "turn off" the pattern of hyperkinesis, the discontinuance of drugs, and the accompaniment of rapid improvement in scholastic achievement is strong evidence to support the relationship between H-LD and the ingestion of artificial flavours and colours. In most cases a review of the diet diary reveals a larger than usual ingestion of artificial flavours and colours. In view of these observations the question is raised, "Is it possible to attribute the increase in H-LD among the children of school age to the increased consumption of these chemicals in foodstuffs?"

It is not difficult to recognize the increased consumption of artificial flavours and colours when the ingredient labels on food packages are examined. What is the average child in America given for breakfast? Usually a cereal charged with non-essential flavours and colours which have been added to entice the child; a beverage—either chocolate, a fruit punch, "Kool-Aid", "Funny Face", etc.; pancakes made from a mix; frozen waffles dyed with tartrazine; frozen French toast with syrup. Most of these are rich in many of the artificial flavours and colours. Then, having a conscientious and concerned mother, the child is given vitamins, usually chewable, which are also charged with additives. To cap the ironical situation, the child is given a dose of either Ritalin or amphetamine before he goes to school. At school the same ritual is continued at lunch, with hot dogs, luncheon meats, ice cream and various beverages. It is not surprising that children are failing to learn.

Except for terminology, there is no difference between artificial colours, flavours and many drugs. They are all low molecular weight chemicals. Recognizing this relationship, the observations on adverse drug reactions in clinical medicine, and particularly in the field of pharmacogenetics, can be drawn upon for an interpretation of the mechanism that may be involved in H-LD induced by artificial colours and flavours.

Studies in the field of genetics over the past few decades have demonstrated that each person has a unique "biological individuality" that determines a "pharmacological individuality". The pharmacological reactions of drugs depend to a great degree upon proteins that have a high degree of specificity. The quantity and the quality of these proteins can be altered through genetic mutations which influence drug metabolism, their binding abilities and drug receptor interactions (McKusick and Claiborne, 1973; Legator, 1972).

There are a number of metabolic variations which are actually not abnormalities, since under normal conditions the individuals manifest no disturbances. However, in the presence of certain drugs they express their potentially dangerous character. For example, the abnormal haemoglobin Zurich is characterized by the replacement of a histidine residue by arginine at the 63-position of the amino acid sequence of the beta chain of haemoglobin (Childs, 1972). The molecule is abnormally sensitive to oxidative denaturation but not to the point where this occurs spontaneously at an appreciable rate. Under normal conditions heterozygotes show no unusual symptoms, apart from a slightly shortened life span of the erythrocytes. However, when such patients are given sulphonamides or other oxidant drugs, methaemoglobinaemia develops. The haemoglobin denatures and precipitates which results in a fulminant haemolytic anaemia. Similar adverse effects have been observed with some other abnormal haemoglobins.

Another example is inherited deficiencies of the enzyme glucose-6-phosphate dehydrogenase (G-6-PH), a condition thought to affect some tens of millions of people (LaDu, 1972). Here again the pathology is essentially drug dependent, and haemolysis results from a number of compounds, e.g. the anti-malarial primaquine, para-amino-salicylic acid, phenacetin, the sulphonamides and also certain constituents of the broad favus bean. It is interesting to note that the gene carrying the determining characteristics for this enzymatic disorder is on the X-chromosome, which explains the greater frequency of the enzyme deficiency and drug sensitivity among males. This observation is highly suggestive that in H-LD the X-chromosome may be involved, which could explain the overwhelming preponderance among boys, as well as the occurrence in only one boy in a family.

A still further example of the contribution of genetics to the variability of drug metabolism is that observed with Isoniazid (INH) which is currently in common use for the treatment of tuberculosis (Valentine, 1972). Very early in the use of INH clinicians observed wide variations in the metabolism of the

TABLE 8

Genetics of isoniazid (INH)

	R	= Rapid inactivation
	r	= Slow inactivation
50%	Homozygote (RR) Heterozygote (Rr)	= Rapid inactivation
50%	Homozygote (rr) (recessive)	= Slow inactivation

drug, whether measured by the decrease in serum level of INH or by the rate of urinary excretion in the form of acetyl INH. The problem was resolved following the demonstration that the general population is divided into two genetic groups, namely "slow inactivators" and "rapid inactivators". INH inactivation is controlled by two autosomal alleles at a single genetic locus identified as R (rapid) and r (slow). Both homozygotes and heterozygotes for the rapid allele (RR and Rr) are rapid inactivators, while only the slow homozygotes (rr) are slow inactivators (Table 8). In other words, slow inactivation of INH is a recessive trait.

It is also interesting to note that the slow inactivators (rr) are also more likely to show toxic effects from two drugs chemically related to INH—the antidepressant phenalzine, a monoamine oxidase inhibitor, and the antihypertensive hydralazine.

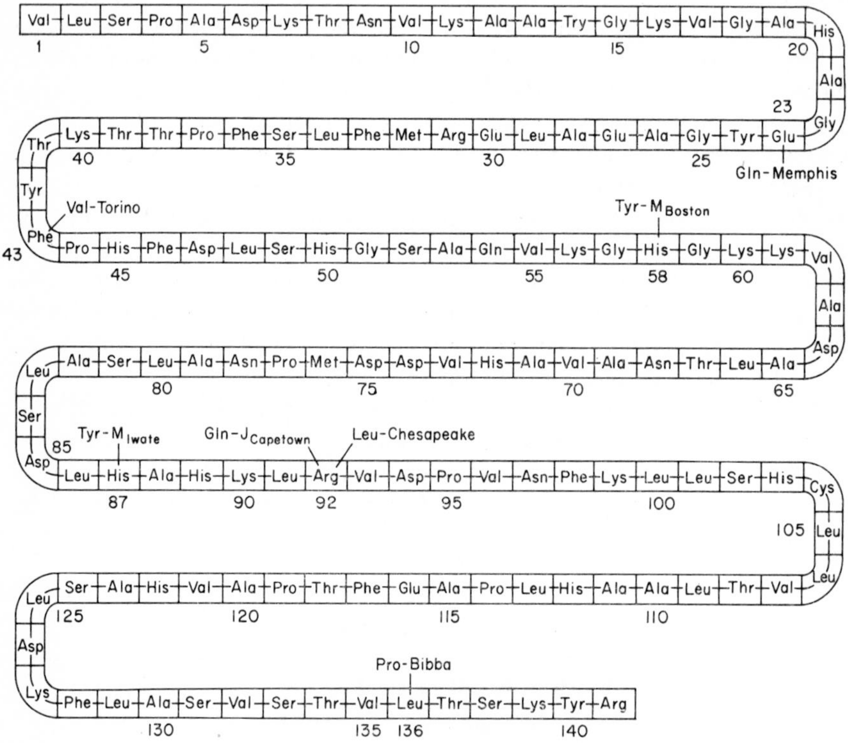

Fig. 1. Sequence of amino acid residues in polypeptide chains of human haemoglobin• Sequences of the 141 amino acid residues in the alpha (left) and the 146 in the beta (right) chains of normal human haemoglobin (Hb A) are shown schematically on these pages. (The normal haemoglobin molecule includes two alpha and two beta chains, or a total of 574 amino acid units.) Indicated at their appropriate positions are the substitutions or

This observation raises another important point relative to H-LD and the artificial colours and flavours, namely the possibility of cross-reactivity among each group of chemicals, resulting in more than one colour or more than one flavour to be at fault in the same individual. This is supported by the recognition that the colours are derived from four basic structurally-related groups, while the flavours although occurring in their thousands also show a close structural relationship. Accordingly, the broad exclusion provided by the salicylate-free diet is necessary for successful management.

The Lesch-Nyhan syndrome, which was described less than ten years ago, may also serve as a guide in studying the possible genetic basis for H-LD as related to artificial colours and flavours. In this disease the defect which involves a deficiency of the enzyme hypoxanthine guanine phosphoribosyltranferase (HPRT) is an X-linked recessive condition that occurs exclusively

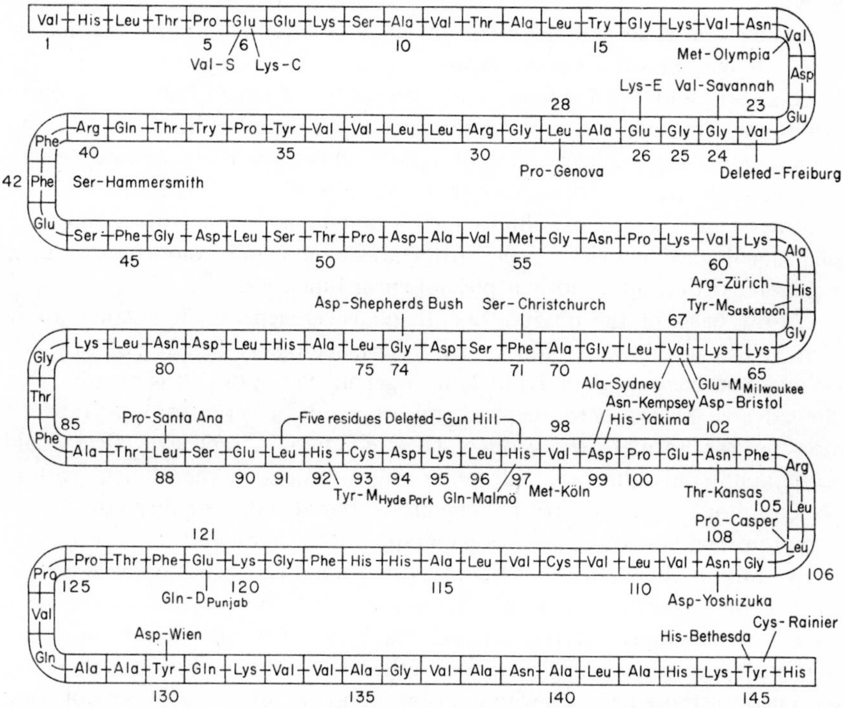

deletions responsible for the abnormal haemoglobins named. Many other abnormal haemoglobins have been indentified, most of which do not affect the functioning of the haemoglobin molecule. This rendering emphasizes (but is not necessarily a complete listing of) those in which the mutations produce clinical symptoms. From McKusick and Claiborne (1973).

in males. The importance of the Lesch-Nyhan syndrome as a guide in studying H-LD is twofold:

1. the involvement of the X-chromosome with the exclusive implication of males.
2. this is the first disease in which an identified biochemical abnormality can be associated with a specific aberrant pattern of behaviour, namely, compulsion and aggression. Although environmental influences have not been demonstrated for Lesch-Nyhan disease, nevertheless, it is conceivable that other variations of the X-chromosome or perhaps polygenic alterations may be responsible for environmentally induced behaviour patterns, e.g. the artificial colours and flavours in H-LD.

In addition to metabolic disturbances and enzymatic variations, anomalies of the receptor sites can be at fault. Receptors may exhibit either increased or decreased sensitivity as is observed in coumarin tolerance and vitamin K activity.

It is also possible that the involvement of children with either normal or high IQs may be on a genetic basis.

Educators and child psychologists generally recognize that in the early years and through the pre-school years girls exceed boys in learning achievement. By the beginning of school, however, there are no longer consistent differences. It is also at school age that the pattern of H-LD becomes apparent in most children. This could also be an expression of the pharmacological activity of the artificial flavours and colours exerting a repressive action upon normal physiological functions.

On the basis of the observations in pharmacogenetics, it is conceivable that H-LD is an expression of the pharmacological activity of artificial colours and flavours in individuals with genetic variations. It is possible that the adverse response to these chemicals exerts a repressor effect which prevents the normal expression of these children. A repressor effect could explain not only the rapid, dramatic improvement in the clinical pattern which follows elimination of the chemicals, but also the speedy recurrence of symptoms, within hours, following ingestion of the additives.

In addition, the rapid improvement observed both in the behavioural pattern and scholastic achievement would indicate that food chemicals induce a functional derangement due to the pharmacological activity, rather than persistent organic changes. On the other hand, this position cannot be assumed for those children who fail to respond favourably. Is it possible that children who fail to respond experience irreversible damage induced by the chemicals? This raises another aspect of the problem for consideration; what is the effect on a foetus of food additives taken by the mother during pregnancy?

Investigators in the field of foetal development and pharmacology suspect that drugs taken during pregnancy may have a subtle effect upon the child, which may be manifested later in life as behavioural disturbances. Food additives, like drugs, are low molecular weight chemicals which also have the capacity to cross the placental barrier, and may have similar adverse effects upon the child following ingestion during pregnancy.

The control of hyperkinesis with subsequent improvement in scholastic achievement has been demonstrated following management with the salicylate-free diet. The precise identification of the specific factors among the thousands of food additives has not been determined. The nature of the pharmacological behaviour of these chemicals is also undetermined. The incidence of H-LD among school children is not known but is generally recognized as being high and consistently rising. Nevertheless, with the recognition that this basic data is lacking, in view of the critical state of the problem and its extremely wide distribution among the school children, it would seem advisable that a broad-based programme for the management of H-LD with the salicylate-free diet should be developed. The gains are many, and the risks are nil. The programme involves no danger to the health and behaviour of the child, nor are any drugs involved.

In order to implement the effectiveness of the programme, it is essential to have widespread public awareness of the universal distribution of additives in the food supply and the potential of these chemicals for causing adverse reactions. A campaign for diligent scrutiny of package labels would alert the public regarding the imminence of the problem.

The recognition that food additives are linked to H-LD should open many areas for investigation, particularly in the fields of pharmacogenetics and neurophysiology. The availability of specific food additives as research tools could be valuable in determining the underlying genetic variations. Such observations could explain the predeliction of H-LD for boys and also the selective involvement of only one child in a family. The food chemicals could also be helpful in studying the neurophysiological responses associated with other emotional and behavioural disturbances.

Confirmation of the thesis for H-LD would justify an extension of the studies to other areas of emotional and behavioural disturbances, not only in children but also in adults. And further, the same concept could be applied to the study of the possible role of foods in the behaviour of ethnic groups.

Such an extension of the investigations would necessitate increased knowledge concerning all the accessory natural compounds occurring in various foodstuffs. Presently, such information is lacking. Is it not possible that many emotional and behavioural disturbances of Man may be due to the pharmacological behaviour of accessory food chemicals which are still unknown, some in gross quantities, while others may occur only in trace amounts?

Such studies can be of extreme importance in future planning of food supplies for a growing population which will become more and more dependent upon synthetic food products, many of which will be flavoured and coloured with artificial additives. In addition, as the studies are extended to include all food chemicals, both natural and artificial, a new dimension could be available for evaluating the Man/Food Equation.

References

AAAS, (1970). "Research for The World Crisis". A symposium presented at the meeting of AAAS, Publication No. 92 Am. Assoc. Adv. Sci., Washington, D.C.

Bannatyne, A. (1971). "Language, Reading and Learning Disabilities". Charles C. Thomas, Springfield, Illinois.

Childs, B. (1972). *Ann. Rev. Med.* **23,** 373.

Farr, R. S. (1970). *J. Allergy* **45,** 321.

FDA, (1973). "Primer on Food Additives". US FDA Consumer, p.11.

Feingold, B. F. (1968). *Ann. Allergy* **26,** 309.

Feingold, B. F. (1973). "Introduction to Clinical Allergy". Charles C. Thomas, Springfield, Illinois.

Ferreira, M. S. and Vane J. R. (1971). *Nature New Biology* **231,** 237.

Furia, T. E. (ed.) (1968). "Handbook of Food Additives". The Chemical Rubber Company, Cleveland, Ohio.

ISFP, (1962). "Clinical and Biological Hazards in Food". International Symposium on Food Protection, Iowa State University Press, Ames, Iowa.

LaDu, B. N. (1972). *Ann. Rev. Med.* **23,** 453.

Legator, M. S. (1972). *Ann. Rev. Med.* **23,** 413.

McKusick, V. A. and Claiborne, R. (eds) (1973). "Medical Genetics" pp.54–55. HP Publishing Company Inc., New York.

NRC, (1965). "Chemicals Used in Food Processing". Food Protection Committee, Food and Nutrition Board, National Academy of Sciences—National Research Council, publication 1274, Washington, D.C.

Pyke, M. (1970a). "Man and Food". World University Library, Weidenfeld and Nicolson, London.

Pyke, M. (1970b). "Synthetic Food". John Murray, London.

Samter, M. (1969). *Ann. Int. Med.* **71,** 208.

Samter, M. and Beers, R. J., Jr. (1968). *Ann. Int. Med.* **68,** 975.

Valentine, W. N. (1972). *Ann. Rev. Med.* **23,** 93.

Vane, J. R. (1971). *Nature New Biology* **231,** 232.

Vane, J. R. (1972). *Hospital Practice,* 61 (March).

The Protein Myth

M. A. CRAWFORD and J. P. W. RIVERS

Nuffield Institute of Comparative Medicine, Zoological Society of London

Summary

Human evolution has been in progress for some four million years, with the earliest evidence of meat-eating and tool-making going back some 2·6 million years, but scientific knowledge of nutrition is barely 50 years old. Assumptions are now being made that all the answers to human nutrition are known, and decisions on future food and agricultural policies in both developed and developing countries are being taken on this basis.

The current design of food and agricultural policies contains an elementary error which could affect future human development. These policies are confined to increasing production of protein and energy; they have overlooked a complete group of structural nutrients involved in the growth of the brain, and the brain is the most outstanding development of the human species.

Introduction

Consideration of nutrient requirements has clearly been dominated by protein and calories. Foods are described as protein-rich or rich in energy. In this paper it is suggested that other nutrients could be as, if not more, important than protein and that the emphasis on protein is misplaced.

In the publications by expert committees which attempt to define human nutrient requirements, specific recommendations can be found for both protein and essential fatty acids (EFA). Protein requirements are quite simply defined. According to current views (FAO/WHO, 1973) they are defined only in terms of inevitable body losses (endogenous losses) and demands made for growth, pregnancy and lactation. The latest estimates of minimal requirements are not very high—that of an adult man being satisfied by a diet providing 4% of its calories as "reference protein", or about 5% from the sort of protein found in a UK diet.

The EFA requirements are defined by the amount necessary to prevent overt deficiency. The minimal dietary concentration (in this paper all concentrations are measured in terms of calories per 100 calories, e.g. protein calories as a percentage of total dietary calories) has been variously estimated as 1–2% (DHSS, 1972), or 3–4% (Soderhjelm *et al.*, 1970) of the calories. The two sets of nutrients are not, therefore, greatly different as far as minimal dietary concentrations are concerned.

However, even a casual survey of the scientific literature reveals that the two nutrients are regarded as of completely different orders of importance. EFAs are considered to be of little practical importance, the common view being that EFA deficiency rarely if ever occurs (Davidson *et al.*, 1972). In contrast protein deficiency is regarded as a major world problem and a voluminous literature exists on protein requirements and deficiency (FAO/WHO, 1973; Davidson *et al.*, 1972). A comparison of their presumed relative importance can be gauged from the DHSS (1972) "Recommended Intakes of Nutrients in the UK". The EFAs are dismissed in eight unreferenced lines whereas protein takes six pages, twenty-one references and a two-page appendix.

This preoccupation with protein is not due to the fact that other dietary constituents are unimportant. In the UK protein supplies 12% of the dietary energy, sucrose 18% and fat 40% (NFSC, 1973). Both of the latter have been implicated in the causation of IHD (Symposium on Diet/Cardiovascular Disease, 1972). Sucrose additionally is thought to be a cause of tooth decay and diabetes mellitus, and saturated lipid of atherosclerosis (Symposium on Diet/Cardiovascular Disease, 1972). There are no DHSS recommendations about these nutrients, nor indeed any statement as to where the 80% of the energy not derived from protein or EFA should come from.

Nor can this concern be convincingly explained by the poor quality of the information about EFAs, sucrose or saturated fat, because the information about protein is not much better. A re-analysis of the data used to support the variation of protein requirements by Man suggests that most of the individual variation in requirements can be attributed to experimental error (Sukhatme, 1974). Furthermore, the data, which are used to estimate the global protein needs, are derived from studies on a small number of American college students (FAO/WHO, 1973).

Much work has been done on protein because it is measurable and it is the ease of protein analysis that has focussed attention on this aspect of nutrition almost to the exclusion of everything else. Nutritionists have been hypnotized by the protein myth.

Protein Essentiality

Protein is essential because it provides absorbable amino acids. Some of these (the "essential amino acids") are necessary because their carbon skeletons cannot be synthesized, or cannot be synthesized fast enough, by the living organism. The rest are needed because their α amino groups permit the manufacture of amino acids *in vivo*. The importance attached to protein is that whereas fat or carbohydrate can substitute for it (within limits) as carbon or hydrogen sources and can completely substitute catabolically, only protein can provide the protein for tissue growth and repair.

The awareness of protein essentiality arose out of the experiments of Magendie and Liebig (in Drummond and Wilbraham, 1964). Liebig divided nutrients into "the plastic elements of nutrition", the flesh-forming foods which he equated with nitrogenous foods, and the "respiratory elements" which were the non-nitrogenous foods. These views reached the UK in about 1840 and were quickly popularized. By 1849, for example, in Chambers's "Information for the People", the "heat-forming principle" and the "flesh-forming principle" are differentiated and "nitrogenous matter" (i.e. protein) is already used as a synonym with "nutritive value". Foods had become divided into protein and non-protein foods. Now, although some non-protein foods were literally that (e.g. honey, beer), others (e.g. bread) were just not good flesh formers—the protein they contained had a low biological value—although they were, in fact, reasonably rich in protein. Proteins differ in their flesh-forming properties, which is measured by biological value. This whole subject will only be touched upon in this paper.

By the end of the nineteenth century physiologists felt able to estimate the human requirements for protein. The estimates were widely disparate. Voit (in Singer and Underwood, 1964) estimated an adult man needed 118g of protein/day; Chittenden (1905) estimated 45g/day, but his work was widely attacked (Drummond and Wilbraham, 1964; Crichton-Browne, 1909; McCay,

1912). In World War I, the UK based its rationing policy, such as it was, on an adult man's "requirements" of 100g/day; the German government used an estimate of 118g/day, much of it of animal origin (Drummond and Wilbraham, 1964).

The evidence then available suggested that low protein diets, especially diets low in animal protein, were often associated with poor nutrition, that is, with reduced growth and specific deficiencies like limb fragility and rickets (Drummond and Wilbraham, 1964). Thus, the concept of a high protein intake, with a high proportion to be of animal origin, was firmly established and was incorporated into rationing policies in the Second World War and afterwards (Drummond and Wilbraham, 1964).

With the wisdom of hindsight it is possible to account for the high protein "requirements" and the protein deficiencies found by early workers by a variety of factors, chiefly the low biological value of some of the proteins and the low intakes of vitamins associated with the poor quality of many of the diets. In Magendie's original experiment, for example, dogs were unable to survive on bread. Magendie (in Drummond and Wilbraham, 1964) attributed this to the low protein content of the diet, but from his description of the dogs, it was probably due to vitamin A deficiency. Dogs can, in fact, survive on bread if vitamin and mineral supplements are given (Payne, 1965). However, when later evidence demonstrated that nutrients other than protein were important, protein had become so enmeshed into nutritional thinking that the classic experiments never underwent a major re-evaluation.

In 1933 Williams described the disease Kwashiorkor, a major cause of death in children in West Africa. It became attributed to a "protein" deficiency, but there is no knowledge of any research then undertaken to confirm this diagnosis except the observation that it occurred in children whose diets contained less protein than was customarily considered necessary. After the war Kwashiorkor was reported from other areas in what the newly-established Food and Agriculture Organization (FAO) regarded as the hungry world, and "the world protein shortage" became, and still remains, an "established fact". This illusion has been self-sustaining. In a world believed short of protein, priority has been given to experiments concerned with it, but not to experiments that question its significance. Although the world's protein shortage has found its critics [for example Sukhatme (see pp.53–75) and Wheeler (see pp.207–213)], the international and national advisory groups on problems of protein nutrition have more often been composed of believers rather than sceptics.

Despite the fact that no diet in the world with a concentration of protein below the minimum requirement has been identified, there is still discussion of the world protein gap and the policy of a major commercial enterprise can be guided by such statements as

"It is now accepted that the world nutrition problem is essentially a problem of proteins." (BP Proteins, 1973.)

A principal nutrition advisory group of the UN is entitled "The Protein Advisory Group".

If the present views of protein-energy inter-relationships are accepted, then the information on diets in the developing world would suggest that the energy restriction (i.e. a shortage of food) leads to reduced protein utilization, but that the protein–energy ratio of the diet is adequate. This view has some impressive backing (Platt *et al.,* 1962; Sukhatme, 1970; McLaren and Pellett, 1970), but it is outside the scope of this paper. It is, however, discussed by Sukhatme (see pp.53–75).

What is of concern here is the effect that a preoccupation with protein has had on our understanding of nutrition.

Protein and Dietary Quality

The protein concentration of food has apparently become synonymous with its quality. Within limits, increasing the protein concentration of the diet increases the rate of growth, so that if growth is the criterion, protein concentration dictates quality. Animal experiments have shown, however, that high protein diets result in obesity (Miller and Parsonage, 1972) and a decreased life span (Miller and Payne, 1968) so that by these criteria the high protein diet is not as attractive. Chittenden's claim (1909) that a high protein intake was without benefit has not yet been refuted and these animal experiments back his claim (based on human experiment) that too much protein is undesirable.

Comparative evidence argues against a high protein requirement for Man. It is difficult to state with confidence what is or is not a "natural" diet for any given species. The only "natural food" is milk and there are species differences in milk composition. In this context, it is of interest that cows' milk contains 21% protein and human milk contains 6% (McCane and Widdowson, 1960).

No-one has yet begun to evaluate foods in terms that might more reasonably reflect the desires of a human population: their effect, for example, on intelligence, beauty, or the ability to win friends and influence people! Growth remains the sole criterion.

It might seem reasonable to propose that instead of physiological measurements the index of quality should be the diet which Man eats given the opportunity, that is, if he can afford it. But increasing wealth is not associated with an increasing protein concentration in the diet, but with increasing concentrations of fat, sugar and animal products (Périssé and Tremolière, 1970). Similarly, in post-war Britain the protein intake has not changed, although there has been an increase in the consumption of fat and sugar. High and low social classes in the UK differ not in protein, but in fat and sugar consumption (NFSC, 1973).

Protein and Public Education

Despite all this, a food is currently advertised in the UK as being very rich in protein and "very, very good for you" (ITONA, TVP, 1973), and protein, as advertising agencies are well aware, can be used as a selling point for bread, milk, peanuts, pet foods and shampoo. The magic of protein, and its use in advertising, probably accounts for the frequent equation of "protein-rich foods" with "protein".

The idea of meat as a "flesh-building" food has become simplified to meat as a protein source and this has been stressed so loudly and so long, that meat has come to be considered in terms of protein only. The sales copy of a packet of TVP (Texturized Vegetable Protein) describes it as "the equivalent of completely lean meat". Only in the widest terms of protein chemistry is that so; the spectrum of lipid nutrients is totally different and no meat contains the carbohydrate and fibre of TVP. But it tastes like meat, it has the texture and cooking properties of meat and is therefore claimed to be equivalent to meat.

The sales syllogism is obvious: meat has much protein, beans have much protein and therefore beans are meat.

Arguably, anyone gullible enough to believe that beans means meat is already a lost cause, but unfortunately, the equation does not stop there. The Chairman of the Protein Advisory Group of the United Nations proclaimed on BBC Television that, to meet the future demand, animal agriculture will have to be replaced by cereals and legumes, because more protein can be produced per acre from beans than animals. It is not just bread and peanut advertisements that are dominated by considerations of protein, but global policies in food and agriculture. The protein myth is alive and well; perhaps deciding the future direction of agriculture and ultimately affecting everyone.

Science and Social Custom

Man is physiologically adapted as an omnivore. It is likely that throughout evolutionary history, human food selection patterns have been diverse rather than narrow, and it is suggested that this has conferred evolutionary advantage. Man is, after all, the product of his own digestion (Brillat-Savarin, 1780). The domestication of plants and animals has led to changes in human evolution (Darlington, 1969; Yudkin, 1969; Crawford and Crawford, 1973) and one can legitimately extrapolate to suggest that future agricultural revolutions will cause further changes.

The replacement of animal products by the use of vegetable, fungal or microbial analogues is just such a revolution. It will cause a fundamental change in the nature of human diets in a very short space of time. It is an attractive proposition inasmuch as the analogue foods are made from organisms that give a greater yield per unit input, and hence a higher profit. It is said to be attractive because they have a higher efficiency than animals, but efficiency is not a totally accurate measure. Beans are more efficient ways of producing food energy or protein than a cow; they are totally inefficient ways of producing, for example, cyanocobalamin or arachidonic acid. Cyanocobalamin (vitamin B_{12}) can be cheaply added to analogue meats, but this cannot yet be done with arachidonic acid, and it probably will not, so long as arachidonic acid is regarded as non-essential.

The authors view the ready acceptance of the idea that the nutrients are all known as an unduly arrogant assertion, and suggest that in fact, nutrition is not an exact science, but a very approximate technology. Only some of the functions of some of the major constituents of foods are known. Virtually nothing is known about nutrient interactions, about the variation in human nutrient requirements, or about the effect of diets fed for more than one generation. The analogue foods are of course tested for their teratogenic or toxic effects, but even this process involves considerable simplification. Most foodstuffs are not intrinsically harmful, but they can become so when they displace other foods. For example, the introduction of margarine led to deficiencies in vitamins A and D because it displaced butter; improvements in cereal milling resulted in B vitamin deficiencies because the "white" flour and rice displaced the relatively vitamin-rich "brown" cereal. Children die from eating bananas, not because bananas are toxic, but because by themselves they are inadequate.

The fact that these mistakes can now be described in scientific terms should lead to criticism rather than complacency. Scientific knowledge is in a state of flux and major advances are still occurring in our understanding of nutrition. In lipid chemistry, for example, it is only within the last 10 years that technical advances have made possible the detailed study of vitamin D or the EFAs. The brevity of the UK recommendations on EFA requirements was not due to any lack of biological significance, but to a lack of information.

What is of particular concern here is that the simplification of animal products to protein completely overlooks the structural fats. The evidence suggests that although the structural lipids of animal tissues are derived from plant lipids they are nevertheless different and the conversion may not always occur fast enough to satisfy the optimum requirements (Crawford and Sinclair, 1972; Sinclair and Crawford, 1972).

According to the authors' admittedly limited knowledge, animal products could be more important for their lipid content than their protein content (Crawford and Crawford, 1973). This could be wrong and the authors do not wish to destroy the protein myth simply to erect a lipid myth. The chemistry of meat and milk is more than protein or lipid—there is a vast range of constituents, the nutritional implications of most of which are unknown. Lipids are of concern because, although they are almost totally disregarded nutrients, they are quantitatively the most important structural group in the brain and the second most important in all other soft tissues of the body.

Chronic Degenerative Disease, Environment and Industrialized Food Production

It is obvious that something is profoundly wrong with the present Man/Food Equation. In today's affluent society profit is made from making people fat and another profit from making them thin again! The chronic degenerative diseases of the vascular and nervous systems are peculiar to those countries dependent on an industrialized agriculture. Coronary artery disease, diverticular disease, cancer of the large gut and multiple sclerosis are rare in other communities but in time migrants to the industrialized countries develop the disease pattern of the host country. This must mean that such diseases are environmentally induced and preventable. It has been estimated that nutritionally induced disease in the USA cost $70 billion in one year (Briggs, 1972). From the number of deaths in adults under retiring age it has been calculated that in 1968 alone the UK lost 60 million working days as a result of diseases of the vascular system.

Masland (1972) has stated that

"prenatally determined injury or abnormality of the nervous system surpasses all other conditions as a cause of long-term disability in the United States".

Many workers suspect that poor nutrition of the mother is associated with such conditions (Crawford and Crawford, 1973; Stewart, 1971; Higgins *et al.,* 1972; Winick, 1970; Lowe, 1972; Iyengar, 1967; Habicht, 1973); but in the UK no public health campaign has been aimed at nutrition during pregnancy and lactation and many of the pressures of society have been allowed to coerce mothers to have a restricted food intake during pregnancy and to relinquish breast feeding. One of the most significant nutritional principles to emerge from the laboratory is that dietary changes which have very little effect on an adult can have a marked and permanent effect on the young. Like "running in" a car, the early years of life are most critical.

One would be better advised to pay attention to the mother and child and to prevent disease rather than to indulge in the drama of its cure. This area of prevention deserves the greatest priority and is currently afforded the least. In general it would be better to have preventative food programmes rather than preventative nutrition programmes. Simply bringing in the word nutrition introduces a form of technical jargon which encourages the next step of protein programmes with its attendant risk of overlooking all the other essential nutrients. One should relearn to talk of greens, maize, beans, meat, offal, milk and eggs rather than protein-rich foods which run the risk of simplification to dried casein or extracted soya beans.

Conclusion

The answer to human nutrition is not known and neither are the factors with which to write a Man/Food Equation. Urgent action is needed to re-evaluate our attitude to food and nutrition.

In 1920 in Scotland 6,042 people died from tuberculosis and action was taken; the problem was solved by the construction of sanatoria, improvements in hygiene, the development of effective medicines, and the introduction of appropriate legislation. In 1969 17,798 people died from heart disease and nothing was done.

In this paper it has been argued that there is insufficient knowledge to give confidence in the dietary changes being planned. It has also been argued that bad nutrition may be a major underlying cause of much serious disease.

During the last two centuries there has been a continuous change in Man's diet, a continuous increase in his knowledge of nutrition but at the same time a continuous increase in nutritionally induced chronic disease. The authors are not against change, provided it is supported by adequate research and knowledge. Only when it has been shown that dietary manipulation can eliminate diseases suspected to be caused by nutritional imbalance will people be qualified to discuss the introduction of fundamental and novel changes in the basic biology of food.

References

Briggs, G. H. (1972). Evidence given to Congressional Hearing, Washington, USA.

Brillat-Savarin, C. A. (ca 1780). "Physiologie du Goût". Paris.

British Petroleum Proteins Ltd. (1973). "The Toprina Story: The Protein Famine". Portsoken Press, London.

Chambers, W. and Chambers R. (1849). "Information for the People", 2 vols. W. and R. Chambers, Edinburgh.

Chittenden, R. H. (1905). "Physiological Economy in Nutrition". Heinemann, London.

Chittenden, R. H. (1909). "The Nutrition of Man". Heinemann, London.

Crawford, M. A. and Crawford, S. M. (1973). "What We Eat Today". Neville Spearman, London.

Crawford, M. A. and Sinclair, A. J. (1972). *In* "Lipids, Malnutrition and Brain Development", CIBA-Nestlé Symposium, pp.267–292. Elsevier, Amsterdam.

Crichton-Browne, J. (1909). "Parsimony in Nutrition". Funk and Wagnall, London.

Darlington, C. D. (1969). "The Evolution of Man and Society". George Allen and Unwin, London.

Davidson, S., Passmore, R. G. and Brock, J. F. (1972). "Human Nutrition and Dietetics". Churchill Livingstone, Edinburgh.

Department of Health and Social Security (1972). "Recommended Intakes of Nutrients in the UK". HMSO, London.

Drummond, J. C. and Wilbraham, A. (1964). "The Englishman's Food", revised edition by Hollingsworth. Jonathan Cape, London.

FAO/WHO, (1973). Tech. Rep. Ser. Wld. Hlth. Org. No. 522.

Habicht, J. P. (1973). "Proceedings of a Workshop on Maternal Nutrition". National Research Council, National Academy of Sciences, Washington.

Higgins, A. C., Crampton, E. W. and Moxley, J. E. (1972). "Nutrition and the Outcome of Pregnancy". IV. Int. Congr. Endocrinol., Washington.

ITONA TVP, (1973). Sales copy, ITONA Products Ltd., Wigan.

Iyengar, L. (1967). *Ind. J. Med. Res.* **55**, 84.

Lowe, C. U. (1972). *Am. J. Clin. Nutr.* **25**, 2, 245.

Masland, R. L. (1972). *In* "Women and their Pregnancies" (K. Niswander and M. Gordon, eds), (US Dept. of Health, Education and Welfare, Washington) W. B. Saunders Co. Philadelphia.

McCane, R. A. and Widdowson, E. M. (1960). *In* "The Composition of Foods", MRC. No. 297. HMSO, London.
McCay, D. (1912). "The Protein Element in Nutrition". Edward Arnold, London.
McLaren, D. S. and Pellett, P. L. (1970). *World Rev. Nutr. Diet.* **12,** 43.
Miller, D. S. and Parsonage, S. R. (1972). *Proc. Nutr. Soc.* **31,** 31A.
Miller, D. S. and Payne, P. R. (1968). *Exp. Geront.* **3,** 231.
National Food Survey Committee (NFSC), (1973). "Household Food Consumption and Expenditure". HMSO, London.
Payne, P. R. (1965). *In* "Canine and Feline Nutritional Requirements", (O. Graham-Iones, ed.), pp.19–31. Pergamon Press, Oxford.
Périssé, J. and Tremolière, J. (1970). *Proc. Nutr. Soc.* **29,** 288.
Platt, B. S., Miller, D. S. and Payne, P. R. (1962). *In* "Recent Advances in Human Nutrition" (J. F. Brock, ed.), pp.351–374. Churchill, London.
Sinclair, A. J. and Crawford, M. A. (1972). *Febs Lett.* **26,** 127.
Singer, C. and Underwood, E. A. (1964). "A Short History of Medicine". Clarendon Press, Oxford.
Soderhjelm, L., Wiese, H. F. and Holman, R. T. (1970). *Progr. Chem. Fats Lip.* **IX,** 555.
Stewart, R. J. C. (1971). *Nutrition* **25,** 147.
Sukhatme, P. V. (1970). *Br. J. Nutr.* **24,** 477.
Sukhatme, P. V. (1974). *Proc. Nutr. Soc.* **33,** 36A.
Symposium on "Diet as a Risk Factor in Cardiovascular Disease", (1972) *Proc. nutr. Soc.* **31,** 297.
Tremolière, J. (1970). *Proc. Nutr. Soc.* **29,** 285–292.
Williams, C. D. (1933). *Archs. Dis. Childh.* **8,** 423.
Winick, M. (1970). *Pediat. Clin. N. Amer.* **17,** 1, 69.
Yudkin, J. (1969). *In* "The Domestication and Exploitation of Plants and Animals" (P. S. Ucko and G. W. Dimbleby, eds), pp.547–552. Duckworth, London.

Some Diseases Related to Fibre-depleted Diets

DENIS P. BURKITT

Medical Research Council, London

Summary

A number of the most common diseases in the UK and North America are rare or unknown throughout rural Africa. These diseases are associated one with another in geographical distribution and sometimes in individual patients. The close associations between particular diseases have been used as possible pointers to common causative factors.

The way in which the geographical grouping of crimes or the association between known criminals points to the likelihood of a master mind directing them all, has been used here as an analogous situation. Particular crimes can represent specific diseases and the criminals are the causative agents, which in each case have their origins in fundamental causes.

Epidemiological and other evidence points to diets deficient in fibre, and in particular cereal fibre, as being in some way causative factors in all the diseases under discussion, and mechanisms whereby such diets could be at least partly responsible are considered. In view of the evident advantages of restoring cereal fibre to the diet in the form of wholemeal flour and added unprocessed bran (and this seems to have no disadvantages) this simple measure is strongly recommended.

Introduction

A number of the most common diseases found in the Western world today are characteristic of, and in many instances largely confined to, more economically developed communities (Trowell, 1960; Cleave *et al.*, 1969).

These include the commonest cause of death in Western Europe and North America—ischaemic heart disease; the second most common cause of cancer death after lung tumours—cancer of the large bowel; non-malignant bowel tumours which, though only occasionally harmful, are present in at least a quarter of the population over the age of 50; some of the commonest indications for abdominal surgery—appendicitis and gallstones; diverticular disease—the commonest disease of the gastrointestinal tract; hiatus hernia which may be present in a quarter of the adult population; and the most common venous disorders—varicose veins and haemorrhoids. Also included are the most prevalent of all disorders—constipation and obesity.

There are other diseases characteristic of modern Western civilization which will not be considered since there is no evidence to relate them to dietary factors. These include lung cancer (associated with cigarette smoking), automobile and machinery accidents, and a number of diseases of unknown cause, such as multiple sclerosis and thyrotoxicosis.

Possible Approaches to the Problem of Causation

Searches for the cause of disease can be conducted in a number of different ways. One of the most fruitful approaches has been in determining the geographical areas, communities or individuals in which a certain disease of unknown cause is unduly prevalent or unusually rare, and then looking for environmental factors which are maximum in the areas or communities with the highest incidence of the disease and minimum in the areas where the disease is rare.

Studies of this nature enable the building up of a hypothesis showing that a disease may be the result of certain environmental factors. Experiments can then be conducted to prove or disprove the hypothesis. There are numerous examples of the success of this approach. Snow (1936) related cholera to the drinking of sewage-contaminated water by plotting the distribution of the disease in a London epidemic long before the causative organism was identified. A causal relationship was postulated between malaria and mosquitos before their role in transmission was demonstrated, and soot was was related to skin cancer on epidemiological evidence before the carcinogenic effect of hydrocarbons was recognized.

Alternatively, the search for causes can be directed primarily to individual patients, looking for evidence of causative factors such as bacteria, viruses, parasites of various kinds, poisons, or deficiencies of, for example, minerals or vitamins in essential requirements.

I propose to adopt yet another approach, putting emphasis on the significance of relationships between one disease and another, in their geographical distribution, the times when they increased in prevalence in different communities, and sometimes as coexistent diseases in individual patients.

A Criminal Investigation Approach Applied to Medical Research

The successive clues followed in criminal investigation from the crime committed to the apprehension of those primarily responsible, have an obvious application in epidemiological studies. A fictitious situation will be followed, each crime being represented by a disease.

The Problem to be Studied

Let us suppose that within a limited area a number of specific crimes are all being committed much more frequently than elsewhere. These might represent the specific disease whose prevalence is maximum in the developed world and minimal in rural communities in developing countries (Fig. 1). It is not necessary to include all of these diseases to illustrate the reasoning and deductions that suggest there may be some causative factor which is common to each disease and which could therefore account for the observed associations. Diverticular disease of the bowel, which could be represented by bank robberies, is present in about a third of those over the age of 50 years in the UK and North America, yet it is virtually unknown in Africa and is very rare in countries like India, Pakistan and Iran, to mention but a few (Painter and Burkitt, 1971; Cleave *et al.,* 1969). Appendicitis, which might be depicted by petty theft, is still very rare in rural Africa, but is becoming increasingly prevalent in Westernized and urban communities (Burkitt, 1971a). Its prevalence rises before that of the other diseases listed and analogously petty thefts might be known to have become common in the community envisaged before any increase in other crimes. Large bowel cancer, which might be represented by houseburning, is more closely related

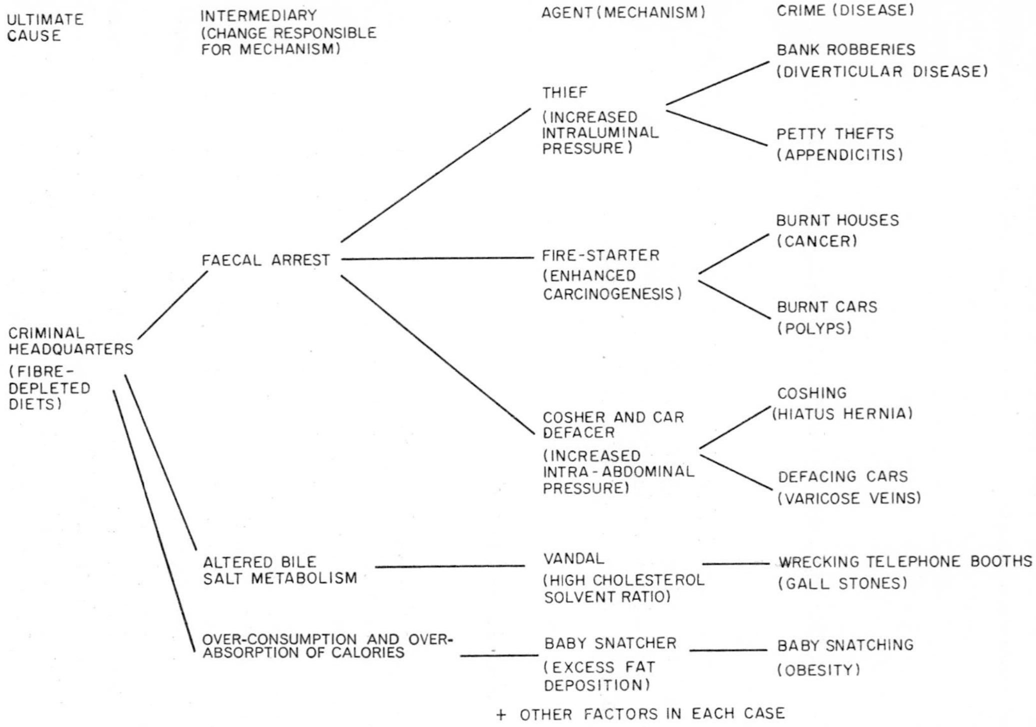

Fig. 1. Ultimate cause of range of disorders deduced by analogy with a criminal investigation.

to economic development than is any other form of cancer, and benign bowel tumours represented by car burning are exceedingly rare in all communities investigated in developing countries (Burkitt, 1971b, 1972a).

Hiatus hernia, depicted as coshing, is rare in all developing countries investigated and almost unknown in Africans (Burkitt and James, 1973); varicose veins, represented by car defacing, are rare in communities living close to their traditional pattern (Burkitt, 1972b; Cleave *et al.*, 1969); gallstones (wrecked telephone booths) are almost universally rare in developing countries, and are virtually unknown in rural Africa (Cleave *et al.*, 1969; Burkitt, 1973), and obesity (baby-snatching) is rare in communities living almost exclusively on traditional diets.

Not only are all these diseases together common in the developed countries, together very rare or absent in rural Africa, and together have an intermediate incidence in partially developed communities, but their historical emergence as clinical problems in different communities has also been related.

They have all tended to increase in communities who have emigrated from a country where the incidence of these diseases has been low to one where it is high, as for example among Japanese who have emigrated from Japan to Hawaii. Available information indicated that most if not all of these diseases were much less common in black than in white Americans a quarter of a century ago, whereas the incidence of each in the two races is comparable today.

All these observations point strongly to environmental rather than genetic factors as primarily responsible.

The Identification of Factors Directly Responsible

As with the detective approach, the next step in the investigation is to find the criminals responsible for these crimes. There is good evidence to suggest that both diverticular disease (Painter, 1964, 1967) and appendicitis (Short, 1920; Burkitt, 1971a) are largely the result of unnaturally raised pressure within the lumen of the large intestine and appendix respectively. Thus increased intraluminal pressure represents the thief who in the analogy is responsible for both the major and the minor robberies (Fig. 1).

Similarly it is generally accepted that malignant and non-malignant tumours of the large intestine have some causative factor or factors in common (Morson and Bussey, 1970; Burkitt, 1971b) and these can be labelled "enhanced carcinogenesis" represented by a fire-starter responsible for both major and minor arson. Evidence has been presented suggesting that both hiatus hernia—an upward protrusion of the stomach through the diaphragm, (Burkitt and James, 1973) and varicose veins (Burkitt, 1972b) are related to raised intraluminal pressures which could be represented by the man responsible for both coshing and car defacing (Fig. 1). Gallstones (wrecked telephones) result from alteration in the ratio between cholesterol and solvent (bile acids) in the bile, represented in the diagram (Fig. 1) by the vandal; obesity (baby-snatching) is caused by excess fat deposition (Fig. 1).

A Search for Associations

Having identified the responsible criminal agents the next step in criminal investigation would be to look for any associations between them. Similarly in epidemiological studies attention must be paid to any associations between the agents directly responsible for the different diseases. Increased intraluminal pressure in the intestine and the disease most closely associated with it, diverticular disease, is very closely associated epidemiologically with intra-abdominal pressure and its postulated results hiatus hernia and varicose veins (Fig. 1). The geographical and age distribution, and time of emergence as clinical problems in different communities of both diverticular disease and hiatus hernia are almost identical, and although the prevalence of varicose veins rises long before that of diverticular disease both these conditions tend to be associated not only geographically but also in individual patients (Latto *et al.,* 1973), an observation that suggests some common causative factors. These agents, raised intraluminal pressure and raised intra-abdominal pressure, in analogy with their criminal counterparts, can thus be said to "talk to one another". Similarly the epidemiological relationships between bowel tumours and diverticular disease and between each of these diseases and hiatus hernia is a "talking together" between the different agents responsible (Fig. 1).

The Role of Faecal Arrest

Both "raised intraluminal pressures" and "raised intra-abdominal pressures" are fundamentally caused by faecal arrest. Abnormally strong contractions of the intestinal muscle are required in order to propel along the colon the viscid faecal masses which are associated with the delayed passage of intestinal content through the large bowel. The straining of abdominal muscles needed to evacuate constipated stools is the most potent cause of raised intra-abdominal pressure.

The cause of faecal arrest must now be considered. It is widely accepted that this is the result of a fibre-depleted diet (Avery Jones, 1972; Burkitt *et al.*, 1972; Cummings, 1973) which could be represented in the analogy by an intermediary linking a criminal syndicate (fibre-depleted diets) with the agents directly committing the crimes (raised intra-luminal and intra-abdominal pressures).

The source of fibre in food is probably of great importance. Cereal fibre and to a lesser extent that of potatoes and legumes appears to be much more effective than that of fruit and green vegetables in maintaining normal bowel function (Walker, 1961).

Not only is faecal arrest, which implies constipation, the intermediary responsible for the local factors inducing some large bowel and associated diseases, but constipation is itself a major ailment in this country. Extensive studies have shown that food passes through the gastro-intestinal tract, from mouth to anus, in about 35 hours in rural Africans who live on unrefined foods and are virtually free of the diseases in question. It takes about two days in communities on mixed diets and with an intermediate prevalence of these diseases, and over three days in most North Americans and Britons accustomed to refined diets. This transit time commonly exceeds a fortnight in the elderly. Moreover, average stool weights in Britons are less than half those of Africans and their stool consistency is much more firm than those of people living in a more traditional manner (Burkitt *et al.*, 1972; Walker, 1947; 1971).

Postulated Relationship Between Bowel Tumours and Faecal Arrest

The evidence thus far presented indicates some link between bowel tumours (the effects of "enhanced carcinogenesis") and the diseases related to raised intraluminal and intra-abdominal pressures. Since there is good evidence that these latter two are related to faecal arrest, it is reasonable to postulate that some of the factors responsible for bowel tumours might also be in some way influenced by faecal arrest, and possible mechanisms must be considered. It has been shown that faecal bacteria in communities with high rates of bowel cancer differ from the bacteria in stools from communities with a low cancer rate. These bacteria, which it has been postulated result from diets rich in fat, can apparently produce potentially carcinogenic substances from normal faecal constituents such as bile salts (Aries *et al.*, 1969; Hill *et al.*, 1971). Faecal arrest will not only provide more time for such mechanisms to operate, but will result in concentration of any carcinogens thus formed, and ensure their prolonged contact with the intestinal mucosa.

It must be emphasized that incriminating fibre-depleted diets as playing a possible role in the cause of bowel cancer in no way whatever suggests that refined foods contain any carcinogens or co-carcinogens, or that white flour plays any role other than that of replacing less refined flour or other foods more rich in fibre, and so predisposing to constipation.

Some other Postulated Results of Fibre-depleted Diets

The evidence outlined above could explain the observed links between the first six diseases and a fibre-depleted diet (Fig. 1).

To turn to the other diseases (crimes), gallstones (telephone vandalism) are now believed to be the result of a high ratio of cholesterol (the main content of gallstones) to bile salts (the solvent) in the bile (Heaton, 1972). This represents the vandal. The intermediary linking this agent with the crime syndicate (fibre-depleted diets) is altered bile salt metabolism. It has been shown that the fibre content of the diet influences both the absorption of dietary cholesterol and the re-absorption of bile acids from the lumen of the small intestine (Heaton, 1972).

In respect of obesity, the excess fat deposition results largely from intake of energy in excess of requirements. This represents the intermediary with headquarters—"fibre-depleted diets"—which inevitably tend to increase energy intake on two counts. In the first place foods rich in fibre have a higher satiety content making over-consumption less likely. In the second place there is with such food incomplete absorption from the alimentary tract of the calories consumed.

Thus the three "intermediaries"—faecal arrest, altered bile salt metabolism and excess energy intake, can be traced to "fibre-depleted diets", and moreover they tend to be associated with one another, i.e. in the analogy used they tend to "talk together".

The appearance of appendicitis in Westernized Africans and its increasing prevalence in other developing countries, suggests, like the early appearance of petty thefts in the analogy, that the other diseases will follow in due course if the changes in dietary habits believed to be responsible proceed unchecked.

Recommended Action

Evidence, much of it by association and similar to that outlined above, would have warranted the arrest of the criminal gang in the analogy, and their confinement on remand pending trial, to safeguard the public.

The evidence suggests the implication of fibre-depleted diets in the causation of the diseases enumerated and warrants caution with regard to these diets, similarly to protect the public. Proof is still required and the evidence needs careful examination before final judgement can be given. The lawyers who would sift and interpret evidence in a legal setting might in the medical research context be experimental workers, whereas the detectives would be represented by the epidemiologists.

It would seem wise therefore in the medical, just as in the legal situation, to recommend custody on remand pending final judgement, since much might be saved and nothing lost by advising removal of the factor postulated to be at least in part responsible for a high incidence of these diseases. This would involve a return to a diet richer in cereal fibre, a measure which will quickly remedy constipation (Avery Jones, 1972) and also, it appears, the symptoms of diverticular disease (Painter *et al.,* 1972). Moreover, a recent paper suggests that such a diet lowers the incidence of appendicitis (Walker *et al.,* 1973) and there is some evidence that it reduces obesity, but it is the next generation which will be most likely to benefit from the lower prevalence of the other diseases, since these take longer to develop.

In practical terms cereal fibre replacement is best achieved by liberal consumption of wholemeal bread, and the addition of unprocessed bran to the daily diet. Requirements vary from one dessertspoonful to several tablespoonsful.

Conclusions

The only hypothesis that accounts for the associations between the diseases discussed above is that each is related to a fibre-depleted diet, which does not imply that this is the sole cause of any, merely a factor common to each. This concept was first enunciated by Surgeon Captain Cleave who must be considered as the pioneer in this field.

Evidence is much stronger in respect of some of these diseases than others, and there can be little doubt that diets deficient in cereal fibre are the commonest cause of constipation. Over 5 million Britons are estimated to be regular laxative users, and over £15 million, more than three times the total health expenditure in many developing countries, are spent annually on laxatives in the UK. This is only a fraction of the cost of constipation in

North America. It would seem that there is much to be gained—but how much is not known—by the return of cereal fibre to our food. On the other hand there is nothing to be lost, and the betting odds would appear to be "Heads I win and tails I don't lose".

References

Aries, V., Crowther, J. S., Drasar, B. S., Hill, M. J., and Williams, R. E. O. (1969). *Gut* **10,** 334.

Avery Jones, F., (1972), *In* "Management of Constipation" (F. Avery Jones and E. W. Godding, eds), pp.97–131. Blackwell Scientific Publications, Oxford.

Burkitt, D. P. (1971a). *Br. J. Surg.* **58,** 695.

Burkitt, D. P. (1971b). *Cancer* **28,** 3.

Burkitt, D. P. (1972a). *In* "Medical Annual" (R. B. Scott and R. M. Walker, eds), Ninetieth Year, pp.5–16. John Wright, Bristol.

Burkitt, D. P. (1972b). *Br. Med. J.* **2,** 556.

Burkitt, D. P. (1973). *Br. Med. J.* **1,** 274.

Burkitt, D. P. and James, P. A. (1973). *Lancet* **2,** 128.

Burkitt, D. P., Walker, A. R. P. and Painter, N. S. (1972). *Lancet* **2,** 1408.

Cleave, T. L., Campbell, G. D. and Painter, N. S. (1969). "Diabetes, Coronary Thrombosis and the Saccharine Disease". 2nd ed. John Wright, Bristol.

Cummings, J. H. (1973). *Gut* **14,** 69.

Heaton, K. W. (1972). "Bile Salts in Health and Disease". Churchill Livingstone, Edinburgh.

Hill, M. J., Crowther, J. S., Drasar, B. S., Hawksworth, G., Aries, V. and Williams, R. E. O. (1971). *Lancet* **1,** 95.

Latto, C., Wilkinson, R. W. and Gilmore, O. J. A. (1973). *Lancet* **1,** 1089.

Morson, B. C. and Bussey, H. J. R. (1970). "Predisposing Causes of Intestinal Cancer". Current Problems in Surgery—a series of monthly clinical monographs. Year Book Medical Publishers Inc. Chicago.

Painter, N. S. (1964). *Ann. R. Coll. Surg. Eng.* **34,** 98.

Painter, N. S. (1967). *Am. J. Dig. Dis.* **12,** 222.

Painter, N. S. and Burkitt, D. P. (1971). *Br. Med. J.* **2,** 450.

Painter, N. S., Almeida, A. S. and Colebourne, K. W. (1972). *Br. med. J.* **2,** 137.

Short, A. R. (1920). *Br. J. Surg.* **8,** 171.

Snow, J. (1936). "Snow on Cholera". The Commonwealth Fund, New York.

Trowell, H. C. (1960). "Non-infective Diseases in Africa". Arnold, London.

Walker, A. R. P. (1947). *S. Afr. Med. J.* **21,** 590.

Walker, A. R. P. (1961). *S. Afr. Med. J.* **35,** 114.

Walker, A. R. P. (1971). *S. Afr. Med. J.* **45,** 377.

Walker, A. R. P., Walker, B. F., Richardson, B. D. and Woolford, A. (1973) *Postgrad. Med. J.* **49,** 187.

Dietary Deficiency and Disease with Special Reference to Diverticular Disease of the Colon

NEIL S. PAINTER

Manor House Hospital, London

Summary

Several diseases have appeared in this century to plague the citizens of the industrialized nations of the Western world. Among them is diverticular disease of the colon. This disease was almost unknown in 1900 but in less than seventy years, the traditional life-span of Man, it has become the commonest affliction of the colon in the populations of Europe and the USA. This paper puts forward the proposition that it is caused by the over-refining of carbohydrates and in particular the removal of plant fibre from the modern diet. The beneficial effects of replacing this fibre in the diet are described.

Introduction

This paper discusses one of the ideas put forward to help explain the sudden increase of certain diseases which affect the Western world and which have become a clinical problem only in this century. Among these conditions are diverticular disease of the colon, appendicitis, constipation, cancer of the colon and rectum, varicose veins, haemorrhoids, hiatus hernia and gall-bladder disease. These diseases are still almost unknown in those communities of Africa and Asia who have not changed their traditional eating habits and adopted the over-refined foodstuffs of the West. There is a great deal of evidence to support the view that dramatic changes occurred in the diet of the industrialized nations towards the end of the last century and that these, by altering the environment of the intestine and affecting the metabolism, have led to the appearance of many diseases that afflict their citizens (Cleave *et al.*, 1969). Burkitt (see pp. 247–256) discusses the importance of dietary fibre, and in particular cereal fibre, and in this paper diverticular disease of the colon will be described. I will explain why I believe a deficiency of dietary fibre is responsible for the sudden appearance of this disease as a major clinical problem, and relate how the symptoms of this condition can be relieved by simple dietary means, namely, adding bran to the diet.

Historical Review

The affluent societies eat more protein, fat and refined sugar than do the citizens of the developing countries, and pride themselves on eating better food. However, their rich and varied diet is eaten at the expense of unrefined foods some of whose constituents are essential to health. Around the years 1870 to 1880, the diet in the UK and the USA altered dramatically. Improvements in rail and sea transport and the introduction of refrigeration, coupled with the opening up of the North American prairies, resulted in a greater variety of food becoming available at a price which all but the very poorest could afford. The true value of wages rose due to the Industrial Revolution, and the reduction of import duty allowed more sugar to be imported from the West Indies while the introduction of sugar beet processing further lessened its cost (Barker *et al.*, 1966). Formerly, most people had eaten a large amount of wholemeal stoneground bread and vegetables supplemented by a little meat, but the increase in their real incomes caused foodstuffs which formerly had been the prerogative of the rich to be eaten in the place of these unrefined cereals. At the same time, the roller-milling of grain replaced stonegrinding and even more cereal fibre was removed from the flour. As a result of these changes the consumption of bread and flour products began to fall and this trend has continued to the present day in the UK except for the years of the two World Wars.

Stonegrinding has made "white" bread available to the rich for centuries but it only removes some of the bran, whereas metal rollers remove not only almost all the bran which covers and protects the wheat germ, but also some of the cellulose that surrounds the individual grains of starch. Hence, modern white bread contains only a trace of cereal fibre whereas stoneground 100% wholemeal bread contains over 2% of fibre by weight. A century ago many Englishmen ate 3–8 g of fibre a day of which $1\frac{1}{2}$–3% was cereal fibre derived from wholemeal bread, or bread of 80–85% extraction. The rest of the fibre was derived from potatoes, legumes, fruit and vegetables. Today's diet includes about the same amount of plant fibre derived from fruit, vegetables, potatoes and legumes but as much less bread, which in any case is made from highly refined white flour, is eaten, the intake of cereal fibre has dropped to a negligible amount.

The consumption of fat has risen in the last century by about 50% and sugar consumption has doubled, but the most dramatic change has been a ten-fold fall in the consumption of cereal fibre.

Previous Experience with Bran

Fibre has been the one fraction of food that has been ignored by most nutritionists, presumably because it yields no calories and is thought to have no nutrient value. While this may be so, it affects the behaviour of the bowel profoundly. It has a much greater laxative effect than do the various fibres derived from fruit and vegetables (Dimock, 1936). This may well be due to the fact that for centuries Man has been able to store only grain and seeds, such as lentils, for his sustenance during the winter months. It is only recently that he has been able to store fruit and vegetables; hence it is reasonable to suppose that the digestive system of Western Man may well have adapted to, and become dependent upon, an adequate intake of unrefined cereals, and that the modern over-refined carbohydrates are so new in the time-scale of human nutrition that our metabolism has not had time to adapt to them.

Many feeding experiments have been performed in which bulk has been added in the form of pure cellulose as if this is interchangeable with bran, but bran is not a negligible food fraction. Hurst, quoted by Dimock (1936), attributed the absence of constipation in German soldiers in World War I to their unrefined coarse bread. All-Bran given to patients cured constipation, mucous colitis and relieved the symptoms of spastic colon (Dimock, 1936), and Cleave used unprocessed bran to cure constipation in the Royal Navy for many years both afloat and when serving as a physician in naval hospitals (Cleave, 1941 and personal communication). Recently, bran has been shown to alter the stool weight and the transit times (Burkitt *et al.*,

1972). Unfortunately, roughage was once thought to irritate the gut and this idea prevailed throughout the profession from 1925 until about ten years ago. In particular, roughage was thought to be harmful in diverticulosis as it might damage the mucosal pouches. Consequently, a low residue diet was prescribed in the treatment of the disease. This was an error as it is now thought that diverticular disease of the colon is caused by a fibre-deficient low-residue diet (Painter, 1969; Painter and Burkitt, 1971; Painter *et al.*, 1972), and it should be treated by replacing the bran that is missing from the modern diet. Diverticular disease will be discussed as it has the distinction of being the first common condition that has been shown to have benefited from the addition of fibre to the diet.

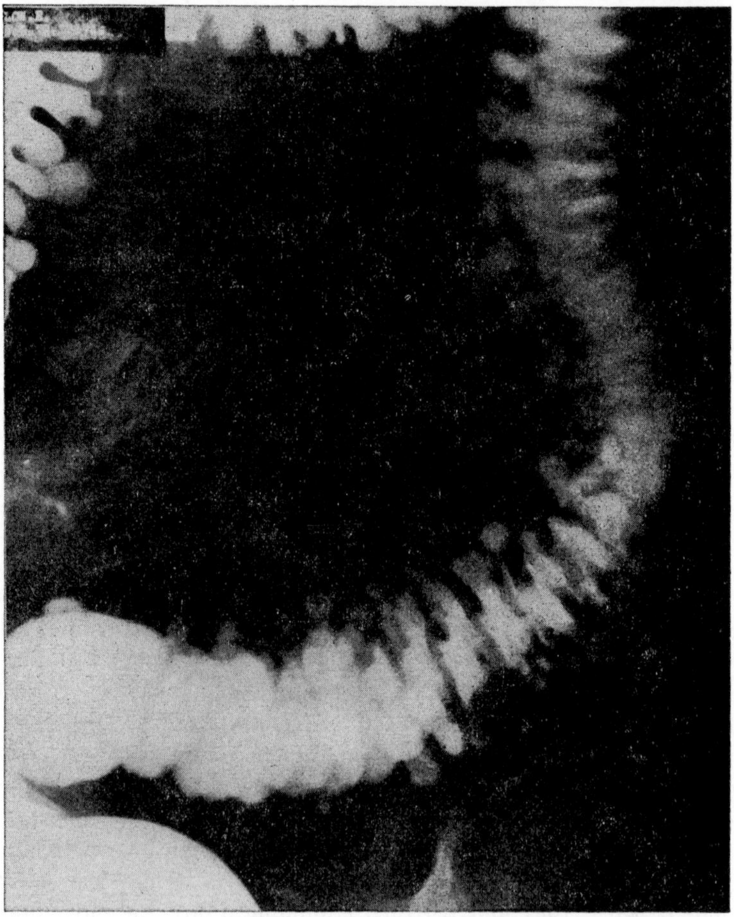

Fig. 1. Barium enema radiograph of sigmoid colon which bears diverticula.

Diverticular Disease of the Colon

Anatomy and Pathogenesis of Diverticulosis

This disease was almost unknown in 1900 and yet the X-ray appearances shown by barium enema (Fig. 1), would be recognized by any student to-day as it has since become so common. On the left is the rectum and above this is the sigmoid colon with the descending colon to its right (this is the left side of the patient). Instead of being a smooth tube gently indented by haustral folds, the sigmoid is grossly deformed with its muscle thrown into ridges

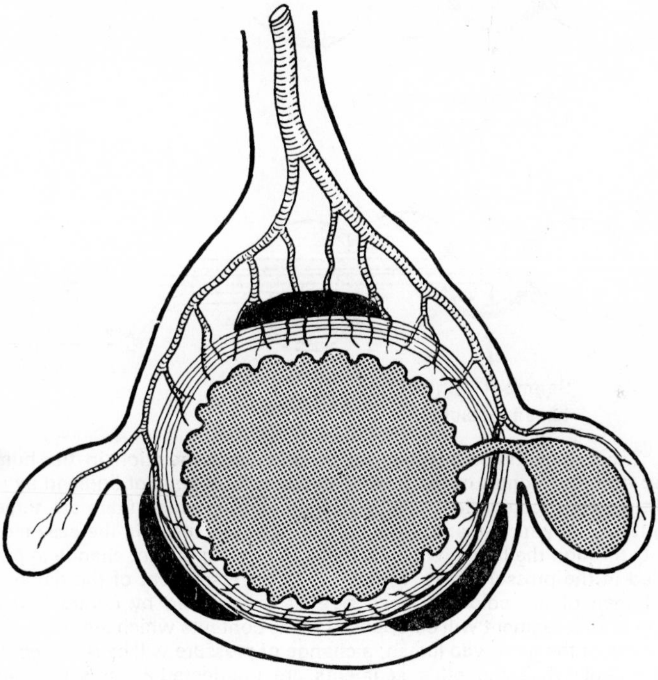

Fig. 2. Cross section of colon (after Hamilton Drummond).
The muscle of the colon consists of a complete tube of circular muscle surrounding the mucous membrane. Outside this tube, the longitudinal muscle is not continuous but is gathered into three bands or taenia between which the muscle coat is obviously weaker. The coat is still further weakened by the passage through it of the segmental blood vessels which form tunnels in the muscle. This point of weakness only determines the commonest site of diverticula, that is herniations of the colonic mucosa through the muscle, but does not cause them.

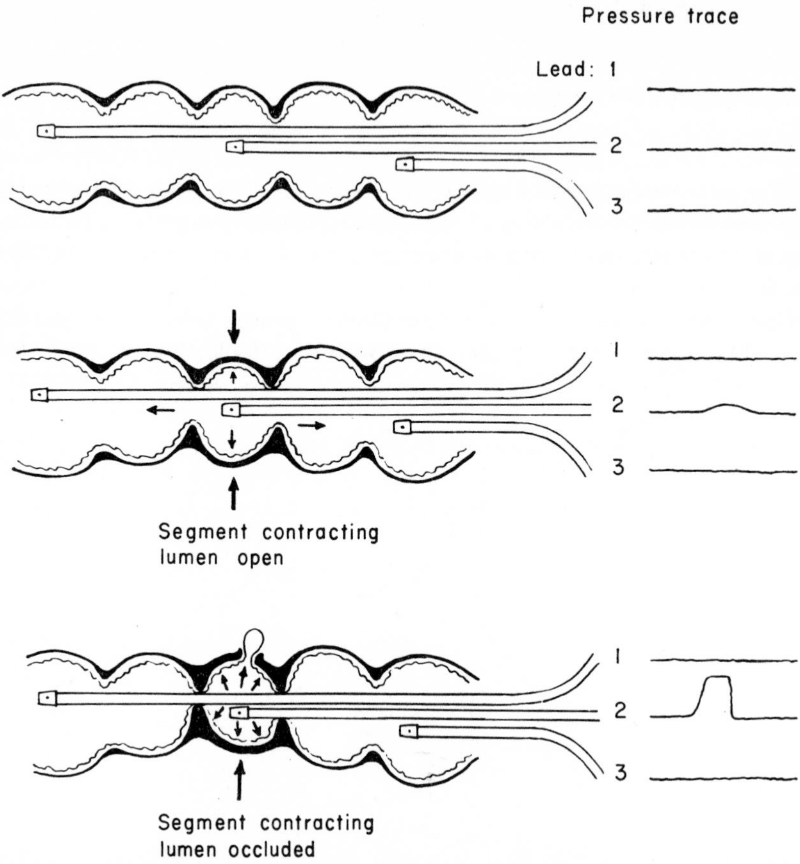

Fig. 3. The segmentation mechanism of pressure generation in the human colon (Reprinted from the Annals of the Royal College of Surgeons of England by permission of the Editor.) Top: longitudinal section of the colon in which there are three pressure recording tubes. Any movement of the colonic wall will result in the easy movement of its contents through the lumen which is open and no significant change in pressure will be recorded in the pressure trace. Middle: the centre segment of the colon contracted with the lumen of the colon on each side of it narrowed by contraction rings. The contraction of this segment will be opposed by its contents which are not entirely free to move because of the narrowed lumen; a change of pressure will be recorded by the tube in this segment while the other segments are unaffected by this pressure change. Lower: the centre segment is fully contracted so that it is almost isolated from its fellows by the occlusion of the colonic lumen that has been brought about by contraction of the colonic muscle. The outflow of this segment is obstructed in both directions and any further contraction of this segment will result in a sharp rise of pressure which will remain localized to this segment. The living colon does not function as a tube when segmenting, but as a series of "little bladders" whose outflow is obstructed; in these isolated segments, high pressures develop which force the mucosa through the muscle coat. The pathogenesis of colonic diverticula is therefore essentially similar to that of diverticula in the urinary bladder.

which narrow the lumen, between which are balloon-shaped projections. These are diverticula which consist of herniations of the mucosa through the muscle wall. They may be likened to blow-outs on a tyre. The outer muscle coat of the colon is gathered into three bands or taenia (Fig. 2), so that between them the mucosa is contained only by the circular muscle and this is pierced by the segmental arteries which supply the colon. These vessels further weaken the circular muscle and form tunnels through which diverticula mainly emerge. This anatomical arrangement determines the commonest site of diverticula but obviously does not cause them as normal colons have the same anatomy.

Diverticula are hernia and must be caused by high intracolonic pressure or weakness of the colonic muscle. No congenital weakness in the muscle coat has ever been demonstrated, but recording of the intracolonic pressures combined with simultaneous cineradiography has shown that diverticula are produced by segmentation of the colon. By segmenting, the colon produces localized pockets of pressure that can exceed 90 mm of mercury. The mechanism responsible for this is shown diagramatically in Fig. 3.

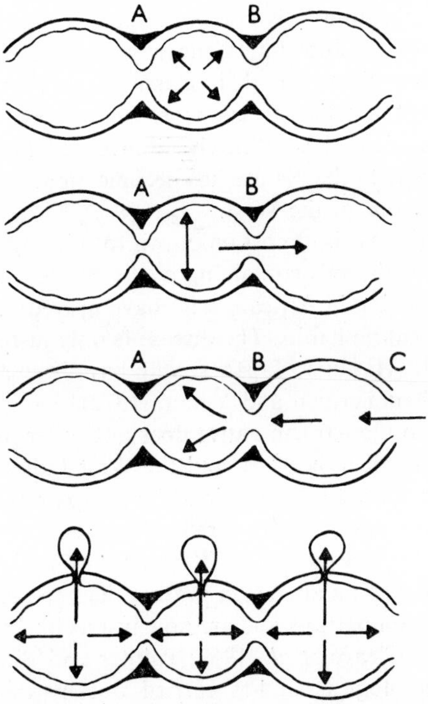

Fig. 4. Role of segmentation in the physiology of the sigmoid colon and its relationship to the pathogenesis of diverticula.

Segmentation plays an essential part in colonic physiology as it is involved in the transportation and in the mixing of the colonic contents, (Fig. 4). (Painter, 1964, Painter *et al.,* 1965).

It is obvious that the amount of pressure required to propel soft semi-liquid faeces through the colon would be less than those required to propel hard viscous stools. The African or Asian who does not get diverticulosis passes soft bulky stools, while the Englishman who is prone to the disease produces small viscous stools and often has to strain to void them. Consequently, the more viscous the stools, the more the pressure that the colon has to withstand over many years. By contrast, the swiftly passed soft stool subjects the sigmoid to less strain and does not favour the development of diverticula (Painter and Burkitt, 1971).

Epidemiology and History of Diverticular Disease

Diverticular disease was almost unknown in the UK in 1900 but in the next ten years its complication, diverticulitis, was recognized as a surgical emergency. By 1917 Telling and Gruner were able to describe all the complications of the disease in their classic paper; and in 1920, Bland-Sutton remarked that diverticulitis is now recognized with the same certainty as is acute appendicitis and is a "newly discovered bane of elders" (Bland-Sutton, 1920). Since then the disease has become an ever-increasing problem in industrialized nations of the West.

By contrast, the disease is almost unknown to this day in rural Africa and Asia, where traditional foods containing plenty of plant fibre are still eaten. It is, however, appearing in Africans who have moved into towns and have adopted European eating habits. The disease is only just appearing in Japan but is rife among the Hawaiian Japanese who have been reared on American processed foods (Stemmerman and Yatani, 1972). The disease is not racial in origin as although the African native does not suffer from the disease, his descendants, the American negroes, and the West Indians living in the UK are as prone to the disease as are their white compatriots. Thirty years ago, black Americans did not eat such a refined diet and they did not develop diverticula as often as did the whites (Kocour, 1937). Since then, increasing affluence has resulted in an alteration in their diet, so that they eat the same food as their white compatriots and are now just as likely to be afflicted with diverticular disease (Cleave *et al.,* 1969; Painter and Burkitt, 1971).

Extensive epidemiological studies carried out by these authors, which included data from over two hundred hospitals throughout the world, revealed that the disease is almost unknown where the population eat an unrefined diet containing plenty of fibre. At Shiraz University Hospital, Iran, two thousand barium enemas are performed annually and in eight years only five patients with the disease have been found. All were wealthy professional or business men who ate a European diet (Burkitt, personal communication).

Eating habits are changing rapidly south of the Sahara, and appendicitis, which heralds the advent of diverticulosis, is already being recognized. If a lack of fibre is the cause of both appendicitis and of diverticulosis, then the disease should appear in this area after a similar time interval which separated its appearance from that of appendicitis in the UK. In order to settle this point, a close watch must be kept on the changing incidence of these diseases in countries where the diet is changing rapidly (Painter and Burkitt, 1971).

The Use of Bran in the Treatment of Diverticular Disease

If a lack of fibre causes the disease, it is logical to add fibre in the form of millers' bran to the diet of patients suffering from the disease. Bran has been shown to cause no complications and to render the stools soft and easy to pass. Consequently, it was given to seventy patients who had symptomatic diverticular disease at Manor House Hospital (Painter, 1971; Painter, *et al.*, 1972). Each patient was told to restrict his intake of brown or white sugar, as these substances contain no fibre and merely yield energy, and they were asked to avoid eating white bread and flour and also brown bread made from refined flour. They were asked to eat 100% wholemeal stoneground flour, All-Bran, Weetabix, porridge and plenty of fruit and vegetables. They were told that, as most people have to eat away from home and hence cannot control their diet completely, they must replace the cereal fibre which is missing from the modern diet by taking two teaspoons of unprocessed millers' bran three times a day. Bran is dry and can be washed down with milk or other fluids, sprinkled on cereals or mixed in soup. These patients were all warned that bran might give flatulence but that this would be temporary and disappear in two or three weeks, and they were not to stop taking bran on this account. After two weeks they were told that they must increase the dose of bran until they opened their bowels once or twice without straining. It is obvious that if defaecation involves straining at stool, then the intestine must have had to exert itself unduly to propel its contents. Hence it is essential to take sufficient bran to render the stools soft and easy to pass.

This trial began in December 1967 and in April 1971 information was obtained from these patients. Three had been made so comfortable on wholemeal bread and cereals that they did not take bran. Four did not like bran for various reasons and were improved with Normacol (Movicol in the USA), which is a bulk former. One had taken Senna for over twenty years and his myenteric plexus was found to have degenerated when his sigmoid was resected. Thus only one case came to surgery in this series.

The average amount of bran required was two teaspoons three times a day but some patients required several tablespoons. It is divided into three portions so that the bran would be mixed evenly throughout the intestinal contents. Each patient was given a sheet of instructions together with a packet of bran on his first visit, but after this forty-nine obtained further supplies at their own expense. Forty-nine of the seventy had taken laxatives when first seen and twenty-seven of these had bought them at their own expense. Only seven of the sixty-two who took a high fibre diet regularly required laxatives and then only occasionally. This represents a great financial saving not only to the Exchequer but particularly to old-age pensioners who otherwise squandered their limited means on expensive laxatives, some of which may be dangerous if taken over many years. The effect of the "bran diet" on the bowel habit is shown in Fig. 5; bran absorbs water and softens the constipated stool and often increases the frequency of defaecation in constipation. Those who pass hard small stools, like "sheep droppings", several times a day, often produce one or two huge soft motions a day without straining at stool once they have taken bran for two or three weeks (Painter *et al.*, 1972).

The symptoms of diverticular disease can be divided into three groups:

1. vague dyspeptic symptoms such as nausea, heartburn, flatulence and distension which might well be attributed to some upper intestinal disorder;

2. symptoms referrable to the bowel such as constipation, the passage of frequent hard small stools, episodes of diarrhoea or incomplete emptying of the rectum;

3. more severe symptoms such as abdominal pain, usually in the left iliac fossa, which may sometimes be so severe and recurrent that it was formerly cured only by surgery. This has been termed, "painful diverticular disease" by Painter (1968) to distinguish it from true inflammatory diverticulitis. It is caused by excessive segmentation of the sigmoid causing intermittent functional obstruction.

Some patients had more than one symptom and it was found that the seventy patients among them had a total of 167 presenting symptoms. The high fibre diet relieved or abolished 158 of these symptoms, and only six patients did not respond to bran. These were made comfortable with Normacol.

To sum up, over 85% of the symptoms were abolished or relieved by the simple dietary changes outlined above and the addition of unprocessed bran to the diet. On average, 12 to 14g of bran a day containing about 2g of cereal fibre was all that was required to relieve not only constipation and mild dyspeptic symptoms but also severe colic that had been mis-diagnosed as left renal colic. No less than twelve patients had suffered recurrent attacks of

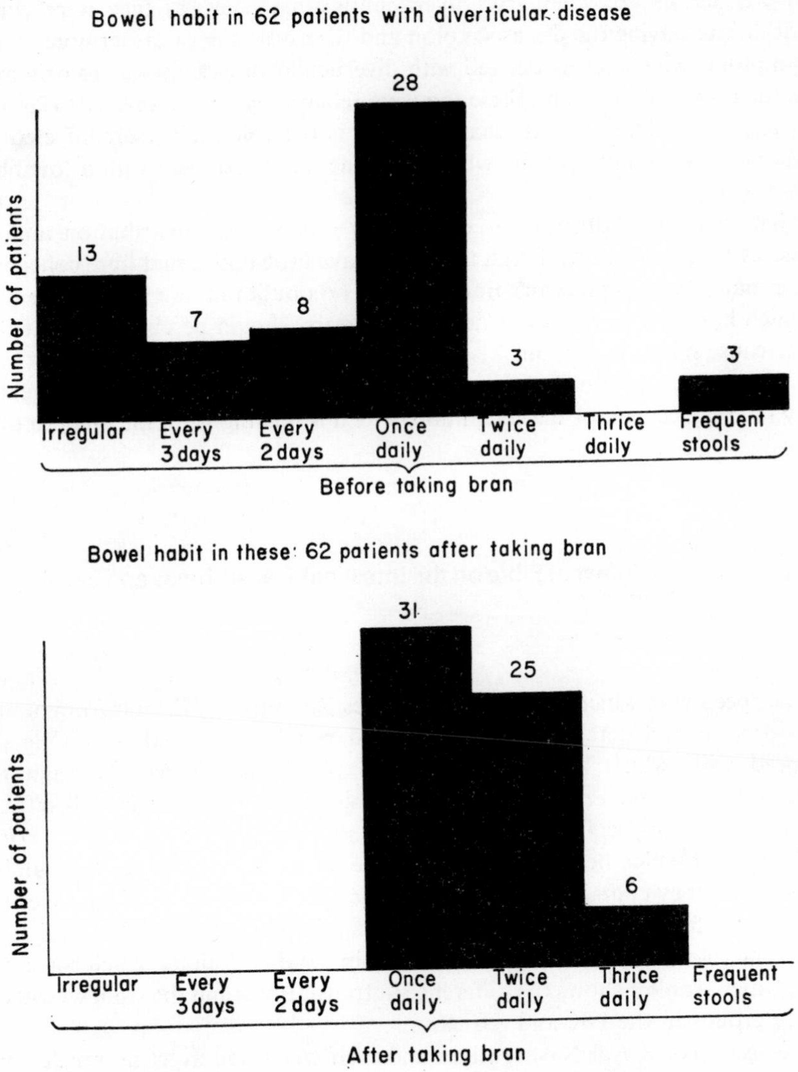

Fig. 5. The effect of bran on bowel habit in sixty-two patients with diverticular disease (from Painter *et al.*, 1972).

severe pain that made them into potential candidates for surgery. Eleven were relieved by bran and the twelfth was made comfortable by Normacol. Thus, the addition of cereal fibre to the diet will lessen the need for surgery in this disease.

The efficacy of the high fibre diet is not only of practical value but also of theoretical interest. The symptoms of the disease are obviously not due to diverticula, except when true diverticulitis supervenes, as they were cured without removing the diseased colon and the diverticula. Furthermore, some symptoms which are associated with diverticular disease appear to originate in the upper intestine and these too were relieved by a high fibre diet (Painter *et al.*, 1972). This suggests that not only is the colon adversely affected by fibre deficiency but that the whole intestine has to struggle with a low fibre diet.

The history of diverticular disease, its geographical distribution and its successful treatment by a high fibre diet leave little doubt that fibre deficiency is a major factor in its causation. There is no doubt that the low residue diet, which has been in vogue for nearly fifty years, should be abandoned as it is the cause of the condition.

Thus diverticular disease is caused by fibre deficiency and should be treated by the replacement of the cereal fibre which is missing from the modern diet.

The Effect of Fibre on the Intestinal Transit Times and Stool Weight

The speed with which food and its residues pass through the gut from mouth to anus is called the "transit time" and can be measured by timing the speed with which barium impregnated plastic pellets pass through the intestine (Hinton *et al.*, 1969). The subject swallows plastic pellets at a known time and collects his subsequent stools in plastic bags, and records the time at which he passes them. The stools are X-rayed to see the number of pellets they contain. In this manner the speed at which food traverses the intestinal tract can be calculated without subjecting the patient to irradiation. Furthermore, this method can be used in small hospitals which have few facilities. Table 1 shows the difference in transit times and the stool weights of five groups in the UK and Africa.

A group of Royal Naval ratings and their wives had average transit times of 83·4 hours and passed just over 100g of faeces a day. Their stools were well formed and hard. The transit times of British sixth form schoolboys were nearly as long and their daily weight of stool was similar. By contrast, Ugandan villagers had transit times of 35·7 hours and they passed no less than 470g of unformed wet stools a day without straining. This is not a racial characteristic as United Kingdom vegetarians, who eat more fibre, had transit times of 49 hours and passed over 220g of soft stools daily. Similarly, Ugandan boarding-school children who had a partly European diet were found to have much the same transit times and passed nearly 200g of stools. In these and other groups investigated there was an inverse relationship between the weight of stool and the transit time. Where refined diets are eaten the transit time is prolonged and less than 150g of stools are passed daily. Where unrefined foods are consumed the transit time is shorter and the large soft bulky stools are passed. The British vegetarians and the African boarding school children might be said to have a "mixed diet", and the values obtained for their transit times and stool weights were between the two extremes. Furthermore, when patients on a British refined diet were given bran in addition to their normal diet, their transit times were reduced to just over 40 hours and their stool weights increased to around 200g (Burkitt *et al.*, 1972).

TABLE 1

Transit times estimated by Hinton's method

Group studied	Average time first marker passed (in hours)	Average transit time (in hours) 80% of markers	Average weight of stool (g)
British Royal Navy personnel	45·7	83·4	104
British sixth form schoolboys	57·4	76·1	110
British vegetarians	22·1	49·0	223
African Ugandian villagers	19·8	35·7	470
African boarding-school Children (partly European diet)	27·6	47·0	185

Payler (1973) added bran to the diet of nineteen schoolboys aged sixteen to nineteen. On their school diet containing white bread, the average transit time was 64·5 hours and the average stool weight 135g. After eating wholemeal bread, together with two dessertspoons of millers' bran daily for three weeks, the average transit time had fallen to 44·9 hours (29% fall), and the average stool weight had risen to 163g (21% rise).

These findings prove beyond doubt that the cereal fibre content of food affects the behaviour of the colon profoundly. It appears that the addition of a few grams of cereal fibre to the diet cures not only constipation and the symptoms of diverticular disease, but might also lessen the incidence of colonic cancer which is almost unknown in communities who eat a high fibre diet.

Discussion

Certain diseases made their appearance in Western countries soon after the refining of carbohydrates became widespread. These same diseases are beginning to appear in the developing countries as their diet undergoes the same changes after a similar interval of time. Cleave has put forward the concept that they are all caused by a diet which contains an excess of refined carbohydrates, in particular sugar and white flour, and which, consequently, is deficient in dietary fibre (Cleave *et al.*, 1969). The relative effects of fibre deficiency and of the over-consumption of refined carbohydrates are not yet known. Historically, both factors usually operate together, but as regards diseases of the large bowel fibre deficiency appears to be the more important.

Fibre deficiency has only recently attracted attention and so it is interesting to speculate as to how it may contribute to the causation of disease.

Conditions which are Related to Small Stools and Prolonged Transit Times

Diverticular Disease of the Colon

This is caused by fibre deficiency and can be successfully treated by adding fibre to the diet, and requires no further discussion.

Appendicitis

Short (1920) produced evidence that appendicitis was due to a lack of fibre; recently Burkitt (1971) has shown that it has the same epidemiology as diverticular disease, and suggested that a deficiency of fibre causes viscous faeces by eliciting excessive pressures in the appendix that may devitalize its mucosa.

Constipation

This is rare in the rural African, although he may use the term if he passes only one large motion a day. In the UK, 36,000 gallons of liquid paraffin are consumed annually and nearly £5 million is spent on laxatives over and above the three and a half million National Health Service prescriptions (Painter, 1972). The addition of bran to the diet will almost always cure constipation safely and cheaply. It has now been used for nearly seven years at Manor House Hospital without any complications.

Benign and Malignant Tumours of the Large Bowel

These tumours are second only to lung cancer as a cause of death from neoplasm in Western nationals, but are almost unknown in rural Africa (Burkitt, 1973). In the former countries, small stools move slowly through the gut and allow bacteria to degrade the bile salts into compounds which are carcinogenic (Aries *et al.,* 1969; Hill *et al.,* 1971), which are then in contact with the bowel mucosa for a longer time than would be the case if a high fibre diet had been eaten. In the developing countries, these tumours are rare and bacteria do not produce these carcinogens from the rapidly moving faeces.

Conditions Indirectly Associated with Fibre Deficiency

Varicose veins are common in countries where refined carbohydrates are eaten. Cleave (1960) believes that this diet caused a loaded colon to press on the pelvic veins and hinder blood returning from the lower limbs so that the leg veins become varicose. Burkitt (1973) points out that a viscous stool requires abnormally high intra-abdominal pressures for its evacuation, and this pressure is transmitted to the leg veins and may damage their valves. Either of these mechanisms would explain the prevalence of haemorrhoids in developed countries, and intra-abdominal straining may play a part in the causation of hiatus hernia.

Diverticular disease is closely associated with gall-bladder disease and hiatus hernia (Saints' Triad, as it is called), and also with coronary disease (Showengerdt *et al.,* 1969). Coronary disease, diabetes mellitus and obesity have the same epidemiology and are almost certainly caused by eating refined carbohydrates (Cleave *et al.,* 1969). A deficiency of fibre may also alter the metabolism of the excretion of cholesterol, and hence an intake of a sufficiency of fibre may help to prevent the incidence of ischaemic heart disease and of gallstones (Trowell, 1972 and personal communication).

Conclusion

The changes that occurred in the British diet after 1870 are so new in the time-scale of human nutrition that the human organism has not adapted to them, with the result that many diseases have appeared on the clinical scene and have since increased in incidence until they have endangered the health of the nation.

One of these diseases is diverticular disease of the colon, which is caused by a deficiency of dietary fibre. The role of cereal fibre has been largely ignored, presumably because it has no nutrient value. Evidence has been presented to show that this attitude is wrong. It would appear that there is an urgent need to replace the cereal fibre that is removed in the processing of carbohydrates.

I believe that a return to a less refined diet containing the natural amount of cereal fibre would achieve more than all our surgical endeavours.

References

Aries, V., Crowther, J. S., Draser, B. S., Hill, M. J. and Williams, R. E. O. (1969). *Gut* **10,** 334.

Barker, T. C., McKenzie, J. C. and Yudkin, J. (1966). "Our Changing Fare". McGibbon and Kee, London.

Bland-Sutton, J. (1920). *Proc. R. Soc. Med.* (*Surgery*), **13,** 64.

Burkitt, D. P. (1971). *Br. J. Surg.* **58,** 695.

Burkitt, D. P. (1973). *Br. Med. J.* **1,** 64.

Burkitt, D. P., Walker, A. R. P. and Painter, N. S. (1972). *Lancet* **2,** 1408.

Cleave, T. L. (1941). *Br. Med. J.* **1,** 461.

Cleave, T. L. (1960). "On the Causation of Varicose Veins". John Wright and Sons, Bristol.

Cleave, T. L., Campbell, G. D. and Painter, N. S. (1969). "Diabetes, Coronary Thrombosis and the Saccharine Disease". 2nd ed. John Wright, Bristol.

Dimock, E. M. (1936). "The Treatment of Habitual Constipation by the Bran Method". MD Thesis, University of Cambridge.

Hill, M. J., Crowther, J. S., Draser, B. S., Hawksworth, G., Aries, V. and Williams, R. E. O. (1971). *Lancet* **1,** 95.

Hinton, J. M., Wennard-Jones, J. E. and Young, A. C. (1969). *Gut* **10,** 842.

Kocour, E. J. (1937). *Am. J. Surg.* **37,** 433.

Painter, N. S. (1964). *Ann. R. Coll. Surg. England* **34,** 98.

Painter, N. S. (1968). *Br. Med. J.* **3,** 475.

Painter, N. S. (1969). *Lancet* **2,** 586.

Painter, N. S. (1971). *Proc. R. Soc. Med.* (*Suppl.*) **63,** 144.

Painter, N. S. (1972). *Nutrition* **26,** 95.

Painter, N. S. and Burkitt, D. P. (1971). *Br. Med. J.* **2,** 450.

Painter, N. S., Truelove, S. C., Ardran, G. M. and Tuckey, M. (1965). *Gastroenterology* **49,** 169.

Painter, N. S., Almeida, A. Z. and Colebourne, K. W. (1972). *Br. Med. J.* **2,** 137.

Paylor, D. M. (1973). *Lancet* **1,** 394.

Schowengerdt, C. G., Hedges, G. R., Yaw, P. B. and Altemeier, W. A. (1969). *Arch. Surg.* **98,** 500.

Short, A. R. (1920). *Br. J. Surg.* **8,** 171.

Stemmerman, G. N. and Yatani, R. (1972). *Cancer* **31,** 1260.

Telling, W. H. M. and Gruner, O. C. (1917). *Br. J. Surg.* **4,** 468.

Trowell, H. (1972). *Europ. J. Clin. biochem. Res.* **17,** 345.

Conclusion

In their very different ways the contributors have presented us with a view of the world from the standpoint of their own disciplines and experience, though within the context of the whole of the problem of Man and his food supply. I do not pretend that we have anywhere near solved or balanced the Man/Food Equation but what we have done is to cut away some of that undergrowth that was occluding our vision. We began with a confusion of ingredients which we have pared down to more manageable proportions, to the basic materials of our daily existence.

It seems likely that the world food situation will worsen. The natural and energy constraints are already operating to our disadvantage, and our alternative methods of producing food might have concomitant risks. We need to know more about the dietary needs of Man although we have, I think, from several points of view exploded that myth of protein—this is perhaps the most important factor to come out of the Symposium.

We have not solved the Equation, but we have each in our own very individual ways perhaps brought the solution into a clearer light than hitherto. In one sense, of course, the Equation is already balanced, and if we are willing to accept that two-thirds of the peoples of the world should live at a subsistence level of nutrition and that the "well fed" citizens of the industrial communities should continue to run the risks of faulty diets, it will continue to balance.

However the problem of more mouths to feed tomorrow remains; as each day passes the world's food resources will have to be even more thinly spread until only the very wealthy will be able to afford a diet that ensures a healthy body. Such a situation would lead to what ecologists call intraspecific competition and the politicians call warfare and dictatorship.

If this Symposium has highlighted the conflicts it has also spotlighted the endeavour of those few people that are trying to solve one of Man's most intractable problems.

ARTHUR BOURNE

Index

C

G

R

Y

Z

303833482Y